The Moral Question of Abortion

The Moral Question
of Abortion

Stephen D. Schwarz

A Campion Book

Loyola University Press
Chicago

Loyola University Press
3441 North Ashland Avenue
Chicago, Illinois 60657

Photos on pages 9, 10, 11, 126, and 127 used with permission,
"Life or Death," Hayes Publishing Co., Cincinnati, OH.

Library of Congress Cataloging in Publication Data
Schwarz, Stephen D.
    The moral question of abortion/Stephen D. Schwarz.
       p.   cm.
    Includes bibliographical references.
    ISBN 0-8294-0623-9
      1. Abortion—Moral and ethical aspects. I. Title.
HQ767.15.S38   1990   90-31261
363.4'6—dc20   CIP

Dedication

To my father and mother
in deep gratitude
for the gift of life

Contents

Foreword

by Bernard N. Nathanson, M.D.

This is truly an encyclopedic work, spanning as it does the spectrum of the abortion dilemma, from the anatomy and physiology of the unborn child to the complex legal and ethical questions involved in the wanton destruction of that child. It will serve as an invaluable guide through the moral thickets of the abortion question.

The book correctly emphasizes that the mere size of a human being is no measure of his/her value; it has long been my contention that in the tiny, almost invisible thirty-two cell blastocyst—in that one gram or so of tissue—there is a physical potential and moral density unparalleled in our universe. Next to it, a gram of plutonium is a triviality: plutonium cannot compose a symphony, cannot cure cancer, cannot plan our course to the stars.

I unhesitatingly recommend this book as an indispensable Baedeker through the tortured landscape of the abortion wars. It should be read by every thinking, morally responsible citizen in the country.

Preface

The aim of this book is to present a clarification of the moral question of abortion, by a careful and thorough analysis of all its essential aspects. What does abortion involve? Is it a private matter? Does it have a victim? Is it ever morally justified? Should it be legal? The analysis starts at the beginning and pursues these questions to their logical conclusions.

The book is addressed to a variety of readers:

To Those Who Have Mixed Feelings About the Morality of Abortion. For example, those who oppose some abortions but approve others; or who believe a child is present and are unsure how to balance the rights of the child and those of the mother; or who are uncertain when the child begins her existence. The book is intended to provide you with a clear picture; with conclusions based on careful reasoning.

To Those Who Are Pro–Life. You will find a confirmation of your position, a carefully reasoned analysis to support and defend it. You will, hopefully, find answers to some of the questions you have, as well as replies you can offer to those who ask you questions or challenge your position. You may wonder whether exceptions should ever be made; that question is carefully considered.

To Those Who Are Pro–Choice. My hope is that this book will give you a new perspective on this most important life-and-death issue.

In another direction, the book is addressed to a wide audience:

To The General Public. The book does not assume any familiarity with philosophy, natural science, medicine or law.

To Philosophers. The book is intended to be a careful and thorough philosophical defense of the "pro-life" position. It offers detailed replies to some major recent "pro-abortion" positions, notably Warren-Tooley and Thomson (chapters 7 and 8), including an analysis of an important distinction for the Philosophy of the Person, being a person and function-ing as a person.

To Those Concerned With The Law: Judges, Legislators, Other Gover-ment Officials, Professionals in the Social Sciences and Medicine. The book is intended to help clarify the essential moral and legal questions so important to your profession.

The argument makes no appeal to religious faith, only to reason, including basic moral principles. It pursues the moral question of abortion as a philosophical question.

The fundamental premises of the book are that intentionally killing an innocent person (someone who is not an aggressor) to benefit oneself or others is wrong; and that all persons as persons have an equal intrinsic value, and an equal right to live, which must be respected by all. The idea of equal treatment of all persons is consistently carried through to its various conclusions.

The basic aim of the book is to see abortion as it really is. Certain points, explained in earlier parts of the book, are stressed and repeated later to help develop the total picture of the reality of abortion (and to remind the reader of things that are easily forgotten or overlooked).

There is a sad chapter in the history of America: slavery. How could something as horrible as slavery be practiced and approved in a country based on human dignity and equal rights for all people? How could we have been so blind to this evil? If some people at that time were blind to a great evil, is it possible that some of us now are blind to a similar evil?

Acknowledgments

I wish to express my grateful appreciation to my many friends who encouraged me in the writing of this book: Ronda Chervin, Alice von Hildebrand, Peter Kreeft, Balduin Schwarz (my father), Wolfgang Waldstein, and Fritz Wenisch. Two of my friends deserve very special thanks. They not only encouraged me but also read the manuscript and made very helpful suggestions. They are Kiki Latimer and Ron Tacelli. Roy Heyne, M.D. provided valuable help with the medical and scientific aspects in several chapters, and also made helpful suggestions for strengthening the argument.

To all those who typed portions of the manuscript, my heartfelt thanks: Ede Williams, Mary Lee Harrington, Terri Russo, my wife Sherry, and my three daughters, Elizabeth, Margaret and Mary.

A special expression of gratitude is due to the late Dietrich von Hildebrand, whom I was privileged to have as a friend and teacher from my earliest youth until his death in 1977. It is mainly from him that I learned the art of philosophizing as careful analysis of and faithfulness to reality. His inspiration guided me throughout this work.

1

Is the Being in the Womb a Real Child?

The moral question of abortion focuses on the central question: What is the nature of the being in the womb that is destroyed by an abortion? Is it mere tissue? Is it a part of the woman's body? Is it a potential person? Is it something that will become a child? Or is it already a child, a small baby not yet born? The purpose of this chapter is to answer these questions on the basis of authoritative scientific findings and careful philosophical analysis, and thereby to show—as a foundation for everything else in this book—that what lives in the womb is a real child, a small person, a human being essentially like us, in the first phase of his or her existence.

The reality of the child in the womb will be established on the basis of four main considerations, four mutually supporting lines of argument:

First, the scientific facts about the child in the womb will be considered, a brief account of his early development. We will see how rapid this development is, how quickly the bodily organs and parts come into place as distinct and identifiable elements and develop as active functioning units, and how soon he or she becomes recognizable as a small baby.

Second, pictures of the being in the womb make it clear that this being is a small child.

Third, reflection on these matters reveals an elementary point: the child who is born and later grows into an adult is the very same being who before birth was in his mother's womb. He is a person later, he is a person earlier, the very same person. This is the continuum of human life.

Fourth, we will see that none of the differences between a preborn child and a born child or other born person make a difference with respect to the reality of their being as persons.

1

These four lines of argument provide a basis, which will be confirmed, and further developed, in chapters 4 through 7. What exists in the womb is not something that develops into a person, but the person himself, in the first phase of his existence. When I speak of the child as a person, I mean a person in the sense that a small born baby is a person, the same human person who is later an older child and still later, an adult. (A full analysis of personhood appears in chapter 7.)

First: Scientific Facts about the Child in the Womb

The reality of the child in the womb as a real human being in the first phase of existence is brought out in a statement entitled "The Unborn Person Is Also a Patient." It was presented by a group of more than two hundred doctors, many of them members of the American College of Obstetrics and Gynecology, in a Friend of the Court Brief filed before the United States Supreme Court.

From conception the child is a complex, dynamic, rapidly growing organism. By a natural and continuous process the single fertilized ovum will, over approximately nine months, develop into the trillions of cells of the newborn. The natural end of the sperm and ovum is death unless fertilization occurs. At fertilization a new and unique being is created which, although receiving one-half of its chromosomes from each parent, is really unlike either.

About seven to nine days after conception, when there are already several hundred cells of the new individual formed, contact with the uterus is made and implantation begins. Blood cells begin at 17 days and a heart as early as 18 days. This embryonic heart which begins as a simple tube starts irregular pulsations at 24 days, which, in about one week, smooth into a rhythmic contraction and expansion.

Straus, et al. have shown that the ECG on a 23 mm embryo (7.5 weeks) presents the existence of a functionally complete cardiac system. . . . All the classic elements of the adult ECG were seen. . . .

Commencing at 18 days the developmental emphasis is on the nervous system even though other vital organs, such as the heart, are commencing development at the same time. Such early development is necessary since the nervous system integrates the action of all other systems. By the end of the 20th day the foundation of the child's brain, spinal cord and entire nervous system will have been established. By the 6th week after conception this system will have developed so well that it is controlling movements of the baby's muscles, even though the woman may not be aware that she is pregnant. By the 33rd day the cerebral cortex, that part of the central nervous system that governs motor activity as well as intellect may be seen.

The baby's eyes begin to form at 19 days. By the end of the first month the foundation of the brain, spinal cord, nerves and sense organs is completely formed. By 28 days the embryo has the building blocks for 40 pairs of muscles situated from the base of its skull to the lower end of its spinal column. By the end of the first month the child has completed the period of relatively greatest size increase and the greatest physical change of a lifetime. He or she is ten thousand times larger than the fertilized egg and will increase its weight six billion times by birth, having in only the first month gone from the one cell state to millions of cells.

By the beginning of the second month the unborn child, small as it is, looks distinctly human. Yet, by this time the child's mother is not even aware that she is pregnant.

At the end of the first month the child is about 1/4 of an inch in length. At 30 days the primary brain is present and the eyes, ears and nasal organs have started to form. Although the heart is still incomplete, it is beating regularly and pumping blood cells through a closed vascular system. The child and mother do not exchange blood, the child having from a very early point in its development its own and complete vascular system.

Earliest reflexes begin as early as the 42nd day. The male penis begins to form. The child is almost 1/2 inch long and cartilage has begun to develop.

Even at 5 1/2 weeks the fetal heartbeat is essentially similar to that of an adult in general configuration.

By the end of the seventh week we see a well proportioned small scale baby. [Emphasis added.] In its seventh week, it bears the familiar external features and all the internal organs of the adult, even though it is less than an inch long and weighs only 1/30th of an ounce. The body has become nicely rounded, padded with muscles and covered by a thin skin. The arms are only as long as printed exclamation marks, and have hands with fingers and thumbs. The slower growing legs have recognizable knees, ankles and toes.

The new body not only exists, it also functions. The brain in configuration is already like the adult brain and sends out impulses that coordinate the function of the other organs. The brain waves have been noted at 43 days. The heart beats sturdily. The stomach produces digestive juices. The liver manufactures blood cells and the kidneys begin to function by extracting uric acid from the child's blood. The muscles of the arms and body can already be set in motion.

After the eighth week no further primordia will form; *everything* is already present that will be found in the full term baby.[1] As one author describes this period: "A human face with eyelids half closed as they are in someone who is about to fall asleep. Hands that soon will begin to grip, feet trying their first gentle kicks."

From this point until adulthood, when full growth is achieved somewhere between 25 and 27 years, the changes in the body will be mainly in dimension and in gradual refinement of the working parts.

The development of the child, while very rapid, is also very specific. The genetic pattern set down in the first day of life instructs the development of a specific anatomy. The ears are formed by seven weeks and are specific, and may resemble a family pattern. The lines in the hands start to be engraved by eight weeks and remain a distinctive feature of the individual.

The primitive skeletal system has completely developed by the end of six weeks. This marks the end of the child's embryonic (from Greek, to swell or teem within) period. From this point, the child will be called a fetus (Latin, young one or offspring).

In the third month, the child becomes very active. By the end of the month he can kick his legs, turn his feet, curl and fan his toes, make a fist, move his thumb, bend his wrist, turn his head, squint, frown, open his mouth, press his lips tightly together. He can swallow and drinks the amniotic fluid that surrounds him. Thumb sucking is first noted at this age. The first respiratory motions move fluid in and out of his lungs with inhaling and exhaling respiratory movements.

The prerequisites for motion are muscles and nerves. In the sixth to seventh weeks, nerves and muscles work together for the first time. If the area of the lips, the first to become sensitive to touch, is gently stroked, the child responds by bending the upper body to one side and making a quick backward motion with his arms. This is called a total pattern response because it involves most of the body, rather than a local part. Localized and more appropriate reactions such as swallowing follow in the third month. By the beginning of the ninth week, the baby moves spontaneously without being touched. Sometimes his whole body swings back and forth for a few moments. By eight and a half weeks the eyelids and the palms of the hands become sensitive to touch. If the eyelid is stroked, the child squints. On stroking the palm, the fingers close into a small fist.

In the ninth and tenth weeks, the child's activity leaps ahead. Now if the forehead is touched, he may turn his head away and pucker up his brow and frown. He now has full use of his arms and can bend the elbow and wrist independently. In the same week, the entire body becomes sensitive to touch.

The twelfth week brings a whole new range of responses. The baby can now move his thumb in opposition to his fingers. He now swallows regularly. He can pull up his upper lip; the initial step in the development of the sucking reflex. By the end of the twelfth week, the quality of muscular response is altered. It is no longer marionette-like or mechanical—the movements are now graceful and fluid, as they are in the newborn. The child is active and the reflexes are becoming more vigorous. *All this is before the mother feels any movement. . . .*

Every child shows a distinct individuality in his behavior by the end of the third month. This is because the actual structure of the muscles varies from baby to baby. The alignment of the muscles of the face, for example, follow an inherited pattern.

Further refinements are noted in the third month. The finger-nails appear. The child's face becomes much prettier. His eyes, previously far apart, now move closer together. The eyelids close over the eyes. Sexual differentiation is apparent in both internal and external sex organs, and primitive eggs and sperm are formed. The vocal cords are completed. In the absence of air they cannot produce sound; the child cannot cry aloud until birth although he is capable of crying long before.

The taste buds and salivary glands develop in this month, as do the digestive glands in the stomach. When the baby swallows amniotic fluid, its contents are utilized by the child. The child starts to urinate.

From the twelfth to the sixteenth week, the child grows very rapidly. His weight increases six times, and he grows to eight to ten inches in height. For this incredible growth spurt the child needs oxygen and food. This he receives from his mother through the placental attachment—much like he receives food from her after he is born. His dependence does not end with expulsion into the external environment. We now know that the placenta belongs to the baby, not the mother, as was long thought.

In the fifth month, the baby gains two inches in height and ten ounces in weight. By the end of the month he will be about one foot tall and will weigh one pound. Fine baby hair begins to grow on his eyebrows and on his head and a fringe of eyelashes appear. Most of the skeleton hardens. The baby's muscles become much stronger, and as the child becomes larger his mother finally perceives his many activities. The child's mother comes to recognize the movement and can feel the baby's head, arms and legs. She may even perceive a rhythmic jolting movement—fifteen to thirty per minute. This is due to the child hiccoughing. . . . The doctor can already hear the heartbeat with his stethoscope.

The baby sleeps and wakes just as it will after birth. When he sleeps he invariably settles into his favorite position called his "lie". Each baby has a characteristic lie. When he awakens he moves about freely in the buoyant fluid turning from side to side, and frequently head over heel. Sometimes his head will be up and sometimes it will be down. He may sometimes be aroused from sleep by external vibrations. He may wake up from a loud tap on the tub when his mother is taking a bath. A loud concert or the vibrations of a washing machine may also stir him into activity. The child hears . . . his mother's voice before birth.

In the sixth month, the baby will grow about two more inches, to become fourteen inches tall. He will also begin to accumulate a little fat under his skin and will increase his weight to a pound and three quarters. This month the permanent teeth buds come in high in the gums behind the milk teeth. Now his closed eyelids will open and close, and his eyes look up, down and sideways. Dr. Liley feels that the child may perceive light through the abdominal wall. *Dr. Still has noted that electroencephalographic waves have been obtained in forty-three to forty-five day old fetuses, and so conscious experience is possible after this date.*

In the sixth month, the child develops a strong muscular grip with his hands. He also starts to breathe regularly and can maintain respiratory response for twenty-four hours if born prematurely. He may even have a slim chance of surviving in an incubator. The youngest children known to survive were between twenty to twenty-five weeks old.[2]

Note especially the statement: "By the end of the seventh week we see a well-proportioned small scale baby." This is before most abortions are performed. An abortion is not simply a medical procedure performed on a woman; it involves a "well-proportioned small scale baby."

Many facts and experiences illustrate the reality of the child in the womb.[3] Here is one particularly striking experience:

Dr. Liley relates the experience of a doctor who injected an air bubble into an unborn baby's (eight months) amniotic sac in an attempt to locate the placenta on x-ray. It so happened that the air bubble covered the unborn baby's face. The moment the unborn child had air to inhale, his vocal cords became operative and his crying became audible to all present, including the physician and technical help. The mother telephoned the doctor later to report that whenever she lay down to sleep, the air bubble got over the unborn baby's face and he was crying so loudly he was keeping both her and her husband awake.[4]

Second: Pictures of the Child in the Womb

A. Unruptured ectopic pregnancy. Fetus aged between 6 - 7 weeks. © Robert L. Wolfe.

B. Human Life at eight weeks.

C. Tiny human feet at ten weeks.

D. Three and one-half months old, just growing bigger.

A. Unruptured ectopic pregnancy. Fetus aged between 6-7 weeks.
© Robert L. Wolfe.

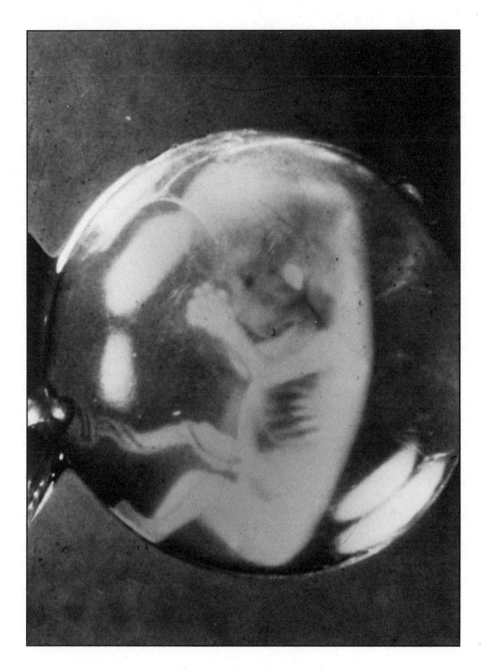

B. Human life at eight weeks

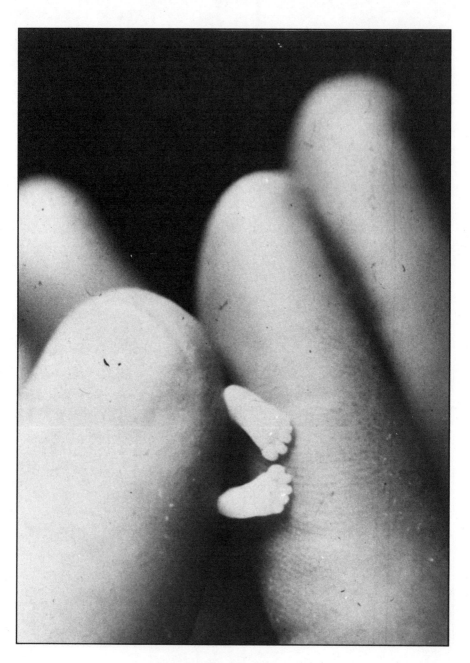

C. Tiny human feet at ten weeks

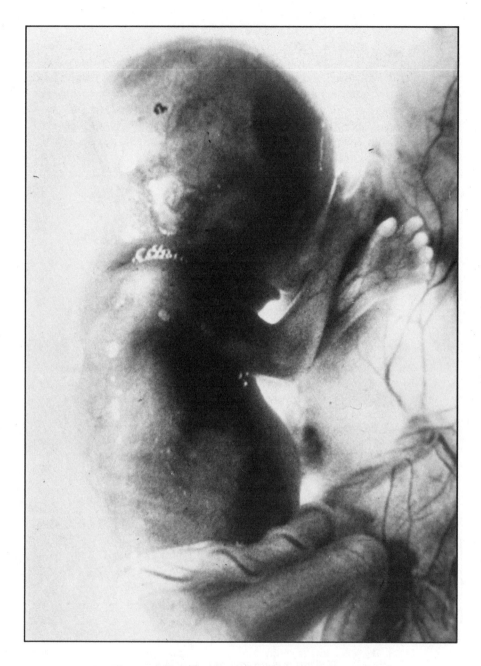

D. Three and one-half months old just growing bigger

The Child Is Not a Part of the Mother's Body. As is clearly illustrated from the scientific facts, the child in the womb is not a part of the mother's body, but a full individual, a distinct being. He is as much his own person (and not part of another) as he will be later in life. He is dependent on his mother, as I would be dependent on you if I were dying from lack of blood and were receiving a blood transfusion directly from you. I would of course remain completely distinct from you. In fact, the child does not even receive such a transfusion from his mother. He has his own independent blood circulation and his blood does not typically mix with that of his mother.

Dr. Bernard Nathanson adds an interesting point:

> I have countered the old pro-abortion slogan, "It's a woman's right to control her own body," by pointing out that the modern science of immunology has shown us that the unborn child is *not* a part of a woman's body in the same sense that her kidney or her heart is. Immunologic studies have demonstrated beyond cavil that when a pregnancy implants itself into the wall of the uterus at the eighth day following conception the defense mechanisms of the body, principally the white blood cells, sense that this creature now settling down for a lengthy stay is an intruder, an alien, and must be expelled. Therefore an intense immunological attack is mounted on the pregnancy by the white blood cell elements, and through an ingenious and extraordinarily efficient defense system the unborn child succeeds in repelling the attack. In ten percent or so of cases the defensive system fails and the pregnancy is lost as a spontaneous abortion or miscarriage.[5]

Third: The Continuum of Human Life

The third of the three mutually supporting considerations to show the reality of the child in the womb is the *continuum argument*: Human life is a single continuum, from conception-fertilization to death (or beyond). I will now examine several aspects of this argument, each in its basic formulation. Taken together—and supplemented by the other lines of argument of this chapter, and completed by the arguments of later chapters—these aspects of the continuum argument form the basic premise for establishing what underlies this book as a whole: the reality of the child in the womb.

(1) The life of a human person is a single continuum, having different phases. Being a child in the womb is the first of these phases; further phases include being a newborn baby, a born baby in his fifth month, his second year, a child of eight, a young adult, a person in middle age, an older person. Life in the womb is part of life. Each of us can say,

I was once a child of three; a newborn baby; a baby two months before birth; six months; and so on. Small children have a perfectly clear understanding of this, remarking, "When I was in Mommy's tummy . . . "

(2) The core of the continuum argument is that the child in the womb is the same person as the born child he will become, as well as the youngster of six, the teenager, the adult, he will become later. I am now the same person I was ten years ago, even though I have changed. That "I have changed" means that I, the same person, have changed; these changes happened to me. I am now the same person who was once a newborn baby; and before that, a preborn baby in the womb. (*Person* means here simply "human being"; in chapter 7, I will analyze these terms carefully, thereby completing the present argument.)

I am now the same person as I was ten years ago. One way to understand this is through memory. I remember, not only events that occurred ten years ago, but myself experiencing these events. To remember an experience is to reach back, not only into the past, but into another phase of one's own life, the life of the same person.

Memory of one's own past experiences presupposes oneself as experiencing them. I who now remember, and I who had those experiences, must be the same person.[6] Memory can stretch no farther back than identity; I cannot remember an experience occurring before I came to be, for obviously such an experience was not my experience. But the converse is not true, for one's identity can, and does, stretch farther back than one's memory. That I cannot remember an experience does not mean it was not my experience. I cannot remember being born, nor any of the moments of my existence before birth. But each of these moments was a moment in my existence, a part of that continuum that is my life on earth.

The function of memory in the continuum argument is to provide a clear and vivid understanding of the meaning of personal identity. Suppose the being in the womb had mental capacities that were far more developed than they actually are. Then she could later say, I now remember experiencing such and such while in the womb. That is—and this is the crucial point—I now remember myself, *the same person,* having these experiences. That means of course that I was already present then. The absence of such developed mental capacities means the absence of such (actual) memory experiences; it does not mean the absence of the real identity that links the person as she exists now and as she existed then, and that is made intelligible by this (supposed) memory experience.

(3) It is not so that there is something in the womb—"a blob of tissue" or a mere biological organism—that turns into a child.[7] The child is already there, the same child, the same person all the way through. There

are significant developmental changes, but these occur in the life of one and the same being who is present throughout; and who is the being to whom these changes occur.

Later chapters will confirm this point. Thus chapter 4 will show that there is no point in pregnancy where one could draw a line to mark the place where something nonpersonal "turns into" a person. Chapter 5 will show that a person does not come into existence gradually; i.e., nothing "turns into" a person gradually. Chapter 6 will show that a person's existence begins at conception-fertilization, as opposed to something else coming into existence then, which later turns into the person. Finally, chapter 7 will show that the being who exists throughout pregnancy is indeed a person, not a potential person who somehow "turns into" a person.

(4) The person is already there in the womb: nothing needs to be added to make him a person. Indeed nothing can be added. This too will be confirmed in later chapters; for example, none of the suggested places to draw the line marks the addition of what is needed for becoming a person.

Before concluding the continuum argument, two points of clarification are in order. First, the argument does not refer merely to the biological continuum of a single organism. Rather, it is the identity of a person through various phases of his existence. The biological continuity is certainly there, and it is an integral part of the continuum of the person. It is not the whole of it or its essence. The biological continuum is a dimension of the personal continuum, as the biological physical is in general a dimension of the human person.

Second, the continuum argument is not the claim, often heard, that one cannot find a clear cutoff point in the life of a human being from conception to birth and beyond, a point marking the line between non-person and person, or merely potential person and actual person. If there is a spectrum, say from A to Z, the fact that no clear, nonarbitrary cutoff point can be found along the way does not mean that A and Z cannot be radically different. Think of such examples as the color spectrum from black to white, or night to day. In each case A shades off into B, B into C, etc. There are no clear dividing lines; there is a continuity. But it is not the continuity of the continued existence of the same being; for example, a baby grows up to be a twenty-year-old, and always remains the same person.

If the continuum argument were merely that one can't find a clear cutoff point, it would indeed be invalid, and would not support the basic thesis, that the being in the womb is the same person who will later be born.[8] Rejection of this argument does not touch the real continuum argument, the continuum of the same person. As already indicated, and as chapter 4 will confirm, there is indeed no line to be drawn. The reason for this is the continuum of human life. Continuum implies no line; no line (by itself) does not imply continuum.

The child becomes an adult, and he is a child no longer. The fetus becomes the born child, and he is a fetus no longer. The stages—zygote, embryo, fetus, newborn baby, toddler, teenager—cease to be, but the person going through these stages continues to be, and continues as the same person. Being a fetus is merely one stage in the life of a person.[9]

Fourth: Four Differences between Preborn and Postborn Persons

There are, of course, differences between the child in the womb and a born person. What are these differences, and are any of them morally significant? Let us examine this question now with regard to the child at seven to eight weeks, described earlier as "a well proportioned small-scale baby." Later chapters (4, 6, and 7) will confirm that what is established here for the older child at seven to eight weeks applies also to the younger child, the same child in earlier phases of her life. There seem to be four major differences between a preborn and a born person:

Size. The child in the womb at seven weeks is normally smaller than the newborn child. The latter is normally smaller than a one-year-old child, who is normally smaller than a five-year-old child. A 100-pound girl is smaller than a 250-pound football player. This is of no moral significance. The larger person isn't any more a person, or more precious, than the smaller. A small newborn baby is just as precious as an older child, or an adult. The child in the womb is simply a still smaller child.

Level of development. A baby is less developed than a teenager. Is he or she less a person? Being less developed, as well as being smaller, represents earlier phases on the human life continuum. But he is equally a person; he is the same person at his earlier stage of development as at the later stages, or else it would not be his development.

The child at seven to eight weeks is less developed than later, but he is already very well developed. As noted earlier, "After the eighth week no further primordia will form: *everything* is already present that will be found in the full term baby." For example, "a human face with eyelids half closed . . . hands that will soon begin to grip, feet trying their first gentle kicks" (see note 2).

Environment. If one person is in one environment and another person in another environment, nothing changes concerning the reality, or dignity and worth, of the two persons. Being inside his mother, nesting in her womb, represents being in a different environment than the familiar environment we know. But the being in the womb is as much a real person, a real child, at that time as after birth.

A child in an incubator is no less a real child than one in natural surroundings. The preborn child is in the incubator of his mother's womb, a warm, protective nesting place. It is the necessary environment he needs while still small and fragile, what he needs for protection, nourishment, and growth. It is the environment he needs to develop into a being who can survive the rigors of life in the outside world. The difference between the preborn and postborn child is one of needs, not of reality or worth and dignity.

Degree of dependency. We are all dependent on one another, physically and psychologically. Some are more dependent than others: children, the sick, the handicapped. A more dependent person—someone in an intensive care unit, for example—is not less of a person, than someone who is relatively more independent.

To see clearly the moral irrelevance of degree of dependency for the reality, dignity, and preciousness of a person, consider the following:

(1) Degree of dependency is relative. It is, precisely, a matter of degree, of more or less. Everyone is dependent on others to some extent, physically and psychologically. At certain times, each of us becomes, or can become, more dependent on others than usual: if we are lost, if we've had a serious accident, if we are blinded. Clearly these conditions do not affect our being as persons, our preciousness and dignity, our right to live.

(2) Specifically, it is important to remember that when you are dependent on others, that is, more dependent than usual, you are the same person as you were before, and will be later. So, too, is the child in the womb. He is at this stage of his life the same person who will later be born and grow up to be less dependent.

(3) Suppose that you are now healthy, thus relatively independent. Then you have a serious accident that leaves you paralyzed, thus very dependent on others. The continuation of your life depends on others for protection and nourishment, parallel to the child in the womb. You are still the same person. You have the same dignity and right to live.

Suppose someone were to say to you, "You don't count; you are too dependent." This would be an outrage. If this were used as a reason for killing you—that you were perceived as being in the way— it would be regarded as a terrible injustice.

Precisely this is what is said to the child in the womb by those who defend abortion on the grounds that the child is too dependent. The fact that the child can't hear and understand what is being said, or that it is not said in so many words, or out loud, surely is of no moral significance.

(4) Physical dependency, as it applies to the child in the womb or to a person who is paralyzed, concerns a person's bodily dimension, and not

the person as a person, or his right to live. I remain myself through the various changes, phases of growth and development, phases of relative dependency or independence, that pertain to my body. I am not any less *me* because my body may be in a state of greater dependency than at another time. Thus we see that dependency through connection to another person has nothing to do with being a person. It has only to do with how the body is sustained.

In short, to hold that a more dependent person—whether normally (in the womb) or not normally (as in paralysis)—is less of a person, less worthy of being treated like the rest of us is sheer prejudice, ungrounded in fact and reason. It is like the prejudice that asserts that certain people in distant lands, of different cultures and ethnic groups, are different in an odious sense, less human, not fully persons, whose death doesn't matter, or matters much less than the death of a familiar person. A person who is different—whether it is because he belongs to a different culture, or because he is more dependent—is above all a person, like you and me, with the same right to live as we have. The class of preborn persons is simply one instance of this. Such a person should be treated just like any other person, with respect for his dignity and right to live.[10]

To kill a normal child sleeping in his crib is a terrible evil. Killing a child in an incubator, dependent on that incubator, is no less evil. Abortion is killing a child in the incubator of his mother's womb. A more dependent child is a more fragile child. He deserves more care and protection, not less.

That the child in the womb is dependent on another person, while the prematurely born child is dependent on an incubator has nothing to do with the status of the being who is thus dependent. If person A is being sustained by, and thus dependent on, a direct blood transfusion from another person, while person B is similarly being sustained by a blood transfusion through a machine, then both are equally sustained, equally dependent; both are persons nevertheless. That is, the kind of dependency, whether it is on another person or on a machine, has nothing to do with the person's being and his moral status. (dignity, right to life, etc.)

These four features that differentiate preborn persons and born persons can be conveniently put together and easily remembered by the acronym SLED:

	For the child is:
S: Size	smaller;
L: Level of development	less developed;
E: Environment	in a different environment;
D: Degree of dependency	more dependent;

A brief word about some of the other differences between preborn and post-born babies. Preborn babies cannot be seen, they have no name, and they are incapable of social interaction. These differences are of no moral significance.

That preborn babies cannot be seen really refers to the fact that we cannot see them, not to anything about their being. A person enclosed in something—whether it is a closet or a womb—cannot be seen, for obvious reasons. That says nothing about him as a person.

That a preborn child has no name says nothing about him as a person. An unnamed orphan is as much a baby as a named child.

No social interaction, to the extent that it applies, is an obvious consequence of the child's level of development and environment. Even if he were more developed, he couldn't very well carry on a conversation with us in his present position. But again, that says nothing about him as a person.

Finally, the child in the womb lacks mobility: he cannot move about. First, this is only partly true. Beginning in the third month he becomes very active, and moves about in his amniotic sac.[11] Second, where it is true, it is due to his lack of development at the beginning, and later, his cramped quarters as he grows larger. Third, it is in any case morally irrelevant. A paralyzed person is as much a person as one who is fortunate enough not to be so afflicted. Mobility, to the extent that it pertains to the child in the womb, is a matter of development, environment, and degree of dependency.

The Child in the Womb Is Not a Potential Person. It is false that the being in the womb is merely a potential person. He is not a potential person, but an actual person, a fully real person, the same person he will later be. He is only smaller, less developed, in a different environment, and more dependent, in comparison to a born baby. Just as the small born baby is not a potential person but an actual person, so too is the preborn baby, who is simply a baby at an earlier phase of development. Both the postborn baby and the preborn baby are persons with potential, which is true of older children, and to a large extent, of all adults. We are actual beings with varying potentials for growth and development. In short, the child in the womb *has* potential, but he is an actual person, just like the rest of us.

Being a Person and Functioning As a Person. Persons under anesthesia cannot feel pain, think, or communicate intentionally. That they cannot do these things means they cannot *function* as persons. But they have the *being* of a person. The child in the womb has a potential capacity to function fully as a person; in terms of being, the preborn is an actual person.

The greater the level of development, the greater the capacity to function as a person. Level of development is relevant only to functioning as a person not to being a person.

Concluding Remark. The term *fetus* is in itself a perfectly proper term, meaning "young one," and in the context of human persons, a young human person. But in recent times it has come to be understood in a very different, even an antithetical way, as something other than a person, a child. For some people it is a fetus instead of a child that a woman is carrying. It is psychologically easier to speak of the destruction of a fetus than of a child. Defenders of abortion object to the use of the term *child*: they generally do not want to appear as defending the killing of a child. So it is a fetus; destroying a fetus does not sound so bad. It is for this reason that it is imperative that we speak of the child and not the fetus. The reality of the child in the womb must be emphasized and conveyed to others.

Suppose a woman suffers a miscarriage. A sympathetic doctor will not tell her, "You have lost your fetus"; he will say, "You have lost your child." If the child is marked for destruction he may well be referred to as a fetus, for this term has a cold scientific neutrality that effectively obscures the reality and preciousness of the small preborn child. For this reason I shall always use the term *child (or baby)* rather than *fetus* (except in quotation marks)

A woman is walking down the street carrying a child in her arms. She is with child. Another woman is walking down that street. She is pregnant. She too is carrying a child, only in a different way. She too is with child, an expression often used, and most aptly, of a pregnant woman. The child carried in the arms is dependent, so is the child carried in the womb, only it is a different kind of dependence.

The woman and the child in her arms make two persons, two distinct individuals. The pregnant woman and her child also make two persons, two distinct individuals—one seen and one hidden from view, but each as real as the other.

2

Is Abortion the Killing of This Being?

Methods of Abortion

Abortion is generally described as the termination of pregnancy. It is terminated by the removal of the child from the womb. That is done by several methods:

D & C or Dilation and Curettage:

Performed between 7 and 12 weeks, this method utilizes a sharp curved knife. The uterus is approached through the vagina. The cervix, or mouth of the womb, is stretched open. The surgeon then cuts the tiny body to pieces and cuts and scrapes the placenta from the inside walls of the uterus. . . .

One of the jobs of the operating nurse is to reassemble the parts to be sure the uterus is empty, otherwise the mother will bleed or become infected.[1]

Suction or Vacuum Aspiration: A powerful suction tube is inserted through the cervix into the womb. The baby is violently torn to pieces and sucked into a jar. Used between 7 and 12 weeks.[2]

D & E or Dilation and Evacuation: Used between 12 and 24 weeks. Here, too, the child is cut to pieces by a sharp knife, as in D & C, only it is a much larger and far more developed child, weighing as much as a pound, and measuring as much as a foot in length. A newspaper report on abortion and live births describes it:

It involves dismembering the fetus while still in the womb, which eliminates any possibility of live birth. It is a relatively new procedure in late abortions and is generally believed to be among the safest for

20

women and the least psychologically painful. However, it is also generally considered the most traumatic for doctors and staff. . . . [The use of this method] in second trimester abortions [twelfth to twenty-fourth week] has increased greatly in recent years.[3]

While in these three methods the child always dies, there are other methods that generally result in the death of the child, but occasionally result in a live birth:

Saline Solution or Salt Poisoning:

This method is generally used after thirteen weeks of pregnancy. A long needle is inserted through the mother's abdomen and a strong salt solution is injected directly into the amniotic fluid that surrounds the child. The salt is swallowed and "breathed" and slowly poisons the baby, burning his skin as well. The mother goes into labor about a day later and expels a dead, grotesque, shriveled baby. Some babies have survived the "salting out" and were born alive.[4]

"It takes over an hour to slowly kill a baby by this method."[5] Another description of this procedure explains:

A very long needle pierces the skin near the belly button and is driven through the abdomen into the womb and amniotic sac (the bag of water surrounding the swimmer). If the preborn does not push the needle away (which they are often known to do) about one hundred and fifty cc's of his fluid environment are removed to be replaced by the deadly saline solution.

Sometime during the next hour comes the most difficult part (and the part most likely not to be told to the woman considering abortion). More difficult than making The Choice, more difficult than seeing that huge needle bearing down on the stomach, is the time when the saline begins to affect the preborn and s/he begins to react to it with the basic tools for survival used by every living creature—fight or flight. The preborn kicks, thrusts, and writhes. Soon, since s/he can neither fight the poison nor run from it, the convulsions begin. The death throes of the preborn can be very uncomfortable for the mother; she can . . . feel . . . them [if the child is 20 weeks old or more]. There is no escape for her either. After the preborn dies labor begins, followed by delivery of the infant and the afterbirth (that is, if all goes according to plan).[6]

Prostaglandin Chemical Abortion:

This . . . form of abortion . . . uses chemicals developed and sold by the Upjohn Pharmaceutical Company. . . . These hormone-like compounds are injected or otherwise applied to the muscle of the uterus, causing it to contract intensely, thereby pushing out the developing baby. Babies have been decapitated during these abnormal contractions. Many have been born alive.[7]

Hysterotomy or Cesarean Section Abortion:

Used in the last trimester of pregnancy, the womb is entered by surgery through the wall of the abdomen. the tiny baby is removed and allowed to die by neglect or sometimes killed by a direct act.[8]

Is Abortion Killing?

Is abortion the killing of a preborn child? That it is called removal does not mean that it is not also killing. There are essentially three types of cases here.

First, abortion may be removal of the child by killing him or her. The ultimate intention is removal, but it is carried out by a method that is in fact killing, such as dismembering or poisoning. Hence abortion in such cases is killing: the method of "removal" kills the child.

It is sometimes said, "We only want to remove the child, not kill her, though she may die as a result." Where the first three methods are used (D & C, suction, D & E), this is hardly plausible. One "removes" the child by a method that cannot be anything other than killing, even if one's interest lies in removal rather than in death. And where the next two methods are used (saline and prostaglandin) and result in death, the same applies; for example, one kills the child by poisoning and burning.

Second, there are some cases in which the distinction between removal and killing has meaning, namely hysterotomy, which is very rare, and those cases, also rare, when saline and prostaglandin result in live births. I will deal with these cases shortly. They constitute rare exceptions to the general rule that abortion is indeed the killing of a child.

Third, termination of pregnancy may sometimes be carried out with the explicit purpose of killing the child. This is explained by Steven L. Ross, who points out that abortion is not, in many cases, abandonment of the child, or merely wanting him removed, but rather wanting him dead. He says:

If upon entering a clinic women were told, "We can take the fetus out of your womb without any harm to you or it, keep it alive elsewhere for nine months, and then see it placed in a good home," many would, understandably be quite unsatisfied. What they want is not to be saved from "the inconvenience of pregnancy" or "the task of raising a certain (existing) child"; what they want is *not to be parents*, that is, they do not want there to *be* a child they fail or succeed in raising. Far from this being "exactly like" abandonment, they abort precisely to avoid being among those who later abandon. They cannot be satisfied *unless* the fetus is killed; nothing else will do.[9]

Obviously abortion means killing the child in such cases. On the whole, apart from the rare instances where there are live births, abortion is the killing of the child. It is a deliberate and intentional killing; either because one wants the child dead, or because one chooses a method of removal that in fact constitutes killing.

A Table of Comparisons:
Status of Child and Method of Abortion

The following table provides the baby's stage of development when he is destroyed by the various methods of abortion.[10]

Number of Weeks	Status of Development	Type of Abortion
2.5	Blood cells, heart.	
3	Foundation for child's brain, spinal cord, and entire nervous system. Eyes begin to form.	
3.5	Heart starts first pulsations.	
4.5	The three main parts of the brain are present. Eyes, ears, nasal organs, digestive tract, and gall bladder are forming.	
5.5	Heartbeat essentially like that of an adult.	

6   Brain waves noted.

7   A "well-proportioned small scale
                baby." Brain configuration like
                adult brain sends out impulses that
                coordinate functions of other organs.
                Nervous system well developed.
                The heart beats sturdily. Familiar
                external features and all internal
                organs of the adult. If the area of
                the lips is stroked, he responds
                by bending his upper body to one
                side and making a quick backward
                motion with his hand.

8.5   Eyelids and palms of hand sensitive
                to touch. If eyelid is stroked, child
                squirms. If palm is stroked, fingers
                close into a small fist.

9   All structures completed; only devel-
                opment and growth from now on.
                Entire body sensitive to touch, except
                sides, back, and top of head. Child
                moves spontaneously without being
                touched.

10   Threefold increase in nerve-
                muscle connections. If forehead
                is touched, he can turn his head
                away. Arm movements, bending the
                elbow and wrists independently.

11   Facial expressions similar to his
                parents. Fingernails appear. Eyelids
                close over eyes.

12   Baby can move his thumb in opposi-
                tion to his fingers. He swallows
                regularly. He moves gracefully. (All this
                before the mother feels any movement.)

Suction   D & C

13	He can kick his legs, turn his feet, curl his toes, make a fist, suck his thumb, bend his wrist, turn his head, frown, open his mouth, press his lips tightly together. He drinks amniotic fluid.	
16	Weight increases six times since week 12. He is 8-10 inches tall.	
22	He is now about one foot tall, weighs one pound. Fine baby hair begins to grow on his eyebrows and his head. He sleeps and wakes just as he will after birth.	
38	End of time in the womb; some babies are born before 38 weeks.	

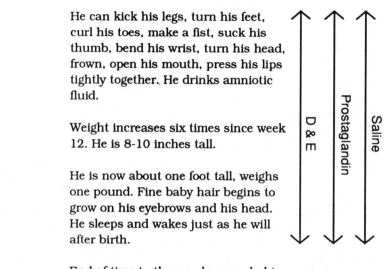

Abortion as a Form of Infanticide

Abortion is a moral evil because it is a form of infanticide: the killing of a small child. One usually thinks of infanticide as the killing of a born child. But the killing of a preborn child is not any different. He is hidden from view, he is smaller, more dependent, more fragile. But he is a real person, just like the born child. He is simply at an earlier stage of his life and development. If it is wrong to kill him later (post-birth infanticide) it is equally wrong earlier (prebirth infanticide).[11]

The moral equivalence of infanticide (after birth) and abortion (before birth) is illustrated clearly in the Kamchadal practice: "The Kamchadal of northern Siberia . . . have practitioners who specialize in killing a fetus through the wall of the abdomen, during the last stages of pregnancy. This may result in a stillbirth or in the birth of an injured but living infant that is killed forthwith."[12]

Is this abortion or infanticide? It is abortion because the child is killed while still in the womb. It is infanticide because a person aims a knife or dagger directly at a child in order to kill him, a child whose presence is obvious by the bulge in the mother's abdomen, a child who could be seen and touched except for the abdominal wall that shields him. It is infanticide because it is killing a baby who is right there.

What this practice shows with unmistakable clarity is a practical identity of abortion and infanticide. It is not really one rather than the other. It is a form of abortion that vividly displays the identity of abortion and infanticide, and precludes any attempt to draw a line between them rationally.

What the Kamchadal practice amounts to is simply early infanticide: one doesn't even wait for the child to be born. What are called abortions, such as saline injections, D & C, and D & E are basically Kamchadal-like practices carried out earlier, and with different instruments. In D & C, for example, the knife has to be carefully inserted into the womb, because the baby is hidden away and not protruding as in the Kamchadal practice. In other words, it is easier to do a late Kamchadal because the baby is protruding in his mother's abdomen; it is more difficult to do an early Kamchadal (e.g., D & C or suction) because the baby is more remote. But morally, there is nothing that differentiates them.

Abortion is infanticide. Whether the child is killed while still in the womb or after she has emerged from the womb is morally irrelevant. It is the same child before and after.

Is Abortion Murder?

Suppose someone intentionally kills an adult to get him out of the way (an innocent person, not an attacker). That surely would be murder. Suppose it was not an adult, but a child. Would that not be equally a case of murder? Size, age, level of development are irrelevant here. Suppose it is a very small child, a baby just born. Suppose the child is not yet born, but about to be born. Suppose he still has a month to go before birth. More than a month. All of these refer to different points on the same human continuum. It is the same person throughout, only smaller, less developed, and sometimes out of sight, in the earlier stages. If it is murder at a later stage, it is also murder at an earlier stage. Merely being in another place (the womb), and smaller, cannot take away the reality of murder. Abortion is the killing of an innocent human being: murder.

To substantiate the thesis that abortion is murder, some points of clarification are in order. First, murder is the *intentional* killing of an innocent person. Not all causing of death of innocent persons is intentional, thus murder. Suppose I'm driving a school bus with twenty-nine children, on a treacherous mountain road, going down a steep incline. The brakes fail, and the bus is about to plunge down the abyss and kill all thirty of us. The only way I can avoid this catastrophe is by quickly veering sharply to one side. Unfortunately a person is walking there, and I will hit him, causing his death. It is too late to warn him. If I veer the bus sharply to the side, I cause his death, tragically. But I do not kill him intentionally. And so I do not commit murder.

Second, murder is the intentional killing of an *innocent* person. If the only way I can defend myself, or another, from a murderous attacker is by killing him, I kill in defense, which is not murder. Innocent in this context means non-aggressor; it does not imply lack of moral guilt in other matters (though that is in fact the case with regard to the child in the womb).

Both of these, intentional killing and killing an innocent person, clearly apply to abortion. The child is absolutely innocent. He is not an attacker. He is in his natural place. Abortion is the deliberate and intentional killing of this innocent person.

Third, it is important to distinguish clearly between murder as applying to *actions*, and as applying to *persons*, making them guilty, or murderers. Thus, to say that abortion is murder is to classify the *action* of killing an innocent preborn child as murder; it does not make a judgment about the *personal guilt* on the part of the woman, the doctor, and those who assist. In saying, quite generally, that A's killing of B is murder, the action is characterized as murder—as opposed to justified killing (e.g., self-defense), or unjustified killing, which is nonetheless not murder (e.g., a soldier who kills in an unjust war). In characterizing the action as murder, the question remains whether the moral guilt of the agent is that of a murderer. It may or may not be, due to extenuating circumstances. A person who is terribly frightened may shoot someone in desperation. The act is murder; the person is less guilty than someone who kills intentionally without being frightened. Thus, two people may perform what is morally the same act (e.g., killing someone to get him out of the way), but one is more guilty than the other. The first may realize with full clarity the wrongness of the action; the second may be in a confused state of mind, half realizing it is wrong, half trying to justify to himself that it is right, or not so bad. The first may act entirely on his own initiative; the second may be under strong pressure to do the killing. Clearly such differences among agents are to be found in the practice of abortion. Therefore, to say that abortion is murder is to say that the action of killing a child in the womb is murder, just as any other intentional killing of an innocent person is murder.

Does a doctor who performs an abortion in order to benefit the woman commit murder if his motive is to help her? Is this not a good motive? How then can the action be murder?[13]

In Dostoyevsky's novel *Crime and Punishment*, Raskolnikov kills an old woman so that he can distribute her money to the poor. Good motive? Perhaps. But the fact that he intentionally kills an innocent person makes it murder, good motive or not. To point to a good motive is to refer to the end; the means are murder nonetheless. If I kill an innocent person for you in order to get him out of the way and thereby save you serious hardship, I may be motivated by good intentions, but my action is still murder. This is exactly what happens in the case of a doctor who performs an abortion: good motives or not, he commits murder.[14]

Does a woman who has an abortion commit murder? Some women are literally coerced into their abortions and are of course entirely innocent of murder. Some women decide voluntarily and then later deeply regret their abortions, exclaiming in some cases, "I have murdered my baby!"[15] They feel they have committed murder. The *action* is murder; were they guilty as *persons*? There are many factors that can mitigate or remove guilt, such as ignorance of what abortion is and altruistic motives; for example, "I would rather abort than cause my parents shame." To a large extent, women are the second victims of abortion, often pressured into it by others, wanting to keep their babies but agreeing to an abortion only because they see no realistic alternative.[16]

Whatever the status of the doctor's motives, and the woman's motives and circumstances, the *action* of abortion, as the deliberate killing of a small child, is murder.

Fourth, in saying that abortion is murder, we speak of such an act in the moral, not the legal, sense. Whether a given act of intentionally killing an innocent person is legally murder or not depends of course on the status of the law. Where such killing is allowed under the law it is, of course, not murder in the legal sense. Thus the Nazi extermination process was not legally murder, but it was obviously murder in the sense that is really important, the moral sense. The Nazi extermination program was the mass killing of innocent persons who could not defend themselves, who were in some respects different or seen as different, in order to get them out of the way—a perfect description of abortion today.

That something is allowed by law, or even mandated by it, does not settle the moral question. Intentionally killing an innocent person, at whatever age, and in whatever location, is morally an act of murder. No law can alter that fact.

Finally, it is important to stress the point that abortion is murder. Otherwise one may have the impression that abortion, though wrong, though it is the taking of a human life, is somehow less wrong than ordinary murder. It is not. It is the same thing, morally, as the deliberate killing of a born innocent person.

Objection and Reply: "He Will Never Know the Difference"

A fundamental assumption underlying much of the support for abortion is the idea that the being in the womb may be aborted because he will never know the difference. "If I kill an adult or a child who realizes what is happening, that is, of course, terrible [so goes the assumption], but if I destroy the child in the womb, he will never know it. So what difference can it make to him? He just won't be born, and will never realize it. How can abortion be wrong?"

If the being in the womb is indeed a child, a person, then whether or not he realizes he is being killed is irrelevant. Murder is murder whether the victim realizes what is happening or not. If I kill a born person painlessly in his sleep, he will never wake up. He will never know the difference. But a murder has been committed nonetheless. If a preborn child is killed in his sleep, his state in the womb, he will never wake up to be born; he will never know the difference.[17] But again, a murder has been committed nonetheless.

This is the primary reply, which grants the objector his assumption that the child in the womb is in a state like that of sleep, and will never know the difference. A second reply is this. We do not know that the child will never know the difference. He may feel terrible pain when the abortionist's knife cuts him to pieces. There is strong evidence that this is so, as I shall show in the next chapter.

"Abortions" Resulting in Live Births

A reprint of an article in the *Philadelphia Inquirer* entitled "Abortion: The Dreaded Complication,"[18] reports:

> Something happens in a very small number of abortions, performed relatively late in pregnancy, that no one wants to talk about. It horrifies many of the medical personnel who have encountered it.
>
> What happens is that about once a day somewhere in the U.S., something goes wrong and an abortion results in a *live baby*.[19]

"When a crying baby emerges instead of a lifeless fetus, doctors have a problem with no easy answer."[20] Some examples:

> A baby girl, weighing 1 pound 11 ounces, was born in February 1979 after a saline abortion at Inglewood (Calif.) Hospital. Harbor General Hospital, which is associated with UCLA and is fully equipped to care

for premature babies, was called to help, but the neonatal rescue team did not respond. The infant died after three hours.[21]

January 1969. Stobhill Hospital, Glasgow, Scotland: A custodian heard a cry from a paper bag in the snow beside an incinerator. He found a live baby. It was taken inside and cared for in the hospital's operating theater but died nine hours later. The infant's gestational age had been estimated at 26 weeks by the physician performing the abortion. It was actually closer to 32 weeks. No efforts were made to check for signs of life before the aborted baby was discarded. No charges were filed.[22]

[In another case,] the abortion, induced by an injection of prostaglandin, a substance that stimulates muscle contraction and delivery of the fetus, was filmed for use as an instructional film. The film showed the three-pound infant moving and gasping. . . . A nurse and a medical student testified that they had noticed signs of life. No charges were filed.[23]

[Finally, there is the case of] an abortion live birth in the mid-70s in a Florida hospital. The infant was dumped in a bedpan without examination, as was standard practice. "It did not die," the nurse said. "It was left in the bedpan for an hour before signs of life were noticed. It weighed slightly over a pound."

The baby remained in critical condition for several months, but excellent care in a unit for premature infants enabled it to survive. The child, now five years old, was put up for adoption. The nursing supervisor, who has followed its progress, said she has pictures of the youngster "riding a bicycle and playing a little piano."[24]

Unfortunately, this last case represents an exception. Most of these babies die. Some are too immature to survive. Some are too severely injured by the abortion process. Some are directly killed. Many are left to die. "This is happening all over the place," says a California prosecutor. "Babies that should live are dying because callous physicians let them die."[25]

The evil of abortion, the moral equivalent of infanticide, is starkly illustrated when we analyze the phenomenon of live births. If a live birth occurs after an attempted abortion (or a hysterotomy), there are basically three things that may be done.

First, the medical staff may deliberately kill the child. As one obstetrician describes it, "You want to know how they kill him? They put a towel over his face so he can't breathe. And by the time they get him to the lab, he is dead."[26] This is obviously murder, infanticide, a clear-cut evil. What should be noted is that if the abortion procedure carried out before was done with the intention of killing the child then the deliberate killing of the child after a live birth is perfectly consistent with it. If one does not succeed before, one does so now, and finishes the job. If the child is to be killed, it makes no difference morally whether this is started and finished in the womb, or started there and finished outside the womb. The moral equivalence of abortion and murder of a born child stares us in the face.

Abortion is sometimes carried out with the explicit purpose of killing the child (see note 9). Essentially the same point is made by Dr. Thomas F. Kereny, a New York expert on abortions: "You have to have a feticidal [fatal] dose of saline solution, . . . It's almost a breach of contract not to. Otherwise, what are you going to do—hand her back a baby having done it questionable damage?"[27]

Second, the medical staff may neglect the child; throw him out alive in the trash for example, and thus let him die. Again, there is a moral consistency. It corresponds to abortion as removal of the child, by the methods described above. Throwing her out in the trash is simply more of the same. It is an expression of the idea that the child is worth nothing, and can therefore be disposed.

In both cases, the procedures after a live birth illustrate the horror and clear-cut wrongness of abortion. They are the logical, natural sequences to the original act. If we are appalled by the deliberate killing of a child or his callous abandonment after a live birth, we should be equally appalled by the procedure that does the same to him before his birth: abortion.[28]

Third, the medical staff may make every effort to save the child. This is of course what should be done. But if it is, it stands in direct contradiction to what was done before in the abortion or the attempted abortion. First one tries to kill the child or one removes him by a procedure that is in fact killing him in most cases. Then one makes an about-face, and tries desperately to save him. Here is an incredible inconsistency. If the child is now worth saving, he should not have been subjected, just moments before, to a procedure that in almost all cases would have killed him. The evil of abortion as death-dealing comes out again, this time in its contrast to concern for the child in trying to save him.

Why the double standard? Because the child is now born? But why should his location have any moral bearing? He is the same child before and after birth. It should not be thought right to kill him simply because he is no longer a burden on the woman. Is it thought right merely because abortion is legal, whereas killing a born child is illegal? Are we going to do whatever the law allows, regardless of its moral status? Slavery was once legal in the United States: that hardly made it moral.

Is abortion the killing of a child? In almost all cases it is, for one either intends to kill him and does so; or one intends to remove him by a procedure that in fact kills him. In a few cases the child is born alive, despite the abortion, but is then deliberately killed, or allowed to die by neglect; or the child dies despite all efforts to save him, after being fatally wounded by the abortion procedure, or because he is born too soon to be able to survive outside his natural habitat. In all these cases it is clear that abortion means killing the child.

The very few cases where an abortion leads to a live birth, followed by intense and successful efforts to save the child, do not constitute a significant exception to this statement. Abortion is still a procedure undertaken with the intention of killing the child or removing him by a procedure that in fact kills him. This is enough to make abortion murder. The few isolated instances in which the victim survives, and is then successfully cared for, does not alter the nature of this action as an act of killing.

There is an outcry today against child abuse. It is plain that abortion is one of the worst forms of child abuse.

3

Does Abortion Cause Pain to Its Victim?

A Review of the Methods

To determine whether abortion causes pain to its victim, I will review the methods of abortion.

(1) *D & C or Dilation and Curettage.* The child, seven to twelve weeks old, is cut to pieces by a sharp knife.

(2) *Suction.* The child, also seven to twelve weeks old, is torn to pieces by a suction machine, twenty-nine times as powerful as a home vacuum cleaner.

Wouldn't any sentient being with functioning nerve endings and a nervous system feel pain, probably excrutiating pain, when subjected to such procedures? As I will show, the child at this stage has functioning nerve endings and a nervous system sufficient for feeling pain.

(3) *D & E or Dilation and Evacuation.* As in D & C, the child, now much larger and more fully developed, is cut to pieces by a sharp knife. "This procedure requires the inflicting of innumerable knife wounds until death results. It takes about ten minutes."[1] In the booklet *Fetal Pain and Abortion: The Medical Evidence,* we read:

> D & E abortions are performed after the 12th week of pregnancy (and are performed up to and including the period of viability) when fetal bones are too large and brittle and the size of the fetus is too great for standard first trimester abortion techniques. D & E involves the progressive dismemberment of the fetus prior to extraction in order to facilitate removal of the fetal parts from the uterus. The slicing and

crushing involved in dismemberment of the fetus in D & E abortions would obviously excite pain receptors and stimulate the neural pathways, thereby evoking an aversive response in the fetus whose central nervous system is functioning. It must be concluded, therefore, that the fetus suffers pain as the result of D & E abortion.[2]

This booklet is by Dr. Vincent J. Collins, with Dr. Steven R. Zielinski and attorney Thomas J. Marzen. Dr. Collins is Professor of Anesthesiology at Northwestern University and the University of Illinois, and author of *Principles of Anesthesiology*, one of the leading medical texts on the control of pain.

(4) *Salt Poisoning or Saline Solution*. Here the child is older (thirteen weeks or more), and thus more developed, and the procedure takes longer (one to two hours), so the amount of pain is undoubtedly much greater. The child is bathed in a chemical solution that poisons him and burns his skin. Curt Young writes of the effect of saline solution on the child:

Because the salt is so concentrated, it chemically burns human tissue. The child assaulted with saline looks as though he has succumbed to an attack with napalm. Much of the outer skin has simply been burned away.

No one can imagine how excruciating the pain is. We do know that physicians recognize immediately the effect of instilling saline into the woman's gut rather than the amniotic sac. The pain is so unbearable the client may throw herself off the table. This is exactly what the unborn child does in his mother's womb. In fact the mother can feel this:

" . . . Once they put in the saline there is no way to reverse it. And for the next hour and a half I felt my daughter thrash around violently while she was being choked, poisoned, burned, and suffocated to death. I didn't know any of that was going to happen. And I remember talking to her and I remember telling her I didn't want to do this, I wished she could live. And yet she was dying and I remember her very last kick on her left side. She had no strength left.

"I delivered my daughter whose name is now Charmaine Marie. She was 14 inches long. She weighed over a pound and a half. She had a head of hair and her eyes were opening."[3]

[Another report tells us that] saline abortions cause the fetus to feel "the same agony as an adult who has suffered burns over 80% to 90% of his body." . . . The fetus squirms, throws himself around, and shows a total grimacing pattern of withdrawal."[4]

(5) *Prostaglandin.* The child is subjected to violent muscle contractions as he is forced out of the womb. Some babies have been decapitated. Another factor: "The method of abortion involving the introduction of prostaglandin into the mother's system may bring about death of the fetus by constricting the circulation of the blood and/or impairing the heart function. Pain analogous to that of a person experiencing a heart attack can be assumed."[5]

Death for the child by prostaglandin may be a long agony: "Another intended effect of this chemical is the induction of labor so that the woman delivers a stillborn infant much as she would be induced to deliver a live one. In this method, then, the infant dies very gradually (maybe over a two-day period) from severe cardiovascular complications."[6]

The Conditions for Feeling Pain

When we see another person brutally cut by an ax, screaming and bleeding, we know he is in pain, even though we do not perceive his or her pain directly. Pain is known to exist, or can be inferred, when (a) functioning neurological structures necessary for pain sensations exist, (b) there is overt behavior expressive of pain, (c) there is a cause for pain.[7]

Elements (a) and (b) are necessary for pain, and they are also sufficient for us to establish or infer its existence; element (b) provides additional evidence, but is not necessary for inferring that pain exists. Condition (c) is certainly fulfilled in these methods of abortion: the sharp knife, the suction machine, the chemical solution that poisons and burns, the violent muscle contractions. Element (b) is also present in some of these procedures: "I felt my daughter thrash around violently while she was being choked, poisoned, burned, and suffocated to death." The crucial question to be examined is whether condition (a) is fulfilled.

The Medical Evidence That the Child Feels Pain

What are the neurological structures necessary to feel pain? The booklet, *The Medical Evidence* states that three elements are required: "Pain receptive nerve cells, neural pathways and the thalamus."[8] The thalamus is a portion of the brain that "lies above the spinal cord and brainstem, but below the cerebral cortex."[9] The cortex is the seat of higher mental functions. It is very significant, in the present context, that

the presence of a functioning cortex is not necessary to pain sensation. Even complete removal of the cortex does not eliminate the
sensation of pain; no portion of the cortex, if artificially stimulated,
results in pain sensation. It follows, therefore, that neither the
presence of the cortex nor transmission of pain impulses to the cortex
are essential to pain sensation. When the cortex (which develops and
functions later in human gestation than the thalamus) is involved in
a pain response, it generates elaborated aversive behavior and adds
psychological and cognitive components to pain sensation.[10]

The functioning neurological structures necessary to suffer pain are
developed early in a child's development in the womb.

Functioning neurological structures necessary for pain sensation are
in place as early as 8 weeks, but certainly by 13 1/2 weeks of gestation.
Sensory nerves, including nociceptors, reach the skin of the fetus
before the 9th week of gestation. The first detectable brain activity
occurs in the thalamus between the 8th and 10th weeks. The
movement of electrical impulses through the neural fibers and spinal
column takes place between 8 and 9 weeks gestation. By 13 1/2
weeks, the entire sensory nervous system functions as a whole in all
parts of the body. . . .[11]

That functioning neurological structures necessary for pain are in
place between eight and 13 1/2 weeks corroborates and supplements the
Amicus Curiae statement that in the seventh week, "the brain configuration is already like the adult brain," that "brain waves have been noted at
forty-three days (6.14 weeks)," and particularly, "After the eighth week
no further primordia will form: *everything* is already present that will be
found in the full term baby."
     If a full-term baby can feel pain, then it is reasonable to infer that a
baby that is essentially like her, one in whom everything is already
present that will be found in the full-term baby, must also feel pain when
she is destroyed by the violence of abortion. Recall also, *"Dr. Still has noted
that electroencephalographic waves have been obtained in forty-three to
forty-five day old fetuses, and so conscious experience is possible after this
date."* [12] With conscious experience, or soon after, comes the possibility
of feeling pain.
     The development of the central nervous system leading to "function-
ing neurological structures necessary for pain sensations" at an age
between 8 to 13 1/2 weeks begins early in the child. As was stated before,
"commencing at eighteen days the developmental emphasis is on the
nervous system"; and "by the end of the twentieth day the foundation of

the child's brain, spinal cord and entire nervous system will have been established."

Turning to element (b), overt behavior expressive of pain, *The Medical Evidence* booklet tells us: "Concurrent with the development of the sensory structures is the emerging responsive behavior of the fetus. By the end of the 5th week a tap on the mouth of the fetus will cause the lips to draw back."[13]

The *Amicus Curiae* states:

> In the sixth to seventh weeks, nerves and muscles work together for the first time. If the area of the lips, the first to become sensitive to touch, is gently stroked, the child responds by bending the upper body to one side and making a quick backward motion with his arms . . .
>
> In the ninth and tenth weeks, the child's activity leaps ahead. Now if the forehead is touched, he may turn his head away and pucker up his brow and frown. . . . In the same week, the entire body becomes sensitive to touch.[14]

The *Medical Evidence* adds:

> By 10 weeks, the palms of the hands are sensitive to touch, and at 11 weeks the face and extremities likewise respond to tactile stimuli. By 13 1/2 weeks, these responses are sufficiently elaborate and sufficiently avoidant to warrant the definite conclusion that the fetus responds aversively, not reflexively. They evidence an integrated physiological attempt to escape noxious stimuli. In response to experiments performed on 12 to 16 week fetuses, movements of the head, body, and limbs have been observed. These movements were vigorous, and consisted of ventro- or dorsoflexion of the trunk, flexion of the limbs, and turning of the head, indicating the presence of acute fetal pain. It is agreed that a fetus must be heavily sedated before intrauterine manipulation, such as transfusions, because such painful stimuli cause the fetus to move, making the procedure difficult.[15]

The *American Medical News* reprint reports, "Physicians know that fetuses feel pain . . . because [among other things]:

> Nerves connecting the spinal cord to peripheral structures have developed between six to eight weeks. Adverse reactions to stimuli are observed between eight and 10 weeks. . . . "You can tell by the contours on their faces that aborted fetuses feel pain," added obstetrician

Matthew Bulfin, M.D., of Lauderdale by the Sea, Florida. He described the case of a 25-year old woman administered a prostaglandin abortion, who expelled her fetus in the middle of the night. Before hospital nurses arrived, she witnessed "the thrashing around and gruesome trauma on his face, and knew that the fetus had suffered."[16]

The Medical Evidence concludes:

When doctors first began invading the sanctuary of the womb, they did not know that the unborn baby would react to pain in the same fashion as a child would. But they soon learned that he would. By no means a "vegetable," as he has so often been pictured, the unborn knows perfectly well when he has been hurt, and he will protest it just as violently as would a baby lying in a crib.[17]

Objections and Replies

First: "Suppose abortion causes pain to the child. Causing someone pain is a frequent occurrence in medicine. It is hardly a reason not to proceed with a medical procedure."

Granted, the causing of pain is a frequent occurrence in medicine. This by itself does not show that a particular instance or type of causing pain (as in abortions) is morally justified. To be justified, at least three conditions must be fulfilled:

(1) There must be an overriding, justifying reason for causing the pain. In a typical abortion, the woman wants to end an unwanted pregnancy. Is this a sufficient reason for cutting a child to pieces, or subjecting her to an hour or more of burning? Suppose we caused the woman that kind of pain to benefit the child. Who would claim that this constituted a justifying reason?

(2) In the normal medical case, the procedure benefits and hurts one and the same person. We do something that causes a person pain but results in an overall benefit for him. If two patients are involved, causing pain becomes much more problematic. Ordinarily, we cannot cause B pain for the sake of A. Only in extreme cases, for example, saving someone's life or preventing permanent paralysis, could one do this. Even then, as the pain becomes greater, the justification becomes more difficult. When the pain for B is very great, such as what may reasonably be inferred from dismemberment or saline burning, and the benefit for A is not commensurate with it, it is clear that this second condition is not met.

(3) Pain should not be inflicted if there is a reasonable alternative. Couldn't an anesthesia be given to the child to eliminate any chance of pain? Killing the child is the primary evil. Causing her needless pain adds to the horror.

Second: "The child in the womb cannot feel pain because he lacks a sufficiently developed physical basis for pain experience. The brain and nervous system may be there but only in rudimentary form; what is missing is maturation."

Third: "The child in the womb cannot feel pain because pain involves not merely physical sensation, but also higher psychological functions, such as a certain degree of self-awareness, memory (of the immediately past sensation), and anticipation (of the immediate future). Pain is a cognitive as well as a physical experience; and for such a cognitive experience to be possible, the cerebral cortex needs to be developed, which is not the case in the preborn child."

In reply to the second and third objections: No one knows that the child cannot feel pain. The possibility of pain is surely there, and must be taken seriously. Specifically:

(1) Look again at the saline procedure described at the beginning of this chapter. "No one can imagine how excruciating the pain is." If the woman is affected by the saline solution, "the pain is so unbearable . . . [she] may throw herself off the table." This solution affects the whole body of the child, for an hour or more, a child that may be fourteen inches long and weigh about a pound and a half. Suppose this child is not sufficiently developed to feel pain to the full extent, quantitatively and qualitatively, that we would feel pain under these conditions. Suppose her pain is only ten or fifteen percent of what our pain would be. Isn't that horrible enough for the child so that we ought to shrink back from inflicting this on her? Hold your hand to a warm-to-hot stove—that is less painful than the pain of being burned all over your body, but surely it is painful enough to shrink back from. Hold your hand to the stove for just ten seconds—that is much less than one hour, but painful enough! Similar consideration applies to D & E, where a well-developed child is cut to pieces. Perhaps she feels much less pain than you would. But ten to twenty percent of that is horrible enough.

(2) In regard to the point that the cortex is not sufficiently developed to allow for the cognitive elements in pain experience, it is possible that this may increase, rather than decrease, the intensity of the pain:

While the likelihood of weak participation by the cerebral cortex will work against the magnification of the pain, there will also be an absence of the inhibitory input from the brain which modulates and balances the sensory input in more developed beings. Consequently, the possibility exists of smaller and weaker sensory inputs having the same effect which later is achieved only by larger and stronger sensations.[18]

(3) The risk argument: Suppose there is some doubt in the minds of some people: "We do not know that the child feels pain." To which we must immediately add: "And we do not know that the child does not feel pain!" The evidence presented here—the presence of nerve endings and a functioning nervous system, the sharp knife or chemical solution, and the child's agitated attempt to escape—makes it at least extremely likely that the child does feel pain, probably excruciating pain. We cannot risk causing such pain!

A deer is eaten alive by a tiger; a baby seal is clubbed and left to die on the ice. One might argue that it is not known for sure if such animals feel pain; perhaps they are not enough like us to feel pain as we do. But they are enough like us to make it overwhelmingly likely that they do feel terrible pain. The same applies to the preborn child.

We shrink back from the risk of causing pain to animals because we identify with them: "If I were in his place I would not want to suffer such pain." If we identify with the child, we must say the same thing.

Would you do something that might cause terrible pain to a loved one? Even if the probability of pain was fairly low? If the probability of pain is as high as it is for the preborn child subject to the knife or chemical solution of abortion, one would certainly not risk the pain. What is true for the born loved one should also be true for the preborn child. It follows that one cannot risk causing the terrible pain probably associated with abortion.

(4) There is some evidence that the child of seven or eight weeks who is the victim of suction or D & C suffers pain in some way. As the child advances to twelve weeks and beyond, the probability that he or she feels pain increases, to the point where it can hardly be doubted. There is an increasing gradation. As the child grows older, the physical elements necessary for suffering pain become more fully developed (brain, peripheral nervous system, etc.). This means that, as the child grows older, there is an increase in: (a) the likelihood that there is pain; (b) the physical intensity of the pain; (c) the psychological intensity of the pain: it is more fully experienced, and at a more conscious level; and (d) the length of time of the painful death, due to the methods of abortion corresponding to the child's size (one to two hours for saline, one to two days for prostaglandin).

Concluding Remarks

This should emphatically not be taken as an argument for early abortions. *There should be no abortions!* For there should be no killing of innocent children. Late abortions simply add a new horror: greater pain. For the same reason, even if all abortions were painless, they would all be wrong. The pain of abortion simply adds a new evil to the evil of killing an innocent child.

> All this [pain] is happening right now, in our own cities, towns, and neighborhoods. If we avert our gaze from this ocean of pain—if we fail to acknowledge the excruciating death agonies of one and a half million tiny victims every year in the U.S. alone (one abortion every twenty-one seconds)—if we close our ears to all those "silent screams," how can we still call ourselves compassionate human beings?[19]

4

On Drawing Lines

Abortion is a moral evil because it is the killing of a child, a person. I have shown (in chapter 1) that the being in the womb is a small child. I now want to reinforce this and show explicitly that he is a child all the way through pregnancy (chapters 4 and 5); that his existence begins at conception-fertilization (chapter 6); and that he is truly a person (chapter 7).

What is in the womb is a real child all the way through pregnancy. A major stumbling block to realizing this is the idea that there is a line to be drawn sometime during pregnancy or at its end, a line marking the end of *potential* human life and the beginning of *actual* human life.

This is not so. Human life is a continuum; all the changes occurring during pregnancy and through birth are changes in the life of one and the same person. I will now develop these points more specifically by examining ten suggested places to "draw a line" between nonperson and person.

Birth

There seem to be four main reasons for suggesting that birth marks the beginning of human life.[1] (1) At birth the child becomes fully independent of his mother. (2) He can be seen and touched. (3) He becomes a member of society. (4) Age is marked from one's day of birth. Are any of these, if true or valid, morally relevant? Do any of them, if true or valid, distinguish persons from nonpersons?

Regarding (1), the dependency of a child on his mother does not make him a nonperson or a lesser person. The dependency of the child on his mother before birth says something about the state of his body, his bodily needs, his fragility; it says something about his phase of existence. It says nothing about him as a person. Dependent persons are persons.

Regarding (2), a child inside an opaque protective shell cannot be seen, nor can any person for that matter. This indicates nothing about the status of his being.

Regarding (3), it is not true that a child in his mother's womb is not a member of society. For a long time preceding birth, the mother knows the child is there, even if she knows little about him. That the child is known to be there and is expected makes him, in a very real sense, a member of human society.

Through instruments of modern technology, especially with fetoscopy and hysteroscopy, we can literally see the child and perform diagnoses and surgery on him. As Dr. Nathanson tells us, "With fetoscopy we are looking at the child eyeball to eyeball, seeing it in living color."[2] Surely anyone whom we can see, and perform surgery on, is a member of our society.

It is true, of course, that the child in the womb is not an active participant in society. He cannot be! Part of the evil of abortion is that it takes unfair advantage of this. He has no voice with which to defend himself. Nonparticipation in society, far from being an argument for abortion, throws further light on its evil. Abortion is the killing of a small person that takes unfair advantage of his not being among us as an active participant—like a shut-in, ignored, out of sight and out of mind.

(4) No one would have a birthday unless he were already there to be born. A birthday is a day of entry. But a person must already *be* in order to enter into something. That we mark our age from our birthday is simply a social custom we have. The Chinese mark a person's age from conception. Ours is a more convenient custom, because one's birth date is easily known. One's conception date is not.

That birth should even be suggested as a line is incredible. For the baby just before birth and just after birth is obviously the same child, and hardly different in appearance. The baby just before birth is fully there, waiting to be born. The doctor listens to his heartbeat, determines his position, and so on. How could a change of location, from inside the mother to outside, change a nonperson into a person? There is also a change in how nourishment (oxygen, food, water) is taken, from direct input to the stomach via the umbilical cord to breathing, eating, and drinking through the mouth. How could such a change transform a nonperson into a person? The irrelevance of birth is clearly explained by Nathanson. Referring to the preborn child as *alpha*, he says:

The most obvious change at birth is breathing, as the lungs are galvanized into activity. Inside the uterus, alpha carries out spontaneous respiratory movements, but the lungs are not expanded since their function is not necessary and they are bathed in amniotic fluid. The routing of blood in the circulatory system and the intake of nutrients and the outgo of wastes are shifted. All other functions of the newborn baby, even crying, may occur within the womb. In terms of metabolism, biochemistry, brain and heart function, and most everything else, birth is an insignificant event, indeed a mythology. At term, i.e., at the end of pregnancy, alpha's growth needs simply outstrip the ability of the placenta to supply food and oxygen, so the lungs and mouth must take over. The organism is put into a different physiological milieu—and nothing more. It is like switching from AC to DC current; the energy connection changes, but the basic mechanics remain the same.[3]

If birth is so irrelevant as a line, why is it nevertheless so widely accepted? I suggest that the reason is not the status of the child, which is the same before and after. Perhaps it is that the preborn child is more dependent on the mother, while after birth he is relatively independent. That is often the reason given for selecting birth as the line. I think it hides a deeper reason; namely, the claim that a woman has "a right over her body," in the sense of "a right to an abortion." If one assumes this right, it becomes plausible to say that a woman may remove a being that is inside her and burdensome to her. But if such a removal is killing, and killing persons is wrong, it must be held that this being is not a person.

Thus the impetus to make birth the line stems not from anything to do with the child, but from the desire to get rid of him. He is in the way, and so he must be labeled the sort of being who may justifiably be terminated. And he is in the way until birth. That is why birth is selected as the place to draw the line.

Viability

A second point suggested to draw the line between person and nonperson is viability. Viability refers to the child's ability to live outside the womb. Why would one think that a postviability child is be be counted as a full person, a real baby, while a previability child should not be counted as a real person?[4] Three possible reasons come to mind. First (it is said), the child in the early stages, prior to viability, is part of his mother's body. In being viable he shows his independence, that he is a distinct being.

Second, the previability child is too intimately involved in the body of his mother to be his own person. Third, the child after viability is too much like a born child to be dismissed as a nonperson, but this is not true of the child in the earlier stages.

The first and second points are simply false. First, the child is not a part of his mother's body. For example, their blood circulations normally do not mix; the child may have a different blood type from the mother; the child may be male, and his male body is obviously not part of his mother's female body. Second, the intimate involvement of the child in his mother's body reflects his dependency on her. But dependency does not affect personhood. He is dependent because he is small and fragile; he needs the protective nest of his mother's womb. This says something about his body, its state of development. It says nothing about his status as a person. Dependence on, and the ensuing involvement in, his mother's body simply reflects the state of his development along the continuum of human life.

In short, a previability child is simply one who has a greater need for his natural incubator, his mother's womb, than a postviability child does; just as a fragile, premature baby has a greater need for an artificial incubator than a stronger baby does. Both are real babies, both are equally persons.

Third, even a child before viability (at ten weeks) looks like a familiar baby. "By the end of the seventh week [long before viability at present] we see a well-proportioned small-scale baby."[5] So this point does not establish viability as the place to draw the line. Much more important, however, is that it creates confusion. The fact that the baby in his very early stages doesn't look familiar to us, does not resemble what we are accustomed to as a baby, says very little about him. He is what he is, regardless of resemblances. That he is noticeably different from the highly developed baby in middle and late pregnancy and at birth is hardly surprising: he is near the beginning of his development. Looking like a familiar baby means having the physical features of a familiar baby, and these take time to develop. Before this time elapses, a less developed, and therefore a less familiar-looking, baby is just what we should expect.

The irrelevance of viability for the real status of the child becomes even more clear when we consider the following points.

First, viability is not a definite line, much less a morally significant one. It can only properly refer to an extended period of time during which the probability of a child's surviving outside the womb increases. Near the beginning of this time, the child might have only a twenty-five percent chance of surviving, later fifty percent, then seventy-five percent, still later perhaps ninety percent. None of these, even assuming the figure could be acurately assessed, is able to mark the point of viability, and with it the alleged beginning of real human life.

Second, viability is not a real line because it is a constantly changing point. According to Nathanson, writing in 1979, viability is around twenty to twenty-eight weeks.[6] With advances in technology, it will be pushed back farther and farther, perhaps even to point zero with the creation of an artificial womb. That is, viability is a function of advances in medical technology; it has nothing to do as such with the child. It measures our ability to sustain human life, not the status of that life. The same child will be viable given one degree of medical technology, not viable given another. Viability, then, cannot be the determining factor for whether the being in the womb is a real person or not.

Referring to the child in the womb as *alpha*, Nathanson says:

> Viability is the current reflection of medical achievement and is too evanescent to deal with such a fundamental issue. An infant could be "viable" in New York City but not in a rural U.S. town, or in the rural town but not in Bangladesh. Everything is potentially viable; there are only limits of technology to overcome. The lines are shifting, and they will shift to earlier and earlier points. In the future, artificial incubation may make alpha "viable" at any time in pregnancy. The whole concept of viability is currently in danger of obsolescence; one might even say that the concept itself is not viable.[7]

The child may be viable if he is New York City, but not if he is in Bangladesh. Is he not the same being in either place? If abortion is wrong in one place, it is equally wrong in the other place.

Third, the arbitrariness—indeed, the unfairness—of making viability the line at which to say that a real person begins to exist is well expressed by Blumenfeld. Referring to a recent determination of viability, he asks:

> Why choose viability as the cut-off point? The human fetus is not viable before the twenty-fourth week merely because its lungs are not sufficiently developed for outside respiration. Nature decided that lung development could wait because it had nine full months in which to do its work. It gave priority to brain, neural, sensory, skeletal, digestive, and circulatory development before it completed its work on the lungs. So why penalize an unborn infant because nature decided to complete its kidneys before its lungs?[8]

Fourth, viability has to do with environment. That is, a previability child can live only in a certain environment, his mother's womb, while a postviability child can live either in his mother's womb or outside it. For the previability child, this is simply an instance of a general truth: every organism needs its proper environment. A fish can live only in water, not in dry air. A cat can live only in dry air, not in the water. Each is nonviable in the other's proper environment. So too, an adult human being would be nonviable inside a uterus (if we imagine one large enough to hold him). Human beings are not viable in most parts of the universe, because they are too hot, or too cold, or lack oxygen, etc. One class of human beings, those in the early stages of their development, are further restricted in regard to their viability. But this concerns the relation of their bodies to an environment, not the reality of their being as persons. "The decisive objection to viability is that there is no reason to suppose that the fact that a given creature cannot live outside a given environment provides a reason why depriving it of that environment should be totally acceptable."[9] There is still less reason why the creature may be killed in its present environment.

Quickening

Quickening refers to the time when the mother first feels the baby inside her, at approximately sixteen to seventeen weeks. Quickening refers to the mother's perception of the baby's movements; it has nothing to do with the baby himself, who is there long before quickening. In the very early phases of his existence he does not move, but he is there, and that is the important point. Later he moves, but the mother cannot feel the movements; the important point is that he is there. Dr. Liley states:

> Historically "quickening" was supposed to delineate the time when the fetus became an independent human being possessed of a soul. Now, however, we know that while he may have been too small to make his motions felt, the unborn baby is active and independent long before his mother feels him. Quickening is a maternal sensitivity and depends on the mother's own fat, the position of the placenta and the size and strength of the unborn child.[10]

Sensitivity to Pain

Sensitivity to pain might be suggested as a place to draw a line between person and nonperson. After this point the baby suffers pain in being subjected to abortion; before he does not. This surely is a morally relevant difference. But the moral relevance of this line is not the difference between murder and non-murder, but rather between painless murder and painful murder. Painless murder is still murder, a moral evil. Painful murder is a greater evil. So this line simply marks the difference between a moral evil and a greater moral evil.

That sensitivity to pain cannot mark the beginning of the person is too obvious to need much elaboration. Someone who loses his sensitivity to pain through nerve damage is not thereby a nonperson. That the very young preborn do not feel pain is simply an aspect of their gradual development. It says nothing about their status as persons.

Sentience

Richard Werner argues "that being a sentient human being is the relevant criterion for being a fully fledged member of the moral community, for having full moral rights. . . . "[11] The argument is based on the idea "that we have no obligations except when some improvement or impairment of someone's life is involved . . . [and] also that we have a prima facie obligation *whenever* this is involved."[12]

Werner states his argument as follows:

> Simply put, one cannot make a creature's life good or bad, better or worse unless that creature is capable of experiencing and, in particular, capable of experiencing pleasure, satisfaction, happiness, pain, dissatisfaction, or anguish. One cannot help or harm another creature unless that creature is capable of help or harm, capable of having experiences consonant with help or harm. Clearly, a creature that has no experiences is not capable of having experiences consonant with helping or harming the creature. If the creature is destroyed before it becomes sentient, appeal to the better or worse condition of its future experiences is irrelevant. Hence, one cannot have moral obligations to a being that is not sentient and will not become sentient and, thereby, such a being cannot have moral rights.
>
> In the case of a being that is not yet sentient but will become sentient, certainly we can help or harm this being by an action we perform today that will affect the future experiences of the being. However, it would seem that our moral obligations are not to the nonsentient being that now exists. So a being would not have rights until it became sentient.[13]

In reply, the mere addition of sentience cannot turn a nonperson into a person. If there is no person before sentience, adding this feature will not transform it into a person. An insentient frog does not become a person by acquiring sentience. And if there is a person after sentience is acquired, that being must already have been there, as the being who acquires this feature, as the same being who first lacks sentience then has it. Sentience comes about through physical development of the being who is there, before and after sentience is attained.

After sentience is acquired, there is a being who can *function* as a person on an elementary level; for example, he can feel pain. But his *being* a person is not affected by this; he was that already. An adult who is awake can function as a person: feel pain, think, communicate, etc. But he is equally a person, the same person, when he is under anesthesia, even though he cannot then function as a person since he temporarily lacks sentience.

Sentience, then, does not affect the *being* in question (whether person or not), but only a capacity of certain beings (persons, animals) to *function* as sentient beings, for example, feel pain.

To kill a small, very young, nonsentient baby in the womb, or to kill an adult under anesthesia, both are cases of killing a nonsentient being who, were he not killed, would wake up to sentience. The only difference is that the child was never sentient while the adult was. But this makes no moral difference. To kill the child is to deprive him of the only sentient existence he would ever have. If anything, abortion is therefore a still greater evil.

Suppose, through some strange disease, a baby were born insentient and did not acquire sentience until, say, age one. Would it be right to kill such a child after birth? But if not after birth, why before birth? If not when the insentience is abnormal, why when it is normal?

That a baby in the very early phases of her existence in the womb is insentient simply means that she is in a kind of deep sleep. This says something about the level of her development; it says nothing about her as a person. Clearly, sentience is not a place to draw the line. It represents merely the acquisition of another characteristic by the child in the womb, a further dimension of her development.[14]

Familiar Human Form

It is also argued that the line between nonperson and person may be drawn at the development of a familiar human form. In the very early stages of his development, a human being lacks certain features. He will soon have, and maintain, these through the remainder of his time in the womb and after birth. These features make him look familiar to us, because he resembles born persons. What is important here is to realize that familiar human form is a relative concept. After certain developments are completed, the child looks familiar to us, because he looks more and more like us. In reality, he is the same being all along. His status as a person is unaffected by these physical developments and by how these developments appear to us.

Before certain developments are completed, the child in the womb lacks *familiar* human form. But he does have human form, he does look human; that's what we all looked like when we were at that stage of our existence. If fetoscopy and hysteroscopy and similar techniques become widespread and more advanced, so that we can all watch tiny babies grow as a matter of course, these babies would begin to look familiar to us. So, familiar human form does not designate a characteristic of the being in the womb, but rather something about us. Since it is not a characteristic of the being in the womb, it cannot mark the time when he becomes a person.

In short, it is not how the child looks to us, or if he is familiar to us, that is important. What is important is his own status, what he really is. He is essentially the same being before and after acquiring (what we now call) familiar human form; if he is a person after, he cannot be a nonperson before merely because he looks unfamiliar to us. Hence, familiar human form cannot be the place to draw the line. It is merely an aspect of the development of the child in the womb, the same child all the way through the various phases of development.[15]

Functioning Brain

Baruch Brody holds that it is the presence of a functioning brain that marks the beginning of a human person's existence. He argues:

> The property of having a functioning brain (or, at least, a brain that, if not functioning, is susceptible of function) is one that every human being must have because it is essential for its being human; by the time that an entity acquires that property, it has all the other properties that are essential for being human; the class of human beings is a natural kind; therefore, when the fetus acquires that property, it becomes a human being.[16]

This, Brody says, occurs at about the end of the sixth week. Before that, he holds, the being in the womb is not a human being. He offers two arguments to support his view "that the fetus becomes a human being about six weeks after conception."[17] Both rest on "the fact that electroencephalographic waves are noticeable at that time, and therefore the fetal brain must clearly be functioning."[18] The first of these arguments is:

> The absence of electroencephalographic waves has come to be regarded by physicians as the indicator of the moment of death, the moment at which the entity in question is no longer a human being. So on grounds of symmetry, it would seem appropriate to treat the appearance of such waves as the indicator of the moment at which the entity in question becomes a human being.[19]

The second argument is:

> One of the characteristics essential to a human being is the capacity for conscious experience, at least at a primitive level. Before the sixth week, as far as we know, the fetus does not have this capacity. Thereafter, as the electroencephalographic evidence indicates, it does. Consequently, that is the time at which the fetus becomes a human being.[20]

The first argument, the *symmetry argument*, states that if the absence of brain waves indicates the death of a person, his ceasing to exist as a human being, then it must be the presence of such waves that indicates his coming into existence. Before that, when he is in the embryo stage of his existence, he is, according to this argument, not a human person. There are several reasons why this argument is fallacious.

First, in an adult, the loss of certain brain waves, indicating the cessation of brain activity, implies (or is taken to imply) death.[21] But the absence of brain waves in an embryo obviously does not indicate that he is dead. Far from it, he is very much alive. In fact, it would be very strange if he did have brain waves. In an adult, brain death (defined with sufficient precision) implies death of the whole body, of the person. This simply does not apply to the embryo. And the reason for this asymmetry is plain: an adult needs a brain to live, an embryo does not. The loss or absence of brain activity is not in itself crucial for deciding life or death, the presence or absence of a person. It is only crucial for certain human beings, namely those who have reached phases of development where the presence of brain activity is essential for life. The embryo has simply not reached this phase, so for him the absence of brain activity is not crucial. That is, it is not the lack of something essential for life but, on the contrary, something perfectly normal.

Second, another aspect of this asymmetry is that in an embryo there is the mere *absence* of brain activity, while in an older person or an adult who no longer has brain activity, there is something essentially different: there is the *death* of the brain, the dying of an organ that had been alive. There is simply no symmetry between a dead brain and the absence of a brain, or between a brain that no longer functions because it has fatally deteriorated and the absence of a functioning brain that has not yet developed, because the time is not ripe.

Third, in an adult the cessation of brain functioning must be irreversible to constitute the death of the person. If the brain is merely temporarily out of order, its role perhaps taken over by machines, then the patient is clearly not dead. If he still has the potential to function as a person (to think, to communicate, etc.), though incapable of functioning at present, then surely he is a person now. But this is precisely what the embryo has: the potential to function as a person, though incapable of this at present. The person with irreversible loss of his brain function has no future on this earth; the embryo indeed has a future. There is clearly a world of difference between no brain activity in the sense of "no more" and in the sense of "not yet." If a human being with irreversible "no more" is dead, it does not follow that a human being whose lack of brain activity has the character of "not yet" is dead, or otherwise not a human being. A human being with "not yet" is simply in an early phase of his existence. He is "not yet" displaying brain functioning because he has not yet reached that phase of his existence where this is appropriate. We throw out food that has lost its nourishing power, that has it "no more"; we do not, however, throw out food that has "not yet" developed its nourishing power. We wait, and give it a chance. This is what we must do with human beings in their embryonic stage.[22]

The second argument advanced by Brody is, "One of the characteristics essential to a human being is the capacity for conscious experience, at least at a primitive level." Since the embryo lacks this capacity, it is not a human being.

This is essentially the same argument as the one previously discussed, that sentience marks the beginning of a human person's existence. We have seen that this is false; that an unsentient person (for example, someone under anesthesia) is as much a real person as one who is sentient. He temporarily lacks a capacity that the rest of us have. This does not change his nature as a person.

We may also say, in a deeper sense, that the child in his embryonic stage does have "the capacity for conscious experience." For he is already the kind of being who normally has conscious experiences. He has the capacity, but it is still dormant, undeveloped. For he now already has what will become his brain; it must unfold, develop, grow, be nourished.[23]

A succinct, and conclusive, refutation of the idea that it is only when a functioning brain is present that a human being comes into existence is that there must already be a human being in existence for the brain to emerge as a functioning organ. *"Only a human being can develop a human brain, a human brain cannot develop before a human being exists."*[24]

Finally, we should be point out that even if Brody's argument for drawing the line at functioning brain were successful, it would be of little help to the abortion cause. That line is at about six weeks, and most surgical abortions take place after that time, beginning at about seven or eight weeks. Such abortions are morally wrong regardless of whether the line should be drawn at six weeks or earlier. The significance of refuting Brody's line is to help gain a clear understanding of the nature of the child in the womb all the way through pregnancy. This applies equally to the three remaining lines to be considered.

Heartbeat

Heartbeat begins by day twenty-five, very early in the life of the child. One might think this an appropriate place to distinguish between a nonperson and a person because it seems that a heartbeat is essential to being alive. But what is really essential to being alive is what results from the heartbeat: circulation of the blood, nourishment of the different parts of the body. If the body can be nourished and sustained in other ways, then a heartbeat is no longer essential to being alive. And this, of course, is what applies to the zygote-embryo before day twenty-five.

A heartbeart is a familiar sign of life, but not an essential one. Even an adult can be alive without a beating heart, if its function is taken over by a heart-lung machine.

A functioning heart is one more aspect of what develops in the growing child as he exists in the womb. He is the same being both before and after; the development of the heart occurs within the growth process that characterizes a child's early existence in the womb. There is no essential difference before and after, just more development after.

Implantation

About seven or eight days after conception, the tiny zygote implants in the wall of the uterus, after floating down the fallopian tube. Nathanson, in *Aborting America*, suggested why implantation might be selected as the beginning of human life: "Biochemically, this is when alpha [the zygote] announces its presence as part of the human community by means of its hormonal messages, which we now have the technology to receive. We also know biochemically that it is an independent organism distinct from the mother."[25]

But clearly the time when a being announces its presence is not identical with the time when it comes into being. It may already *be* before it is *known*; or it may be and be known by one person and not another, or in one way and not another.

Segmentation

The tenth and final point where a line may be drawn between a nonperson and a person is at segmentation. Identical twins develop from a single conceptus, formed at conception-fertilization by the union of sperm and ovum. The conceptus divides and twins result. This can occur up until the time of segmentation, roughly seven to eight days after conception. Hence segmentation marks a real line in human development, but is it the point at which human life begins?

Why might someone think this is so? A human person is essentially one, an absolute individual. A person cannot be split in two. Since the conceptus that divides to form two identical twins obviously does split, it cannot be an individual. Hence it cannot be a person, and a person cannot be said to exist prior to segmentation. Hence (it is argued) segmentation marks the beginning of a human person's existence.

It is certainly true that a person is an individual who cannot be split in any way. But it does not follow from this that segmentation is the place to draw the line, that the individual human person does not exist prior to segmentation.

First, consider the case where twinning does not, and cannot, occur. This is where the conceptus is, and always will be, an individual. Here the problem discussed above does not arise. For there is simply one conceptus who is one individual person. That another conceptus is different, since it has the potential to split, says nothing about the first absolutely single conceptus.

Second, there will be, or can be, twins (or possibly other multiple births) stemming from one conceptus. There is no reason for saying that the individuals who result from the twinning process came into existence at that time, and did not exist prior to it, from the moment of conception-fertilization. Rather, they existed together in one conceptus, and at segmentation (or prior to it) they separated. It is clearly possible for two individual persons to exist somehow bodily joined together, especially at the very beginning of their physical development.

Consider Siamese twins, joined together at the head, or perhaps back to back. There are different degrees of being joined imaginable, and the two individual persons joined together in one conceptus before they divide at segmentation are joined in the closest way imaginable. Just as each of the Siamese twins is an individual person, though joined to another person, so each of the two newly-conceived persons is an individual person, though joined—in this case much more closely—to another individual person. The two individuals joined together in one conceptus are an extreme case of what we see in a much milder form in Siamese twins: two individual persons joined together.

That two individual persons can "co-exist" in one body (hence be present before segmentation) is illustrated vividly in this instance. On the television show "That's Incredible!" on March 2, 1981, an interesting story was told. A person had recurring headaches, which resisted the usual cure. Diagnosis revealed a kind of tumor, which was then removed from his brain area by surgery. It was benign, and it turned out to be a misplaced twin, stunted in growth.

This story is very significant. Consider two sets of twins, and designate them case A and case B. Case A refers to the case on "That's Incredible," from whose brain area this "tumor" was removed. He is a human being from conception; he has a twin who never develops, and breaks off, but remains somehow attached to him. Case B refers to another human being, brought into existence at conception; in his case his twin breaks off at segmentation and develops on his own, into an adult human being, just like his twin. What is different in the two cases is the fate of the second member of the set of twins: in case A this second member remains joined to the first member, while in case B the second member separates and develops on his own. The first members of each set are alike, not only in that each develops into an adult, but also in that each began his life joined to another human being. And, of course, that is the crucial point. In their first days of existence, before the time of segmentation, the twins in cases A and B were not so different. Each was a case of two human beings joined in one body.

If segmentation were the beginning of human existence, it would mean that no human person could exist before segmentation. But the person described on the television show obviously did exist before his segmentation: his being separated from his twin lodged in his brain. It follows that segmentation cannot be held to be the beginning of human existence. Not only is there no reason to believe it is the place to draw the line; there is every reason for saying it cannot be the place to draw the line.

In short, human development is largely a matter of unfolding. The development of the child in the womb, especially at the early stages, up to eight weeks—after which "no further primordia will form; *everything* is already present that will be found in the full term baby"[26]—is a series of unfoldings, of moving from the potential to the actual, on the part of the being who is already an actual reality, whose actual reality underlies these unfoldings, in whom they occur, and of whom they are developments. "Though his parts are not yet fully expressed, a whole new human being is there, and he manifests his fully given reality by growing."[27] The potential for the brain is already there at conception-fertilization, it only needs to unfold. Now this unfolding sometimes includes the unfolding of two separate bodies, in the case of identical twins. Potentially the two bodies are there all along; the actual separation takes some time. Segmentation represents, not the beginning of human existence, but a certain stage of development; when, in the case of identical twins, their bodies actually separate.

Conclusion

Thus at each of the places suggested for drawing the line, the being in the womb is essentially the same on either side of that line. He may be a little larger and a little more developed, but he is the same being, the same human person, before and after. He acquires nothing at any of these suggested places that would transform him into something else, as the fairy-tale frog is transformed into a charming prince. Here would be a radical break, a real place to draw a line.[28] Nothing of this sort occurs at any of these places. Rather, what we have is like the tadpole developing into a mature frog, a development in the life of one and the same being.

What all this means is, among other things, that the often-heard question, "At what point, or stage, in pregnancy does a human person begin to exist?" is a false question. That is, it rests on a false premise: that there is a point or stage during pregnancy (or at its end in birth) at which a human person begins to exist. There is not. The person is there all along.

5

The Agnostic Position and the Gradualist Position

The Agnostic Position

"No one knows when human life begins." Let me call this the *agnostic position.*[1] I offer two basic replies: (1) The position is not tenable. (2) Even if it were tenable, it would not support abortion.

(1) What can it mean to adopt this position? First, it could be said that a person begins to be when the soul is infused into the body (or some similar event), and that no one knows when this occurs. Second, it could mean that we do not know which features make the being in the womb a person or when these features come to be.

First, if a person comes to be at the moment when the soul is infused into the body, then this represents a radical break, before which there is no person, after which there is. That there is such a radical break, and that we can know when it is (conception-fertilization), will be shown in the next chapter. That is one refutation of the agnostic position.

Second, (a) we do know which features make this being a person, namely his identity with the being who is later clearly a person: I was once a being in my mother's womb; I am now that same person. And we do know when this feature comes to be: conception-fertilization.

(b) We also know that a person does not come into being after conception-fertilization, as was shown by refuting each of the proposed lines; none of them marks the beginning of being a person. Thus reply (b) confirms the validity of reply (a).

(c) When those who adopt the agnostic position say we do not know which features make a person or when these features appear, it is likely that they have in mind capacities such as sentience and the relative independence of being able to live outside the womb. But these capacities

57

do not constitute being a person, which is our theme here. (When does human life begin? When does a person come into existence?) Thus, part of the fallaciousness of the agnostic position is a confusion between *being* a person and *functioning* as a person; for example, sentience, thought. This position is agnostic about which features to designate as the beginning of being a person when in fact the features it considers are of significance only with respect to functioning as a person.

(2) Even if the agnostic position were tenable, it would not support abortion. Suppose, for the sake of argument, that we do not know when a person comes into being. There is a gradual development of a being; at an unknown point it becomes a person. Call this point X. Now surely we can specify a point in the life of a human being when it certainly is a person. Call such a point Y. Now consider the stage immediately prior to point Y. Surely there is an extremely high probability that the being is a person already then. As we move backward in time, towards X, that probability, though it diminishes gradually as we go back, still remains very high. It remains a significant probability for the following reasons: (a) It is the same being all the way through, at every point. (b) The changes that occur from point to point are only changes in size and level of development, development of what is already there, the essential structure of the being. This applies to all points. (c) Thus all the points that precede point Y are essentially similar in regard to the significance of the probability that a person is there. Since there is a high probability that the being is a person at the points immediately preceding Y, there must be at least a very significant probability that he is a person at all the earlier points.

Therefore, even if we do not know what point X is, and when it occurs, we do know one very important thing about it: it occurs somewhere along a continuum of development, where every point represents a significant probability that a person is there. So this reply to the agnostic position is essentially very simple: even if we do not have the *certainty* of knowing *precisely* when a person begins to exist (since, by hypothesis, we do not know when X is), we have a continuum—the whole time the being is in the womb—during which there is a *significant probability* that a person exists.

Significant probability can be illustrated in the following way. A person you love is lost at sea. You don't know if he is still alive. But if there is a chance that he is alive, and that he can be found and rescued, you proceed with the rescue efforts. The probability may be small, but you proceed nonetheless. As long as the probability is of some significance, you proceed.

As long as there is a significant probability that human life exists, we must assume it is there, and act accordingly: we cannot kill this being.

If there is someone present, who, as far as you can tell, is either dead or alive, you must treat him as being alive. Even if the probability that he is still alive is low (he has been severely injured and is not moving), you cannot treat him as dead. You must give him the benefit of the doubt. You cannot, for instance, dismember him to get a bodily organ, even if doing so would save the life of another person. As long as death is not certain, a person must be treated as alive. If you were in the position of the victim, and in fact alive, though seemingly dead to an onlooker, you would certainly want to be treated as alive.

Even if it is claimed that the probability is very low that the being in the womb in the early stages is a person, it is still wrong to destroy this being, parallel to the accident victim. We must always give the benefit of any doubt to the presence of human life. Where there is a significant probability, even a low one, that human life exists, we must treat it as such; we must show it respect, we may not destroy it. Therefore, even on the agnostic position, abortions (including very early ones) are wrong, because they destroy a being who deserves our respect.

Any plausibility the agnostic position might have is limited to the very, very early stages of prenatal life, when the being in question is extremely small and does not look like a familiar baby. It is to this time that the argument above mainly applies. Recall that at seven weeks "we see a well-proportioned small scale baby"; and at eight weeks "*everything* is already present that will be found in the full term baby." At this stage it cannot reasonably be doubted that a small child is present. The probability that it is a small person is not just significant, which includes low probabilities as well as high ones, but overwhelming.

The Gradualist Position

Another reaction to the failure to establish a line at which a human person begins to exist is to hold that there is no specific place at which human life begins, that it is a gradual process. At the beginning (so goes the theory) there is no real person, only a potential person; at the end there is a real person. And there is no point at which the one changes into the other. It is gradual development, like day to night and youth to old age. So reads the *gradualist position.*

The gradualist position justifies abortion in this manner: "At the early stages, abortion is either morally justified or only a lesser evil. As one progresses through the stages, abortion becomes progressively more wrong, a more serious evil, until the killing of this being becomes the moral equivalent of killing a born person. Because of this, earlier abortions are more easily justified than later abortions."

The impetus for adopting the gradualist position is not only the recognition of the impossibility of drawing a line, but also the closely related idea that a baby about to be born seems very much like one of us, while a zygote or embryo seems very different and that there is a gradual development from the one to the other. As Foot expresses it:

> One of the reasons why most of us feel puzzled about the problem of abortion is that we want, and do not want, to allow to the unborn child the rights that belong to adults and children. When we think of a baby about to be born it seems absurd to think that the next few minutes or even hours could make so radical a difference to its status; yet as we go back in the life of the foetus we are more and more reluctant to say that this is a human being and must be treated as such.[2]

Corresponding to this is the idea "that abortion . . . become[s] harder and harder to justify as pregnancy proceeds."[3]

The gradualist position is, then, the thesis that "personhood is a quality the developing human creature acquires gradually."[4]

Let me offer three replies to this position. First, the theory is at best a mere hypothesis. It is not known to be true. There is no evidence for it. The quotation from Philippa Foot merely expresses how many people feel about the developing being (namely puzzled). It says nothing about the facts of the matter, whether the being is a person or not, or when and how it comes into being as a person.

To be validly adopted as a theory of the coming into being of persons—and as a basis for deciding the moral question of abortion—the gradualist position would have to be established with an extremely high degree of probability. Failing this, there would be a significant probability that it was false, and therefore a significant probability that human life actually exists during all the stages to which it is applied. As was shown above, we must always give the benefit of any doubt to the presence of human life. Where there is a significant probability (even a low one) that human life is present, we must treat it as such; we may not destroy it.

Second, the theory is not even a reasonable hypothesis. It is false; it cannot possibly be true. Let me bring this out in three closely related ways:

(1) There is a gradual process in the *development* of a person, physical and psychological, but there can be no gradual process in the *being* of a person. Many years ago when I was a child, I was less developed, physically, psychologically, spiritually. But that child was *me*, the same person I am now. No matter how much less developed I was then, I was not less me. I was myself, a fully real person, a whole person. As a small

newborn baby, my development was very incomplete. But it was my development—the development of *me*, a whole person—that was incomplete. If I continue my imaginary journey backward in time, I discover myself as a tiny baby in my mother's womb. Going back farther, I find less and less development, but it is always *me*. The potential for development is all there, and it takes time to actualize. But this occurs in the life of a person. It is I who undergo this development.

The gradualist position points to gradual development. But this refers not to the *being* of a person, but to his capacity to *function* as a person. The growing person gradually becomes conscious, aware of himself and his surroundings, and acquires the capacity to communicate, to think, to make up his own mind, and so forth. So, too, the body gradually develops, mostly during the first seven weeks. All this development takes place in the life of one and the same person, who is there all the way through, who is the being to whom this development applies.

A less developed person is not less of a person. A child of four is not less of a person because he has not yet matured sexually. So too, a baby in the early phases of his existence is not less of a person because he has not yet matured, as he will later on, in the womb and after birth.

(2) There can be no such thing as half a person. If a person does not exist fully as a person, he does not exist at all. He may be only half awake, or only semi-rational; but if he exists, he is a full person. Now consider the gradualist position: At the beginning there is no person, there is only potential; at the end there is a person, and in between a person gradually comes to be. Consider what is roughly the halfway point in this process. What would we have there? A being who is "half-person"? But that is impossible; there cannot be half a person, or a "half-person." A being who is fully a person? Then the theory is abandoned. A being who is not at all a person? Again the theory is abandoned.

In short, if a person comes into being at a certain point during pregnancy, we have one of the lines previously refuted. If he comes into being gradually, there must be some point at which he is, roughly, half there: half person, half nonperson. But that is impossible. Since the gradualist position essentially involves an impossibility, it must be false.[5]

(3) What lies behind the gradualist position is, I think, a certain picture of the development of a being, the "assembly line picture." Imagine an assembly line where cars are made. At the beginning there is relatively little, a frame perhaps, but surely nothing that could be called a car. At the end there is a car; it can be driven off the assembly line by its own power. Where, in between, does the car come into being? There is no specific place; it is a gradual process. There is "less car" in the earlier phases, and "more car" in the later ones. When such a picture is applied

to the being in the womb, the gradualist position results. But there is a fallacy here: a person is *totally unlike* a car, and the gradualist picture completely falsifies the being of a person, and with it his gradual development. A car is constituted by its parts, in proper relationship to each other. It comes into being when these parts are all there, assembled properly. A person is not made up of parts; if he were, there could be such a thing as "half a person," namely half those parts.

Consider a newborn baby. The reality of this being is not a sum of parts properly ordered, as in a car. She is a *person*, a small, young person, with a lot of growing ahead of her. Exactly the same applies to the baby in the womb, who is smaller, less developed, in a different environment, and more dependent, but essentially the same, a *person*. She too is not a "sum of parts properly ordered." The assembly line picture is absolutely inapplicable to her. And if this picture is inapplicable to the child in the womb, so is the gradualist position that is based on it.

Third, there is another way of seeing the failure of the gradualist position as an answer to the question of the beginning of a person's existence. That is by confronting it with the "time frame" problem. It is clear that human beings develop, from the beginning of their existence, during the time in the womb, during infancy, through childhood, to puberty, and to maturity. At first it is a development that is largely physical, but soon the psychological development begins and expands. The physical development does not, of course, end with birth. According to the gradualist position, this is a development that is itself the coming into existence of a person. At the beginning (according to this view) there is no person at all, only an "organism." As this organism grows and develops, it gradually becomes a person; as the entity on the assembly line gradually becomes a car, as youth gradually turns into old age. At the beginning, there is no person, at the end there is a full person, in between there is a partial person, or a being that is not a person "in the full sense."

It follows that on the gradualist position a baby is not a real person, only a "person in the making." But of course this is not limited to preborn babies. It applies to post-born babies as well. A baby at birth is a being farther along the path to becoming a person "in the full sense" than a child in the womb, but "he" is not there yet. In fact, at birth he is far from being even half there in terms of psychological development, though his physical development is nearly complete.

Hence the gradualist position implies the thesis that a born baby is "less a person" than an older child or an adult; that a one-year-old child is "less a person" than a two-year-old; a two-year-old, than a three-year-old; and so on. But this is clearly absurd. The younger child is less developed, knows less, has fewer skills, etc., than an older child or an adult. But he is equally a person; he has the same dignity as the rest of us. I was not "less a person" when I was younger and immature; I was *myself*, the *same person* I am now.

The gradualist position correlates the wrongness of killing a being that is (allegedly) "developing into a person" with the degree of development attained.[6] It follows that killing a small baby is less wrong than killing an older baby or an adult. A series of killings of babies would become gradually less wrong as one went from older babies to newborns. This is absurd. But it follows necessarily from the Gradualist Position. We must conclude that a theory which entails such absurd and clearly false consequences must itself be false. Pointing to these consequences provides a *reductio ad absurdum* [7] of the gradualist position.

Philip Devine, in his criticism of the gradualist position, recognized this point when he said, "Moreover, if personhood or humanity admits of degrees before birth, then it would seem that it must admit of degrees after birth as well."[8]

What a defender of abortion who adopts the gradualist position *wants* is a "becoming of the person" limited to the time of pregnancy, so that early killings are less wrong and easier to justify than later ones. But what the gradualist position *actually produces* is a view that implies the same result for a whole class of human beings after birth as well; namely, that they, too, are not "persons in the whole sense," but only "partial persons" who are still in the process of becoming persons, and that earlier killings (e.g., born babies) are less wrong and easier to justify than later ones.

Now the abortion advocate may try to block this by holding that the development of a nonperson into a person is completed at some time within pregnancy. This would require a line marking the end of the *development* of the being of a person before birth. Could there be such a line? Clearly not, for the simple reason that the "development of a person" does not stop within the time in the womb but continues well into the time after birth. A line to mark the *end* of the *development* of a person during the time in the womb is as absurd and arbitrary as one intended to mark the *beginning* of the *being* of a person during this time. Just as in the latter case, the person was already there before any alleged line, so too, in the former, he continues to develop after any such line. That is, just as none of the items (e.g., viability) marking any of the lines are necessary for being a person, so too, none of the lines during pregnancy mark the end of the development of the person. For what we have during the time in the womb is a smooth transition from earlier stages of lesser development to later stages of greater development. The degree of development, physical and psychological, increases gradually without ever reaching the full capacity to think, decide, intentionally communicate, etc. Now if it is the process of developing these capacities that constitutes the process of "developing into a person," as the gradualist position maintains, then clearly one cannot draw a reasonable line during pregnancy.

Can one draw a reasonable line at birth? No, for as I showed in chapter 4, birth marks no change in the being of the child. He simply changes location and method of nourishment intake and is no longer directly dependent on his mother. Clearly none of this affects the status of his being. If he is not a person before birth, he is also not one immediately after.[9] If he is a person immediately before birth, he is also a person immediately after. If he is in the process of "developing into a person," as the gradualist position holds, then he is in that process just before, during, and just after birth. In the same way, he is in that process during any time span of equal length before birth or after birth. Birth is of no significance whatever for the status of a "developing person."

The "No Difference" Argument

I have considered three main hypotheses used by defenders of abortion to try to justify it: One, that there is a line to be drawn, before which there is no person or only a potential person, after which there is a person. Two, that no one knows when a person comes into being, the agnostic position. And three, the gradualist position, that what is in the womb starts out being a nonperson but gradually becomes a person, a smooth transition from the impersonal to the personal. Now, underlying all these is a simple fact. That there is a being in the womb, distinct from his mother, who grows and develops, and is then born: a newborn baby.

Suppose we kill this newborn baby. For one thing, we cut short his life; we deprive him of his entire future. We deprive him of the most basic thing he has, which is presupposed for everything else: his life. Surely this is a great moral evil.

Suppose we kill this being shortly before birth. We deprive him of his whole future. Suppose it is earlier, and then earlier still. The same applies. The crucial point is this: *no matter when we destroy the being in the womb, we deprive him of his entire future.* From this all-important perspective, what difference does it make whether it is earlier or later? Either way, the being in the womb (regardless of how his status is now designated) is robbed of his entire future.

This makes the whole debate about where to draw the line, or whether we can know what the proper place is, or whether there is not perhaps a smooth transition from nonperson to person, totally irrelevant. For the being in the womb, it makes no difference (apart from pain) whether she is robbed of her entire future at an earlier or later date. The effect is the same: she is deprived of her future, and that is a terrible moral evil.

Whether I kill a sleeping person (painlessly) five minutes after he falls asleep at night, or five minutes before the alarm goes off in the morning makes no difference to him. Either way I cut short his whole future life; I deny him his existence as an awakened being. The being in the womb is in a "sleep," relative to the "awakened" state of his later life. What is the difference, for him, whether he is killed early or late in this "sleep"? Either way, his existence is ended.

Even if the "fetus" were only a "potential person," abortion would be wrong. For it means the destruction of the whole of that being's life. (That this does not apply to the sperm and ovum will be shown in the next chapter.)

Summary Statements

The agnostic position cannot rationally support abortion. (1) It is not a tenable position. This is because: (a) We do know when a person comes into existence, namely at conception-fertilization, when his identity as a person begins. (b) We know a person does not come into existence at any later point during the time in the womb (refutation of the alleged lines). And (c) in looking for the features that mark the coming into *being* of a person, the agnostic position generally considers features that are in fact relevant only for *functioning* as a person, thus confusing these two essentially different things.

(2) Even if this position were tenable, it would not support abortion. It says we do not know with certainty and precision the moment when a human person begins to be. But we do know the time frame (pregnancy) during which there is a significant probability that a person exists (at every point). Where there is such a significant probability (as with a motionless accident victim), we must treat the being as a person. We must give "it" the benefit of any doubt.

The gradualist position cannot rationally support abortion. First, it is at best a mere hypothesis, unsupported by evidence. There is, therefore, a significant probability that the position is false, and therefore that a human person is present all the way through pregnancy, a being to which we must give the benefit of any doubt.

Second, when we examine it closely, we see that it cannot possibly be true: (a) "Gradual process" refers to my development, not to my being as a person. No matter how much less developed I was at any time in the past, I was always "me," fully a person. (b) If "gradual process" refers to the coming into being of a person, then at about its midpoint there would be "half a person," which is impossible. (c) A car on an assembly line comes into being gradually. The being of a person is totally unlike that of a car; and the coming into being of the one is totally unlike that of the other.

Third, there is the "time frame" problem. If the full being of a person is not attained until her development is completed, it follows that newborn babies are not fully persons, that younger babies are "less persons" than older ones, and that the younger a baby is, the less wrong it is to kill her. This is absurd. A theory that necessarily implies such an absurdity must be false.

The "No Difference Argument." There is a sense in which all these claims—that there is a known line to be drawn, that we do not know where the line is, that there is no line but rather a smooth transition to being a person—are irrelevant. For the being in question: if she is to be killed by abortion, what difference does it make whether it is earlier or later? No matter when it is, she is deprived of her whole future.

A final point. The agnostic position and the gradualist position both rest on a common false assumption: that development turns a nonperson into a person. The agnostic position says that there is a point in this development when "being a person" begins, but we do not know when this point is. The gradualist position says that there is no such point; that the gradual development is itself the transformation of a nonperson into a person.

On the contrary, development does not turn a nonperson into a person: *a person is there already, the same person, all the way through this development.* This is the continuum argument of chapter 1. It underlies the argument of chapter 4, that there is no break in prenatal development. It is, of course, the basis of the argument of this chapter. In the next chapter it will be established that this continuum begins at conception-fertilization, the one genuine "radical break" in prenatal development. This continuum refers to the being of a person, not to his capacity to function as a person, a point to be examined in detail in chapter 7.

6

When Does Human Life Begin?

Conception-Fertilization As the Radical Break

The life of a human person is a single continuum, whose first phase begins in the womb. But *when* does this phase actually begin? When does a new human person come into existence? To answer these questions we need scientific data, though it is not essentially a scientific but a philosophical question. Consider the following:

> The birth of a human life really occurs at the moment the mother's egg cell is fertilized by one of the father's sperm cells. When an egg is ripe . . . it leaves the mother's ovary and moves slowly down the fallopian tube towards the uterus on a current of special fluid. . . . The male sperm as they enter the cervix are affected by the presence of the egg. If there is no prospect of an egg, they just mill around aimlessly. . . . But while an egg is present—and for a time before and after—they stream purposefully toward it. . . . Swimming upstream by lashing their tails back and forth, they move at a rate of three inches per hour across the cervix, through the uterus and up the fallopian tube to meet the egg. There are actually more than 200 million sperm engaged in this race—but [generally] only one will win and fertilize the egg. The egg, which carries all the food and energy, is about 90,000 times as large as the sperm, but [normally] egg and sperm each contributes exactly half of the new individual's total hereditary material.[1]

The eminent embryologist, Dr. Bradley M. Patten states, "It is the penetration of the ovum by a spermatozoon and the resultant mingling of the nuclear material each brings to the union that constitutes the culmination of the process of *fertilization* and *marks the initiation of the life of a new individual.*" [2]

F. R. Lillie: "The elements that unite are single cells, each on the point of death, but by their union a rejuvenated individual is formed."[3]

Geraldine Lux Flanagan: "A baby begins life as a single cell, smaller than the period at the end of this sentence."[4]

E. Blechschmidt: "A human being does not *become* a human being but rather is such from the instant of its fertilization."[5]

Ashley Montagu: "Life begins, not at birth, but at conception. . . . In spite of his newness and his appearance, he is a living, striving human being from the very beginning."[6]

Science helps to answer the question where to draw the line between what is merely a *preparation* for a human being and that human being himself. Scientific facts reveal that sperm and ovum are each merely preparations for a human being. When they come together, they cease to exist. Their interaction is their transformation into something new, a new individual human being at the beginning of his existence. The penetration of the ovum by the sperm transforms what had been ovum and sperm into something radically different, an individual human being. At this first phase of existence, he or she is called a *zygote*.

But is there not a continuity in the biological process? Yes, for the father's sperm and the mother's ovum each contribute (normally) one half of the final gene complement, as well as other cellular materials, to the new human being. But there is also a radical break, a real line, marking the end of that which is merely the preparation for a human being, and that human being himself.

The radical break at conception is that before this event there are two things: the father's sperm and the mother's ovum. After conception, there is one being: the new human person. The transformation of two into one is surely a radical break, a real line, in contrast to the lines examined earlier, where it was not only one being before and after, but the same human person.

The mother's ovum loses its identity as ovum. After being fertilized by the father's sperm it is no longer an ovum, a *preparation* for a person, but a person. The same is true of the father's sperm.

This change of identity is expressed, in a striking way, by the fact that the ovum that comes down from the ovary is at the point of maturity. It is at the *end* of its *life*, "on the point of death." It dies if it remains unfertilized, and it dies in fertilization because it ceases to exist. The zygote is, on the contrary, at the *beginning* of his life, at the point farthest removed from maturity and death. A more radical break can hardly be imagined than that break between a being at the end of its existence and another being that somehow comes from it, but is at the beginning of his existence.

Sperm and ovum cease to exist. What used to be the sperm and the ovum becomes transformed by fertilization into the new human being in his zygote stage. That a new and different being comes into existence at fertilization is reflected in the fact that this new being has his own specific genetic code, different from that of the sperm (and the father), different from that of the ovum (and the mother).

Sperm and ovum do not really unite. They cease to be and lead to a new being:

> The nuclei of the sperm and ovum dynamically interact, and in so doing they cease to be. One might say they die together, but one really should not say that they unite. That notion suggests they remain and form a larger whole. But the new single-celled individual is not a continuing partnership of the two parent sex cells. In their interaction and mutual causation of the new being, the sperm and ovum are self-sacrificial. Their nuclei are the subject of the fertilization process; the zygote is the result of this process. There is neither sperm nor ovum, once the process of interaction is completed, even though cytoplasmic matter from the ovum remains. It is really a misleading figure of speech to say that the ovum is fertilized by the sperm, fertilized as passively as a farmer's field. It is proper rather to speak of the sperm-ovum interaction process.[7]

Conception-fertilization is the radical break, the coming into existence of an individual human being. Sperm and ovum are merely carriers of human life. Each alone is not a human being, but only a part—though a very special part—of the body of either the father or the mother. It is a part of his body and her body that will contribute toward a new human being who stems from them, who is generated from the union of their bodies, but who is absolutely distinct from both of them. The new human being, the child, is as distinct from the mother as from the father. The child merely resides in the mother, is protected by her womb, is warmed and nourished by processes in her body.

Conception-fertilization is the beginning of a person's existence. More precisely, fertilization itself is the process (the intermingling of the ovum and sperm "nuclear material" from the parents) that culminates in the moment of conception, which is the precise "initiation of the life of a new individual." Since fertilization occurs in the fallopian tube, the term womb can be said to encompass not only the uterus but the fallopian tube as well.

Conception, the culmination of the process of fertilization, marks the beginning of the continuum of human life: I was once a newborn baby, and before that, "a well-proportioned small scale baby at seven weeks," and before that, a zygote, right after conception. I am a person now, I was a person in those early phases.

There Is No Such Thing As a "Fertilized Egg"

Discussions of these matters often use the term *fertilized egg* or *fertilized ovum*. This is a serious mistake, for the result of conception is not a certain kind of egg, namely a fertilized egg, but a new human person. After fertilization, the egg no longer exists, and is therefore not a kind of egg at all.

To speak of unfertilized eggs and fertilized eggs is to suggest that there are two kinds of eggs, as there are, for example, two kinds of tomatoes, unripe and ripe. Both unripe and ripe tomatoes are really tomatoes; they are two variations of the same thing. But unfertilized eggs and fertilized eggs are not variations of the same thing, but two realities that are radically different: one is a mere preparation for a person, and the other is that person himself.

The expression *fertilized egg* (or ovum) is also scientifically wrong. The new human being is no more the egg fertilized than he is the sperm fertilized, or modified. He is as little the one as the other, but a new being. The ovum is merely bigger than the sperm, hence the tendency to speak of it as a fertilized egg, but each contributes exactly one half to the genetic makeup of the new person. And in the process, each ceases to be.[8]

Use of the term *fertilized egg* (or ovum) obscures the radical difference between egg, or ovum, and person. It makes it seem as if there is merely a gradual transition, from one state of the egg (unfertilized) to another (fertilized), when in fact there is a radical break between non-person and person. It also invites the question why we should respect and protect fertilized eggs when we do not accord such reverence to unfertilized eggs. Indeed it is hard to see why one state of an egg should be highly revered when another is not. The solution to all this is simple: the result of conception is not an egg, but (normally) a small human being.[9]

Objections and Replies

Let's now consider a series of objections to conception-fertilization as the radical break that marks the beginning of a person's existence, and replies to them.

(1) "The zygote cannot be a human person because it is too small. It is only barely visible to the naked eye."

Yes, a zygote is tiny—to us. That is, in comparison to our size and what we consider normal, he is very small. But for a conscious being that size, the zygote would be of normal size, and we would appear abnormally large. Going in the other direction, imagine a giant who could hold the earth in his hand like an orange. To him each of us would be tiny, much more tiny than the zygote is to us. But each of us would not be less of a person for our small size, or less valuable. If you were to shrink in size, to the size of a zygote, you would still be the same person, equally a person.

Size is relative, and completely irrelevant for the status of being a person. A larger person is not more a person than a smaller person; the smaller person is not less precious. What is obviously true of, say, an 80-pound person in comparison to a 240-pound person is equally true when the comparison is continued: 80-pound person and 8-pound person, all the way down to the smallest person, the newly-conceived child. In a very short time, she will increase enormously in size. She will develop more, but she will not become more a person through this increase in size and level of development, for she is always, in her very nature, fully a person. In short, size is an irrelevant factor in the being of a person. A person is a person regardless of her size.

The same applies to development. A person at an earlier stage of his development, say age 4, and later, say 24, is the same person, and is equally a person at both stages. In fact, the whole notion of development here means the development of a person. It is not the development of something into a person (as was shown, that is impossible[10]), but a development within a person who is already there. Thus the objection that the zygote cannot be a person because it is too undeveloped rests on a false assumption; namely, that to be a person, one must already have reached a certain level of development. On the contrary, if there is development, then the being who reaches it must already be a person. It cannot be that a non-person reaches this level of development and then becomes a person.

Human life is a series of unfoldings. This can be seen clearly on the psychological and spiritual levels. A child unfolds as a personality. An artistically gifted person unfolds his creativity. A small bud unfolds into a mature flower. On a much deeper level, and in many more ways, a person unfolds. Now the psychological and spiritual unfolding is clearly apparent to us in the child after birth. His physical unfolding before birth is less apparent to us, but it is just as real, and just as much a part of the unfolding that is human life.

The newly-conceived child represents a special moment in the unfolding process: the moment it begins. And the child begins to be at this moment. The unfolding process coincides with the life of the child. The child must really be for the unfolding process to begin, for it is the unfolding of his being. That the child is undeveloped at this moment should hardly be surprising; it is precisely his first moment.

So the development one expects to find later, the development whose absence lies at the heart of this objection, is not there. Of course the person at this stage of his existence does not show development: he is at the beginning of his development process.

(2) "But there must be some structure present for us to be able to speak of a person. The zygote lacks this structure. He/it is merely an ovum changed by infusion of the sperm."

The zygote is not an ovum changed by infusion of the sperm. He is a new being brought into existence by the interaction of two elements, sperm and ovum, which play equal roles, despite the much larger size of the ovum. Sperm and ovum are transformed into a new being. This new being has a specific genetic structure and associated cellular structure, which will progressively unfold as the being develops, from its beginning through subsequent, progressively more complex forms of this structure. The zygote needs time, as well as nourishment, protection, and other environmental factors, to unfold and thereby to develop into what is recognized as a familiar human being.

This is the structure that constitutes the individual person, at that stage of his development. It is a specifically human structure, unlike the structure of an animal zygote, as can be clearly determined by inspection under a microscope. (See also note 5.)

Perhaps the above objection refers to something else: a more developed structure, as is found in a newborn child. A developed structure will come, but it takes time. This objection rests on an unreasonable expectation. The being, the zygote, is at the beginning of his existence. Hence what can only come later as a result of his development cannot be present yet. But the being who is developing, who is just starting his process of development, is there. That is the all-important point. Were he not there, his unfolding as a person, could not begin.

(3) "But the zygote is not conscious, he cannot think and communicate. How can he be a person?" That he cannot think and communicate means merely that he cannot function as a person, not that he lacks the being of a person.

(4) "The zygote cannot be a human person because it doesn't look like a human person."

But it does look like a human person, at that stage of her development. What the objection must mean is that the zygote does not look like a familiar human person. That says nothing about her being, and it is the status of her being that matters. That the zygote has an appearance unfamiliar to us is a function of our limited range of experience, not of her humanity.

Looking like a familiar human person is a function of genetic endowment, level of development, and environment. People look familiarly human because they have human eyes and ears, arms and legs, etc. If we cannot expect the results of development in a being who is at the beginning of her development, we also cannot expect that which accompanies those results—looking like a familiar human person—in such a being. In fact, it would be strange if a human person at the very beginning of her development did look like the more developed human beings we are used to seeing outside the womb.

(5) "The zygote cannot be a human person because it is absolutely unconscious; it does not even have the capacity for consciousness."

That the zygote is absolutely unconscious only means that he is unable to function as a person, not that he lacks the being of a person, and it is of course being a person that counts. In regard to capacity, he does possess the essential structure for having this capacity. What he lacks is the immediate capacity for consciousness, which is simply an aspect of his lack of development, something entirely appropriate for a being at the beginning of his development. The zygote is a person who is *not yet* conscious, not a being who is simply not conscious like a stone.

There is a common element in these first five objections: they are all based on the expectation that what is a person must be like us. It must be the right size (a size like ours); it must have a level of development comparable to ours; it must look like us; it must, like us, be conscious. These are not true criteria for being a person but simply expressions of our expectations, of what we are used to, of what appears familiar to us. It is not that the zygote fails to be a person because it fails these tests; rather it is we who fail by using these criteria to measure what a person is.

To consider a zygote less a person because of his appearance is similar to a white person to whom a black person appears strange because he is different. The white racist measures being a human person by what is familiar to him, namely being a white person. When the black person fails this test, he is considered not fully human. Of course, the failure lies not on the part of the black, but on the part of the white, and his narrow standards. Being a white human person is one way of being a human person; being a black human person is another. Existing outside the womb, having reached a high level of human development is one way of being a human person; being a small person, a zygote inside his mother, is another way.

(6) "The zygote is only a blueprint for a human being, not an actual human being. It is merely an information code for a human being, a guide for the development of that being, and not the being himself."[11]

This is simply false. The zygote, like every other human being, contains, in every cell, a blueprint for his development and structure, and information code, namely DNA. Although he contains this DNA information code, he is not the information code itself.

The small-scale baby in the womb is surely not a blueprint, or an information code, for the full-term infant, any more than the full-term infant is for an older child. Each of them is already a fully real, small human person. The zygote is essentially the same, only smaller and less developed, and different in appearance. And he is the same being as the seven-week-old child, at an earlier phase of development. There is no transformation of blueprint for x into x itself, but rather a child just starting his development, and that same child having reached a later phase in his developmental process.[12]

(7) "The zygote is no more a person than an acorn is an oak tree. Just as an acorn is not a tree, a zygote is not a person, though in each case the latter grows out of the former."[13]

If this objection seems to have some force, it is because it assumes a discontinuity between acorn and oak tree. That is, that the acorn and the oak tree are two distinct things, that the acorn somehow causes the oak tree to come into existence but is in no way the same being, and (perhaps), that the acorn dies in the process. But if this assumption is made, the analogy does not fit. The acorn and the oak tree are not distinct organisms. Rather, the acorn contains the embryonic plant that will become the oak tree.[14] The acorn is the embryonic plant, plus other organic material, such as nutrients. The planted seed does not die; the embryo it contains is the plant that will grow and thereby assume the familiar form of a tree. Essentially the same is true of the zygote. It is the being who will later be a born child.

"The zygote is no more a person than an acorn is an oak tree." On the contrary, the acorn/embryo is the the oak tree, in its earliest phase. And the zygote is the person in her earliest phase. In each case the early phase looks different from the later phases, does not have the same functions (it cannot provide shade; she cannot read), and is in a different location (underground, then both underground and above ground; in the womb, then outside the womb).

If we assume discontinuity, the analogy fails. If we recognize the continuity between acorn and oak tree, then the analogy fits perfectly, and merely points out that the acorn and the zygote are different from the oak tree and the later child, respectively. The force of the objection is then simply to emphasize this difference. "See how different they are." Yes, they are different. The acorn differs from the oak tree in being much smaller, in being less developed, in location, and in appearance. So too, the child in her zygote stage and her later stages. Thus the acorn objection merely recapitulates, in a vivid way, the first three objections.

(8) "An egg after fertilization is a zygote, a single cell that divides if development continues. Since it is not indivisible, a zygote cannot be considered an individual or person."[15] In other words, "To be a person, one must be indivisible, a unity. The zygote is not indivisible, since it does divide; therefore, it is not a person."

The single-celled zygote divides into two cells, then four, and continues, reaching trillions of cells. But this division is in fact his development. Speaking of this, "the first division of the zygote into two equal parts by the process known as cleavage." Shettles and Rugh explain, "It is through this process that a single fertilized ovum will give rise to the more than trillions of cells of the unborn baby."[16] Cellular division, far from negating the reality of the individual person, makes possible the physical development of that individual person.

At the beginning, there is a one-celled being. When cleavage occurs there are two cells, but not therefore two beings (except in the case of identical twins). Rather, cleavage means that the original being is now composed of two cells. Later he will be composed of many more cells, but he is the same single being all the way through this development by cellular division.

The objection would only be valid if division meant separation into two beings. It does not. "Cleavage is not at all comparable to a single knife stroke that cuts an egg in two."[17]

(9) "The answer to this whole question—whether human life begins at conception, or later—is very simple. Human life never begins; except once, long, long ago. It is just passed on from one generation to the next. The sperm and the ovum are forms of human life, the resulting zygote is human life; it is a continual process that goes on and on. Thus, human life (except in the distant past) has no beginning."[18]

Life as a biological phenomenon has no beginning (in our time), it is just passed on. But the life of a person has a definite beginning. The general phenomenon of biological life is a continual process; but the life of an individual person is not. It is a continuum, with a definite beginning, and end. The biological is a dimension of human life but not the whole of it. From the fact that biological life is carried on, it does not follow that personal life is simply carried on. The fact that my biological being has its roots in the distant past, and is in some way continuous with it, does not mean that my identity as a person reaches into the distant past. I surely did not exist at the time of Bach or Alexander the Great, even if my biological heredity is somehow traceable to those who existed at those times.

Once we see that biological continuity is absolutely distinct from individual personal life, which has a definite beginning, we can see a deep and meaningful connection between them. This refers to the begetting of a new person by his parents. My being as a person has an absolute beginning, at conception-fertilization. That event is the union of two things, the sperm from my father and the ovum from my mother: two things that represent my connection with the past. I am not created out of nothing but somehow out of a material (sperm and egg) that already exists. Life is transmitted from one generation to the next. This transmission is not the continuity of one thing, life, but the begetting of a new person by two persons already in existence.

(10) "There is no such thing as the moment of conception, since conception is a process that takes time."

This is inaccurate. *Fertilization* is a process that takes time. But, as Joyce tells us, "It has a definite conclusion. The moment at which this process terminates in the resulting zygote can be called *conception.*"[19] So there is a moment of conception: the culmination of the process of fertilization.

Moore describes the process as follows: "*Fertilization is a sequence of events* that begins with contact between a sperm and a secondary oocyte [mature ovum] . . . and ends with the fusion of the nuclei of the sperm and ovum and the intermingling of maternal and paternal chromosomes."[20] Further, "*Embryonic development commences with fertilization.* The fertilization process lasts about 24 hours."[21] He then describes the six stages of this process, the last stage being "*The male and female pronuclei fuse,* forming a new cell called the *zygote.*"[22]

(11) It is sometimes asked, "If we are to revere and protect fertilized eggs, why not also unfertilized eggs and sperm?"

The answer is simple. Unfertilized eggs and sperm are not persons; each is merely a preparation for the coming to be of a person. A "fertilized egg" is not really an egg, but rather a small new person, a zygote, who should be respected for just this reason.

(12) "Some entities that stem from the union of sperm and egg are not human beings and never will develop into them." Thus:

> 1. The hydatidiform mole, an entity which is usually just a degenerated placenta and typically has a random number of chromosomes (aneuploidy).
> 2. The choriocarcinoma, a "conception-cancer" resulting from the sperm-egg union is one of gynecology's most malignant tumors. Aneuploidy is also common.
> 3. The "blighted ovum," a conception with the forty-six chromosomes but which is only a placenta, lacks an embryonic plate, and is always aborted naturally after implantation.
> Also I wonder, are all fertilized eggs "lives" that must be protected and cherished? Many do not implant and are simply washed away.[23]

Suppose it is true that some entities stemming from the union of sperm and egg are not human beings. Some surely are, and they begin their existence at conception. That other entities may also stem from a sperm-egg union does nothing to show that those entities that are human beings do not begin their existence with the sperm-egg union (i.e., intermingling). All that the objection can show is that not all cases of biological fertilization represent the conception of a new person.

In addition, some persons are conceived who are too weak, fragile, and handicapped to survive, and thus are "washed away." That happens later in life as well; not all human beings survive to maturity. This does nothing to show that they were not real human beings before their death.

(13) "If and when human cloning occurs, is this not a human life because it does not result from the union of sperm and egg?"[24]

Suppose cloning is possible. That would simply mean that there is another way in which human beings can come into existence. It does nothing to show that the first way—normal fertilization—is not a way in which human beings come into existence; or that this process does not represent the beginning of a person. Cloning or not, the rest of us begin at conception-fertilization.

(14) Someone could ask, "Granting all that has been said so far in this book, isn't it still possible that, though a new biological entity comes into being at conception-fertilization, a person does not come into being until some time later, when the soul is infused into the body? By *soul*, I mean that which makes us persons, and not merely biological organisms: the capacity to think, and feel, and love, etc., or at least the basis for this capacity. If the soul is infused only later, then conception-fertilization is not the beginning of a person's existence; and destroying the zygote (and perhaps the embryo) is not the killing of a person, and therefore allowable."[25]

Regarding the thesis that the soul is infused into the individual human organism only at some time after conception, four important points should be made. First, we do not know that this is in fact what happens. We have absolutely no evidence for it, no reason to believe it, nothing that would make it even probable.[26] It is, at best, a pure hypothesis. As such, it offers no basis to anyone seeking a justification for abortions.

Second, even supposing it is true, we do not know when the crucial moment is. To know that it is after conception-fertilization is not enough. We would have to know precisely when the soul enters the body, so that we do not destroy the being after that point. So, even granting the thesis to be true, it provides no practical help to anyone seeking to justify abortion, or wondering whether some abortions might not be justified.

Third, there are many reasons to believe this thesis is false.[27] In addition to what has already been offered here, especially that conception is a radical break, let me suggest two further points.

1. A human person is a whole being, bodily dimension and personal being, deeply united into one. He is not a mere biological organism, nor merely a soul, nor a soul lodged in a body. He is a bodily person. The idea of infusing a soul into an already existing biological organism, with the unity and uniqueness (genetic code) that the zygote certainly has, runs counter to what a human person is. The infusion view is too much like that of an empty bottle that is then filled with something. That is a completely false and distorted view of the human person. Our bodies are not bottles to be filled with our souls. Each human person is a unity, a person with a bodily dimension; for example, my right arm is a dimension of me. The human body is not a mere body, but an aspect of the person. The infusion view seems to require a separation of body and soul (or spiritual person) that is untenable. Body and soul are essentially distinct;

we are not mere biological organisms. But a person is also a unity, a profound unity of the spiritual and the physical. My body is not just a shell in which I live. My body is, in a real sense me, though of course not all of me. My body is a dimension of my being as a person.

Each human person is a unity. The full reality of this unity is in the zygote, though of course not yet consciously experienced as it will be later.

2. The infusion view would have the curious effect of implying that I am not conceived by my parents. For what is conceived by them would be an entity, a mere biological organism, that forms a kind of vessel into which a soul is then infused. But if my parents conceived me, they conceived me when conception took place. This means that I came into existence when conception took place, and not at some later time, when a soul was infused into a body. In short, my parents conceived *me*, not just my body.[28]

A fourth argument is that even if the infusion view were probable, though uncertain, it could not be used as a basis for justifying abortions. For if there is a risk, even a small one, that it is not true, one cannot rely on it. If there is a small though realistic chance that the being in the womb before the point when infusion is thought to occur is a person, we cannot destroy her by an abortion. Where there is uncertainty, all benefit must be given to human life. We must know that the being in question is *not* a living person (either not yet or no longer), before we can destroy her. So, even if the infusion view were highly likely, it could not be used to justify early abortions.

Only conception-fertilization represents the radical change that adequately corresponds to, and makes possible, the change from non-person to person. Only conception-fertilization can represent the physical change necessary to transform what is a biological preparation for a person into that person himself. What preexists on the biological level must be radically altered to become a human body, and thereby the physical dimension of a human person. There is no other place, besides conception-fertilization, where such a radical physical change occurs. None of the suggested places to draw the line marking the beginning of a person's existence were even close to being a radical physical change. They were all merely stages in the development of the same being.

The Role of Natural Science

An individual human person begins his existence at conception-fertilization. Is this something that science can establish? There is no one single answer to this question.

First, it is a scientific fact that human life begins at conception. Here *human life* refers to an individual of a zoological species, part of the proper subject matter for scientific inquiry.

Second, scientific inquiry does not establish the further, crucial point that this individual human life is a person; for the term *person* is a philosophical category, not a scientific one. Personhood is something that must be understood philosophically, rather than be proved scientifically. An abortion advocate who admits that the being in the womb is human life but denies that that human life is a person cannot be refuted on purely scientific grounds. Likewise, science does not establish the personhood of a black person or white person. A racist who acknowledges that a black human being is human but denies that he is a person in the full sense cannot be refuted on purely scientific grounds.

Third, scientific data, though not sufficient to establish that the preborn human being is a person, are nonetheless immensely valuable for understanding his status as a person, and that it is at conception-fertilization that he begins his existence. Science presents a detailed picture of the coming into existence of a new individual human being, and of his early development. That this human being is a person, the same person who will later grow into a recognizable baby, and an adult; that he is as much a person as the rest of us, the differences between him and the rest of us being morally irrelevant; that he has the same preciousness and dignity as any other person—these are matters of philosophical understanding rather than scientific knowledge. But science plays a key role in enabling us to reach this understanding. The detailed picture science provides is a kind of raw material for philosophic understanding. Scientific data provide part of the evidence for that which is philosophically understood. Certain scientifically established facts correspond in an intelligible way to what is understood philosophically. Thus it is science that explains the biological continuity between the zygote and the later child and that the zygote comes into being as sperm and ovum interpenetrate, thereby ceasing to exist. Scientific data show that the zygote has his own specific genetic code, distinct both from that of the sperm and that of the ovum. Again, the scientific facts concerning viability—for example, its relativity to medical technology—play a key role in constituting the philosophical argument that it is not the place to draw the line marking the beginning of an actual human person.

Thus, though science itself does not establish the reality of the human person in the womb, since the whole question of the reality of the person is a philosophical question and not a scientific one, science nonetheless plays a key role in providing data used by philosophy to establish that it is indeed a person, one of us, who inhabits the womb.

In the words of Robert Joyce:

> What is a person? When is a person? These questions are essentially philosophical. They require an integration of our knowledge of certain basic data and conclusions in embryology. But they are not specifically scientific questions. We go beyond the eyeball vision and verification involved in natural science, while taking it carefully into account, and we try to say ultimately what this tiny, microscopic creature called a human zygote really *is*. Biologically viewed, even an adult human being cannot be said to be a person. For a biologist as a biologist, you and I are simply human organisms. But for the biologist as a philosopher—and *everyone* is a philosopher to some extent—you and I can be readily recognized as persons.[29]

Abortion and Contraception

The destruction of a zygote is the killing of a real human person; it is therefore a form of abortion. Abortion is therefore essentially different from contraception, which, as the name implies, means the prevention of conception; no new human being comes into existence. Abortion, in contrast, means that an existing human being is killed. Abortion implies a victim; contraception does not.

Thus devices, such as the I.U.D, that cause the death of the zygote are methods of abortion and not of contraception, though they are often misleadingly labeled as contraceptive devices. They are abortifacients, devices that cause an abortion, and should be labeled as such.

The Significance of Establishing Conception As the Beginning of a Person's Existence

The basic argument against abortion is that it is the killing of a human person. That the being in the womb is really a person is established through the continuum argument: human life is a single continuum whose first phase is life before birth.

It is important to establish precisely when this continuum begins, so that a clear picture emerges: human life is a single continuum beginning at conception-fertilization, continuing through the time in the womb, entering a new phase at birth, and continuing after birth to death. If conception-fertilization is not clearly established as the first point of this continuum then the beginning of a person's existence will be lost in obscurity. This will have serious consequences for an understanding of the moral evil of abortion. A person for whom the early phases (zygote and embryo) are somehow lost in obscurity, who does not see them as the first phases of the life of a person, may be confused about later phases in the continuum before birth as well. "If the very small being (e.g., zygote) is not clearly a human person, then perhaps the larger, later, child is not either." There is a valid point here: if the zygote is not a real person, he cannot become one just by getting bigger and developing more. The conclusion, validly drawn, would be that the being in the womb at later stages is not a real person, but only looks more and more like one; that he is only a potential person, and thus may be aborted. This shows how important it is to establish clearly that the premise is false, that the zygote is a real person. He does not become a person; he only grows larger and becomes more developed, until he is able to change his environment, and become relatively independent.

Many people feel confused about abortion. They clearly recognize the born child as a real person, and that killing her is morally wrong. They somehow realize that the being in the womb is essentially such a child, except that he happens not to have been born yet. As they learn more about the development of the being in the womb, they begin to realize more and more that she is a small child, differing from a newborn baby only in size, level of development, etc. But if the continuum is not clearly established as far back as conception, their whole insight into the reality of the person in the womb is in jeopardy. For, as noted, if the zygote is not a real person, she cannot become one merely by growing bigger; perhaps the larger child in the womb is not (in their minds) a person either. So the confusion sets in, and with it sentiments such as, "It is a complex question, so each person must decide for herself whether abortion is immoral or not." The victim of this liberal sentiment is the innocent child in the womb. To protect her we must establish absolute clarity about her existence in the womb as a real person from conception-fertilization.

There is another reason for establishing clearly that conception-fertilization is the beginning of a human person's existence, and that concerns abortifacients such as the I.U.D., the "morning after" pill, and certain forms of The Pill. All these devices kill an individual person, already conceived, and their use is therefore morally wrong.

Is the Zygote a Person?

The zygote is merely still smaller, and less developed, than the child in the womb at say, seven weeks. That he is smaller and less developed should not deny him personhood; he is simply a tiny person at the beginning of his existence, and therefore of his development. It is then only natural that he is not yet developed.

The zygote does not seem to be a person; he is not what we think of as a person. But that is partly a fact about us, what appears familiar as a person to us, and partly a matter of relationships: the zygote does not live in a social environment as other persons do. The first says something about us, the second about the zygote's environment. Neither says that he does not have the status of a person.

If the zygote does not seem to us to be a person, then we must expand our concept of person to include him. There are, unfortunately, numerous occasions where a person appears unfamiliar in some way (race, nationality, ethnic group, size, level of development, etc.), and is then not accorded full status as a person. But all these factors are equally irrelevant in regard to personhood; the unfamiliar person is as much a person as the one to whom he happens to appear unfamiliar. The failure lies not with the person who appears unfamiliar, but rather with the person who fails to recognize and acknowledge the personhood of the one who appears to him as different.

It is helpful to remember in this connection the simple fact: I was once a zygote, just as I was once a newborn baby, only earlier. I am surely a person now; I was a person when I was newborn, just before that in my mother's womb, and equally before that at the beginning of my existence.

A person in a deep sleep is surely a person. A zygote is a person in a kind of deep sleep. Given time, proper warmth, nourishment, and protection, he will wake up. He will surely be a person then. But if he wakes up, he was also a person before, while in his state of sleep.

Is destroying a zygote then murder? Is killing an innocent person in general murder? Why is it any different for a tiny person? An innocent person is the victim. This suffices to constitute murder. Our concepts must be broadened. If the destruction of a zygote is not thought of as murder, the failure lies with us. We fail to identify with him merely because he is small, undeveloped, and unseen. These are hardly things that make him any less a person, or that make his destruction any less murder.

The "Fertilized Egg" Fallacy

Defenders of abortion sometimes argue their case along these lines: "You mean that a fertilized egg has the same status as a fully mature person? That the rights of an hour old fertilized egg, one-fourth the size of a period on a printed page, would take precedence over the wishes and interests of a mature woman?[30] That to destroy a tiny fertilized egg is the moral equivalent of murdering a child or an adult? Absurd!"

I would like to offer three replies to this argument. First, what is called the fertilized egg seems not to be a person. The important question is not what something seems to be but what it really is. Appearance does not always equal reality. Appearances can be, and often are, deceiving. As this chapter has shown, together with the arguments of the previous chapters, the so-called fertilized egg is a tiny person at the beginning of his existence. He is small and undeveloped precisely because he is at the beginning of his existence. If that is so, then he does indeed have the same status as a fully mature person. Denying him this is a form of discrimination: "You don't count, you're too small, too undeveloped." Or, "You have the wrong size and shape to be a real person." Of course the right to life of any person—whether he is "the size of the period at the end of this sentence," or smaller or larger—"takes precedence over the wishes and interests of a mature woman," or any other person. A person's right to life is not dependent on his size.

So the first reply to this argument for abortion amounts to denying the premise on which it is based, that the "fertilized egg" is not a person; and that killing it cannot be seriously wrong. He is not a fertilized egg, but a small human being in the first phase of his existence. (Notice how the use of the term *fertilized egg* creates the impression that this is an impersonal being, hence can be readily disposed. This is an illustration of the point stressed earlier, that use of this term should be avoided.)

Second, the arguments proposed here clearly establish the personhood of the zygote (in the sense in which any child, large or small, is a person). If this is questioned, it must at least be admitted that there is a high probability that the zygote is a person. If the arguments do not establish certainty, they surely provide a strong probability that a person is there at this stage of human development. If this is so, the same conclusion follows. We cannot destroy what is most probably a human being. If we are not certain that someone is dead, he must be presumed to be alive, and treated as such. So too, if we are not certain that the zygote is non-living as a person (a non-person), he must be presumed alive as a person, and treated with respect, not killed on behalf of the wishes and interests of another person.

The second reply to this argument for abortion says to its advocates, "You claim to know the zygote is not a person. You don't know this! Your reasons—its tiny size, not looking like a familiar human being, being undeveloped—are not good reasons, let alone grounds for claiming to know that the zygote is not a person. If you don't know this, your whole argument collapses. Your conclusion, that the zygote may be destroyed, is based on the premise that he is known not to be a person. This is not known; the premise is false, hence the conclusion cannot be drawn."

Third, if the fertilized egg argument is offered as a defense of abortion in general[31] (and not merely for destroying zygotes, as with abortifacients), it suffers from another, rather serious, defect: it becomes an anti-abortion argument. Suppose it convinces a person that a "fertilized egg" counts for virtually nothing in comparison to a mature person. The reason would be its tiny size and undeveloped status, implying that with development and a more normal size, the being in question would be valued. But that is precisely what is true of a seven-week-old baby in the womb, or that same child in later phases. Thus, if the zygote may be destroyed because it is so tiny, then precisely for this reason the child who is a victim of standard abortion techniques may not be destroyed, because he is not tiny. Therefore abortion is wrong.

When examined carefully, the absurdity of this argument as an attempt to justify abortion confronts us. "It's all right to destroy a tiny 'fertilized egg,' because it is so tiny. Therefore it's all right to take a well-developed child at twelve weeks or more, burn her skin and poison her by saline, or cut her to pieces by D & E."

7

Is the Being in the Womb a Person?

A Theory About Human Beings and Persons

Let us now examine a theory that defends abortion on the grounds that the child in the womb, though undoubtedly a human being, is not a person, and that it is only the killing of persons that is intrinsically and seriously wrong. The theory consists of two major theses: First, that killing human beings is not wrong; second, that the child (in the womb and for a time after birth) is human but not a person. I shall argue that both of these theses are mistaken.

This theory recognizes that abortion is the deliberate killing of an innocent human being, but it denies this is wrong because it denies that it is wrong to deliberately kill human beings. What *is* wrong is killing human beings who are persons. Now, of course, many human beings are persons, for example, normal adult human beings, and it is wrong to kill them because they are persons. But small infants, such as newborn babies or babies in the womb, though they are undoubtedly human, are not, according to this theory, persons. And so it is not intrinsically wrong to kill them. That is, it is not wrong in itself, though it may be wrong because of adverse consequences. A small child, therefore, has no right to life as a normal adult does, and if the child is unwanted, he may be killed.

Thus, the theory allows for abortion and infanticide alike. It rejects the typical pro-abortion lines, such as viability and birth. It agrees that there is no morally significant difference between "before" and "after." But instead of saying that killing a human being is *wrong* on both sides of such a line, it claims that it is *right* (or can be right) on both sides of the line.

Joseph Fletcher expresses this view when he remarks, "I would support the . . . position . . . that both abortion and infanticide can be justified if and when the good to be gained outweighs the evil—that neither abortion nor infanticide is as such immoral."[1]

Michael Tooley has an essay entitled, "A Defense of Abortion and Infanticide." If the idea that killing babies is morally right is shocking to most people, Tooley replies in his essay that this is merely an emotional response, not a reasoned one. "The response, rather than appealing to carefully formulated moral principles, is primarily visceral," he says. And, "It is reasonable to suspect that one is dealing with a taboo rather than with a rational prohibition."[2] His position is: "Since I do not believe human infants are persons, but only potential persons, and since I think that the destruction of potential persons is a morally neutral action, the correct conclusion seems to me to be that infanticide is in itself morally acceptable."[3]

I want to show that the theories held by Fletcher, Tooley, and others are absolutely wrong. Infanticide and abortion are both morally wrong, as wrong as the deliberate killing of an older child or an adult, and thus our emotional response of shock and horror at killing babies is completely grounded in reason and moral principles. I want to show that a small child, after birth or still in the womb, *is* a person, as much a person as the rest of us; that the notion of person as used by these writers is a special one, a narrower concept, and not the one that is crucial for morality. I want to make clear why the attempts to show that a small child is not a person are mistaken, and that all human beings as such are persons.

The Argument of Mary Ann Warren

In an argument for this theory, Mary Ann Warren examines "the traditional argument that since (1) it is wrong to kill innocent human beings, and (2) fetuses are innocent human beings, then (3) it is wrong to kill fetuses."[4] This argument, she claims, is "fallacious," because "the term 'human' has two distinct, but not often distinguished, senses."[5] In premise one, human means person, or full-fledged member of the moral community, a being whom it is wrong to kill. In premise two, on the other hand, the term human refers merely to a member of the biological species human, as opposed, say, to a rabbit or an eagle. Warren's claim is that mere membership in a biological species is morally irrelevant and thus does not confer on the being in question a right to life.[6]

"Yes, a fetus is biologically human (human in the genetic sense), but that does not make it the kind of being who has a right to life. It is only persons (those who are human in the moral sense) who have such a right. It is wrong to kill persons, and if a human being is not also a person he does not have a right to life, and it is, or often can be, morally right to destroy him." This, in essence, is Warren's argument.

Warren offers an analysis of what is a person, a full-fledged member of the moral community:

> I suggest that the traits which are most central to the concept of personhood, or humanity in the moral sense, are, very roughly, the following:
>
> 1. consciousness (of objects and events external and/or internal to the being), and in particular the capacity to feel pain;
>
> 2. reasoning (the *developed* capacity to solve new and relatively complex problems);
>
> 3. self-motivated activity (activity which is relatively independent of either genetic or direct external control);
>
> 4. the capacity to communicate, by whatever means, messages of an indefinite variety of types, that is, not just with an indefinite number of possible contents, but on indefinitely many possible topics;
>
> 5. the presence of self-concepts, and self-awareness, either individual or racial, or both.[7]

This, she acknowledges, is not a full analysis of the concept of a person. It is not a list of necessary and sufficient conditions for being a person. But, she says, this does not matter.

> All we need to claim, to demonstrate that a fetus is not a person, is that any being which satisfies *none* of (1)-(5) is certainly not a person. I consider this claim to be so obvious that I think anyone who denied it, and claimed that a being which satisfied none of (1)-(5) was a person all the same, would thereby demonstrate that he had no notion at all of what a person is—perhaps because he had confused the concept of a person with that of genetic humanity.[8]

We can now see Warren's argument for abortion in its entirety. A fetus is human in the genetic sense; that is morally irrelevant. A fetus is not human in the moral sense: he is not a person since he satisfies none of the criteria she has outlined. Not being a person, he has no right to life, and abortion is morally permissible. The same applies to the child after birth. "Killing a newborn infant isn't murder."[9] Infanticide is wrong, according to Warren, only to the extent that the child is wanted, that there are couples who would like to adopt or keep him. "Thus, infanticide is wrong for reasons analogous to those which make it wrong to wantonly destroy natural resources, or great works of art."[10]

But destroying natural resources or works of art is not always wrong, and certainly not wrong in the sense in which murder is wrong. Warren acknowledges this when she says, "It follows from my argument that when an unwanted or defective infant is born into a society which cannot afford and/or is not willing to care for it, then its destruction is permissible."[11]

Being a Person and Functioning As a Person

The failure of Warren's argument can be seen in light of the distinction between being a person and functioning as a person. Consider Warren's five characteristics of a person: consciousness, reasoning, self-motivated activity, the capacity to communicate, and the presence of self-concepts. Imagine a person in a deep, dreamless sleep. She is not conscious, she cannot reason, etc.; she lacks all five of these traits. She is not functioning as a person; that is part of what being asleep means. But of course she is a person, she retains fully her status of being a person, and killing her while asleep is just as wrong as killing her while she is awake and functioning as a person.

Functioning as a person refers to all the activities proper to persons as persons, to thinking in the broadest sense. It includes reasoning, deciding, imagining, talking, experiencing love and beauty, remembering, intending, and much more. The term *function* does not refer here to bodily functions, but rather to those of the mind, though certain bodily functions, especially those of the brain, are necessary conditions for functioning as a person.

When Warren points out that a fetus satisfies none of the five traits she mentions, she shows only that a fetus does not function as a person, not that it lacks the being of a person, which is the crucial thing.

At this point several objections are likely to be raised: First, the sleeping person will soon wake up and function as a person, while the being in the womb will not.

In reply, neither the sleeping person nor the being in the womb now display the qualities of a functioning person. Both will display them. It is only a matter of time. Why should the one count as a real person because the time is short, while the other does not, simply because in her case the time is longer?

Second, the sleeping adult was already self-conscious, had already solved some problems. Therefore, she has a history of functioning as a person. The child in the womb has no such history. Thus Tooley argues that "an organism cannot have a serious right to life [be a person] unless it either now possesses, or did possess at some time in the past, the concept of a self . . . [what is required for functioning as a person]."[12] The human being sound asleep counts as a person because she once functioned as a person; the child never did, so she does not count as a person.

True, there is a difference with respect to past functioning, but the difference is not morally relevant. The reason the child never functioned as a person is because her capacity to do so is not yet sufficiently developed. It cannot be, for she is near the beginning of her existence, in the first phase of her life.

Imagine a case of two children. One is born comatose, and he will remain so until the age of nine. The other is healthy at birth, but as soon as she achieves the concept of a continuing self for a brief time, she, too, lapses into a coma, from which she will not emerge until she is nine. Can anyone seriously hold that the second child is a person with a right to life, while the first child is not? In one case, self-awareness will come only after nine years have elapsed, in the other, it will return. In both cases, self-awareness will grow and develop. Picture the two unconscious children lying side by side. Almost nine years have passed. Would it not be absurd to say that only one of them is a person, that there is some essential, morally relevant, difference between them? Imagine someone about to kill both of them. Consistent with his theory, Tooley would have to say: "You may kill the first, for he is not a person. He is human only in the genetic sense, since he has no history of functioning as a person. You may not kill the second, since she does have such a history." If this distinction is absurd when applied to the two born human beings, is it any less absurd when applied to two human beings, one born (asleep in a bed), the other preborn (sleeping in the womb)?

In short, when it comes to functioning as a person, there is no moral difference between "did, but does not" (the sleeping adult) and "does not, but will." (the small child).

Third, a sleeping person has the capacity to function as a person and therefore counts as being a person, even though this capacity is not now actualized. In contrast, a child in the womb lacks this capacity, so he does not count as being a person.

This is the most fundamental objection, and probably underlies the preceding two objections. In considering it, compare the following beings:

A. A normal adult, sound asleep, not conscious.
B. An adult in a coma from which he will emerge in, say, six months and function normally as a person.
C. A normal newborn baby.
D. A normal baby soon to be born.
E. A normal "well proportioned small scale baby" in the womb at seven weeks.
F. A normal embryo or zygote.

Case A, the normal adult sound asleep, is someone who has the being of a person, who is not now functioning as a person, and who clearly has the capacity to function as a person. I want to show now that all the other cases are essentially similar to this one. That is, if case A is a person—a full-fledged member of the moral community, a being with a right to life, whose value lies in his own being and dignity, and not merely in his significance for others (like natural resources and works of art), a being whose willful destruction is murder—each of the other cases is a person as well.

The objection claims that the being in the womb lacks the capacity to function as a person. True, it lacks what I shall call the *present immediate capacity* to function, where responses may be immediately elicited. Such a capacity means the capability of functioning, where such a capability varies enormously among people, and normally develops and grows (as a result of learning and other experiences).

The capability of functioning as a person is grounded in the *basic inherent capacity* to function. This is proper to the being of a person and it has a physical basis, typically the brain and nervous system. It is a capacity that grows and develops as the child grows and develops.

This basic inherent capacity may be fully accessible, as in a normal sleeping adult. It then exists in its present immediate form. It may also exist in other forms where it is latent, as in reversible coma. I shall call this the latent-1 capacity, where the basic inherent capacity is present but temporally damaged or blocked. In a small child, the basic inherent capacity is there but insufficiently developed for the child to function in the manner of a normal adult. I shall call this the latent-2 capacity.

Let me turn to the actual refutation of this objection. I will begin with cases A through E (replies 1 and 2), then case F (3), then abnormal or handicapped human beings (4).

(1) The beings on our list, A through E, differ only with respect to their present immediate capacity to function. They are all essentially similar with respect to their basic inherent capacity, and through this, their being as persons.

Thus the adult in a coma, case B, is not essentially different from the sleeping person in case A. Person B is in a deep, deep sleep; person A in a comparatively superficial sleep. Person B cannot be awakened easily; person A can be. Person B is in a very long sleep; person A is in a short sleep, say 8 hours. Both have the basic inherent capacity: in A it is present immediate; in B it is latent-1. That is certainly not a morally relevant difference. If the status of persons is to be viewed in terms of capacity to function as a person, then surely a latent-1 capacity (temporarily blocked—person B) qualifies as much as a non-latent capacity (present immediate—person A).

Consider now the newborn baby, case C. He too has the physical basis for functioning as a person (brain, nervous system, etc.). Only his overall development is insufficient for him to actually function on the level of the normal adult. He has a latent-2 capacity. Thus there is an essential similarity between cases B and C, the adult in a coma and the newborn baby. Neither has the present immediate capacity to function as a person. Both take longer than the sleeping adult (case A) to wake up from their slumber. But both have a latent capacity to function, because they both have the basic inherent capacity to function. In the case of B, the impossibility of eliciting an immediate response is due to an abnormality, which brought on the coma. In the other, case C, this is due to the fact that the being is not yet far enough along in his process of development. In both cases the basic inherent capacity is there, it is merely latent.

Cases C and D, babies just after birth and just before birth, are clearly the same in terms of their capacity to function as persons. Birth is, among other things, the beginning of vast new opportunities to develop the basic inherent capacity to function by seeing, hearing, touching, etc., a capacity that is equally present just before birth.

Case E, a baby at seven weeks, has "all the internal organs of the adult";[13] and "after the eighth week no further primordia will form; *everything* is already present that will be found in the full term baby."[14] It is these "internal organs" and "primordia" that constitute the physical base for the basic inherent capacity to function as a person. They are substantially present in both the very young preborn child, at seven and eight weeks (case E), and the older preborn child (case D). Thus the cases D and E are essentially similar with respect to their basic inherent capacity, and because of this, their being as persons.

In brief, cases A through E are essentially similar. Cases B through E are similar in themselves (each represents a latent capacity); and, taken together, in comparison with A (present immediate capacity). There is no essential difference among cases B through E. If a person whose lack of present immediate capacity to function is due to a disorder (as in case B) should be respected as a person, then surely a being whose lack of this capacity to function is due to insufficient development (cases C through E) should also be respected as a person. Both are beings with the potential to function as a person; and this they can only have if they have the basis for it, that is, the being of a person. Case B represents a latent-1 capacity, cases C through E, a latent-2 capacity; both are forms of the basic inherent capacity to function, proper to the nature of a person. If a latent-1 capacity (B) is a mark of a person, then surely a latent-2 capacity (C through E) is also a mark of a person. Both B and C through E represent beings who will have the capability to function as persons, who lack this capability now because of the condition of the working basis of this capability (brain, nervous system, etc.). In one, that condition is one of disorder or blockage, in the other, the lack of development proper to the age of the being in question.

(2) The essential similarity among the beings A through E is also established if they are imagined as the same being: a being in the womb developing from seven weeks to birth (E to C), then lapsing into a coma (B), then recovering (A). Thus if there is a person at the end (A), there is also that same person at the beginning (E). It is the same person going through various stages, representing first a latent-2 capacity, then a latent-1 capacity, and finally a present immediate capacity.

I am now a being capable of functioning as a person (present immediate capacity). Many years ago I was a small newborn baby, and before that a smaller child in my mother's womb. My capabilities have changed, they have increased as my basic inherent capacity to function as a person has developed; but I remain always *the same person*, the same essential being, the being who has these growing capabilities. If I am essentially a person now, I was essentially a person then, when I was a baby. The fact that my capabilities to function as a person have changed and grown does not alter the absolute continuity of my essential being, that of a person. In fact, this variation in capabilities presupposes the continuity of my being as a person. It is *as a person* that I develop my capabilities to function as a person. It is because I am a person that I have these capabilities, to whatever degree.

And so the basic reality is being as a person. This is what entails your right to life, the wrongness of killing you, the necessity of respecting you as a person, and not just as a desired commodity like a natural resource. It is *being* a person that is crucial morally, not *functioning* as a person. The very existence and meaning of functioning as a person can have its basis only in the being of a person. It is because you have the being of a person that you can function as a person, although you might fail to function as a person and still retain your full being as a person.

(3) Let us turn now to case F, the zygote or embryo. There are three considerations that show the essential similarity between this case and cases A through E.

First: The continuum argument applies here as well. The adult now sleeping is the same being who was once an embryo and a zygote. There is a direct continuity between the zygote at F and the child at E, through to the adult at A. If the being at the later stages should be given the respect due to persons, then that same being should also be given this respect when he is at an earlier stage.

Second: It may be objected that the zygote lacks "a well-developed physical substratum of consciousness"[15]—that it lacks the actual physical basis (brain, nervous system, etc.) for the basic inherent capacity to function as a person. This is incorrect. The zygote does not lack this physical basis; it is merely that it is now in a primitive, undeveloped form. The zygote has the essential structure of this basis; a structure that will unfold, grow, develop, mature, which takes time. As Blechschmidt states, ". . . the fertilized ovum (zygote) is already a form of man. Indeed, it is already active. . . . All the organs of the developing organism are differentiation products of each unique [fertilized] human ovum."[16] That is, the organs that form the physical basis for the more developed basic inherent capacity to function as a person (at various stages, E to A) are "differentiation products" of what is already present in the zygote. Thus the zygote has, in primitive form, the physical basis of his basic inherent capacity to function as a person. In the adult this same basis exists in developed form.

The zygote actually has the basic inherent capacity to function as a person because he has the essential physical structure for this. This structure is merely undeveloped:

> The zygotic self cannot actually breathe, but he *actually has* the
> undeveloped capacity for breathing. Nor can this zygotic self actually

think and love as an adult does, but he *actually has* the undeveloped capacity for thinking and loving. And the human zygote could not actually have such undeveloped capacities unless he actually IS the kind of being that *has* such capacities. Just as it is obviously true that only a human being can have the *developed* capacities for thinking and loving, it should be obviously true that only a human being can have the *undeveloped* capacities for thinking and loving.[17]

Elsewhere, Robert Joyce remarks:

A person is not an individual with a *developed* capacity for reasoning, willing, desiring, and relating to others. A person is an individual with a *natural* capacity for these activities and relationships, whether this natural capacity is ever developed or not—i.e., whether he or she ever attains the functional capacity or not. Individuals of a rational, volitional, self-conscious *nature* may never attain or may lose the functional capacity for fulfilling this nature to any appreciable extent. But this inability to fulfill their nature does not negate or destroy the nature itself.[18]

A being at the beginning of his development cannot be expected to possess what only that development can provide for him. He is already the being who will later function as a person, given time. The sleeping person is also a being who will later function as a person, only he will do it much sooner. What they each have now—a fully developed brain in one case, and a potential brain, that which will grow into a developed brain, in the other—is a basis for their capacity to function as persons. It is the same essential basis, one undeveloped, the other developed. It is merely a matter of degree; there is no difference in kind.

One must already *be* a human person in order to develop the human brain necessary for the present and immediate capacity to function as a person. As we noted earlier, "*only a human being can develop a human brain, a human brain cannot develop before a human exists.*" "Human being" means of course "human person," the same being in different phases of his existence.

Third: Imagine a person J solving new and relatively complex problems (item 2 on Mary Ann Warren's list).

1. Person J *is doing* this.

2. Person K *has the capacity* to do this (like the sleeping person A on the list).

3. Person L *has the capacity to learn* to do this (to learn what is

necessary for having this capacity; for example, a child in school).

4. Person M *has the capacity to acquire*, by natural development, what is necessary for the capacity to learn to do this.

What is true of person M applies to a newborn baby (C), or a baby about to be born (D), or a much younger baby, at seven weeks (E). It applies equally to that same being at a still earlier stage of her development, as a zygote (F).

There is a continuity here. If being a person is approached from the point of view of capacity to function as a person, then clearly persons K, L, and M are essentially alike. Each is removed by one or more steps from the person J, who is actually functioning as a person. None of these steps is of moral or metaphysical significance. In reverse order from M to J, there is, respectively, a capacity to acquire, a capacity to learn, and a capacity to do what the next being represents. If doing is to count for being a person, then surely the capacity to do, the capacity to learn to do, and the capacity to acquire what is needed to learn to do must also count.

This chain argument shows not only the essential similarity between the zygote (F) and the child at later stages (C through E) but also the essential similarity among the beings A through F.

We are now in a better position to understand the real significance of past functioning as a person, which is present in the adult (asleep or in a coma), and absent from the child. It is a sign that the being in question is a person. Because a certain being has functioned in the past, he must be a person. But if he has not, or we do not know it, it does not follow that he is not a person. Other indications must also be examined. In the case of a small baby, born or preborn, including the zygote stage of a baby's existence, there are three such indications.

One, the *continuum of being*, the identity of the person. The baby is now the same being, the same "self" that the child will be later on. "I was once a newborn baby and before that, a baby inside my mother." Since it is a human being's essential nature to be a person, this being—as a zygote, as a seven-week-old baby, as a newborn—is always a person.

Two, the *continuum of essential structure* for the basic inherent capacity to function as a person. The baby as a zygote has the essential physical structure that represents this capacity. Both in the primitive form of development and in all later stages of development, there exists the same essential structure.

Three, the *continuum of capacities*, to acquire, learn, and do. The zygote has the capacity to acquire what is needed to learn to function as a person.

If a being is not now functioning as a person, is he a person? Two perspectives can be used in answering this question: present to past and present to future. An affirmative answer in either case suffices to indicate that the being in question is a person. Present to past: yes, he is a person because he functioned as a person in the past. Present to future: yes, he is a person because he will function as a person in the future, based on the three-fold continuum. The mistake of writers such as Tooley is to ignore the second of these.

(4) Let us turn, finally, to the case of abnormal, or handicapped, human beings. Does the analysis offered here—that the beings A through F are essentially similiar with respect to their being as persons, and their basic inherent capacity to function as persons—apply equally to abnormal, or handicapped, human beings?

It certainly does. A handicapped person (physically, mentally, or both) has the same being of a person as the rest of us who are fortunate enough not to be so afflicted. He has, with this, the same dignity, the same rights as the rest of us. We must "do unto him" as we would want others to "do unto us" if we were afflicted with a handicap. Just as there is no morally relevant difference between a normal functioning person and a small child who cannot yet function as a person because of his lack of development, there is also no morally relevant difference between the normal functioning person and one incapable, or less capable, of doing so. Any one of us who now has the present immediate capacity to function as a person may lose it through a severe illness or accident. If that happened to you, you would still have the same status of being a person, the same dignity and rights of a person.

Even a very severely abnormal or handicapped human being has the basic inherent capacity to function as a person, which is a sign that he is a person. The abnormality represents a hindrance to the actual working of this capacity, to its manifestation in actual functioning. It does not imply the absence of this capacity, as in a nonperson.

The normal adult and child were selected for this analysis because it is in them that the essence of functioning as a person, or its usual absence because of (normal) lack of development, can most easily be seen and understood. Once recognized there, it applies equally to all persons, regardless of the degree to which they are able to accomplish it.

To conclude this part of the main argument: would Mary Ann Warren admit the adult sound asleep to the status of person? If not, she is saying it is acceptable to kill people in their sleep. Suppose she admits sleeping person A. She must then admit sleeping person B, the one in a longer, deeper sleep. The only differences are the length and nature of the sleep. In each case there is a being with a capacity to function as a person, who will, if not killed, wake up to exercise it. Clearly there is no morally relevant difference between them. This proves decisively that present immediate capacity to function as a person is not necessary to being a person. This is plainly true of the newborn baby C. Having then admitted B as a person, Warren is forced to admit C as well, for the two cases are essentially the same: no present immediate capacity to function as a person, the presence of a latent capacity, rooted in the basic inherent capacity.

With this, Warren's whole argument is destroyed. For she herself claims that, in terms of their intrinsic nature, their being (as persons or nonpersons), the newborn baby (C) and the preborn baby (D through F) are morally on a par. Neither (her argument shows) can now function as a person. Both, I have shown, have the basic inherent capacity to function as persons. In all of these cases, there is the same being, with the same essential structure of a person, differing only with respect to the degree of development of the capacity to function as a person.

Views like those of Warren and Tooley do not reach the crucial point: the fact that a human being functions as a person or has the present and immediate capacity to do so, is not the ground for his dignity, preciousness, and right to life; rather, that decisive ground is the fact of his *being* a person.

The Reality of the Person Seen through Love

Imagine a person you deeply love in a coma from which he will emerge in about thirty weeks, perfectly normal. Apply Warren's five criteria. He fails them all. He is not conscious, he cannot reason, he is incapable of self-motivated activity, he cannot communicate, he has no self-concepts or awareness of himself. This doesn't mean he is not a person; that he has no right to life of his own; that he could be killed if no one cared. He is just as real, just as precious, just as much a full person as if he were now capable of functioning as a person. It is just as important and necessary to respect him and care for him as if he were awake.

The child in the womb is in a comparable state, only his "sleep" is normal and is not preceded by a phase where he is able to function as a person. He is also unseen. But none of these makes a morally relevant difference. If one person in "deep sleep" (inability to function as a person) is to be respected and cared for, then the other person should be cared for and respected as well.

The Distinction Applied to Some Pro-Abortion Views

Given our understanding of the distinction between being a person and functioning as a person, we can now come to a better understanding of some of the things put forward by defenders of abortion.

1. *Drawing Lines.* We examined ten suggested places to draw the line between what is supposed to be merely a *preparation* for a person and the actual person. Every line proved false. In each case the same fully real person is clearly present on both sides of it. No line marks any real difference with regard to *being* a person: the person is there before as well as after. But many of these lines do have a bearing on *functioning* as a person. Thus a baby after birth interacts with others in a way not possible before birth. A baby who has reached sentience has developed an important dimension of his capacity to function as a person. And the presence of a functioning brain marks a significant milestone in the child's development as a functioning person. If these lines seem to have any plausibility, it is because one has in mind functioning as a person. But the plausibility evaporates when one realizes that the crucial thing is not functioning as a person, but being a person.

2. *The Agnostic Position.* Realizing that these lines do not work, some people say that it is simply not known when a human person begins to exist. What should be said is, rather, that it is not known when *functioning* as a person begins, for there is indeed no single place on the continuum of human life at which this begins. It is a gradual development. But the *being* of the person is there all along. And the development is what it is because the being of the person is there all the way through: it is the person's development. Agnosticism regarding functioning as a person should not lead to agnosticism regarding being a person.

3. *The Gradualist Position.* False when applied to the *being* of a person, the gradualist position is absolutely valid when applied to *functioning* as a person. That is indeed a matter of degree. We gradually develop our basic inherent capacity to think and to communicate.

4. *The Notion of Potential Person.* False when applied to *being* a person, the notion of potential person has a validity when applied to *functioning* as a person. If by "person" we mean "functioning person," for

example, a normal adult making a complex decision or reading a book, then clearly a child in the womb, or just born, or even at age one, is only potentially such a person. A baby is a potential functioning person; but he is that only because he has the actual being of a person.

Human *Is Not Merely a Biological Category*

The theory advanced by writers such as Fletcher, Tooley, and Warren holds that killing babies is permissible because they are not persons; whereas, in fact, they are nonfunctioning persons. A functioning person is one who either is now actually functioning as a person, or has the present immediate capacity to do so. What the theory holds is that only functioning persons (and those who were once such persons) are truly persons. It may, therefore, be called the *functioning-person theory*.[19]

Advocates of the functioning-person theory hold that it is not in itself wrong to kill human beings; that this can only be wrong when the being in question is a "person," as defined by the theory (one who has the present immediate capacity to function as a person, or has had it in the past.) Such advocates hold that the single fact that a being is human does not constitute any reason for not deliberately killing it. Hence, they say, killing babies, born or preborn, is not in itself wrong. *If* it is ever wrong, it is so because these babies are wanted and would be missed by adults. The thesis, as Tooley puts it, is that "membership in a biological species is not morally significant *in itself*."[20] In the words of Singer, "Whether a being is or is not a member of our species is, in itself no more relevant to the wrongness of killing it than whether it is or is not a member of our race."[21] Warren says that being human in the genetic sense does not give the being in question a right to life.

The thrust of this is to drive a wedge between two categories of beings—persons and human beings—and to hold that it is the former, not the latter, that is of moral significance. There are two fundamental and disastrous errors in this approach. The first concerns the category of persons, and consists in equating this term with functioning persons (present or past), thereby excluding babies who have not yet developed the present immediate capacity to function as persons. The second error, closely related to the first, is to dismiss the category of human being as not (in itself) morally significant.

Proponents of the functioning-person theory are quite right in maintaining that there is a distinction between persons and human beings. They point out that there could be persons who are not human beings, for example, creatures on distant planets who can think, make decisions, feel gratitude, and so forth. They would certainly be persons, without being human beings. In the Christian faith, angels are persons, but not human beings. So, not all persons are necessarily human beings. But, I shall maintain, all human beings are persons (though not necessarily functioning persons). Being human is not necessary to being a person (there could be others), but it is sufficient, for all human beings are persons.

The fundamental error here is the notion that human is a mere biological category,[22] that it designates simply one of many zoological species. If this were so, if the difference between human and other species were like the difference between, say, cats and dogs, or tigers and bears, then of course it would be morally irrelevant. But human—though it may be viewed as a zoological species, and compared to other species in the study of anatomy and physiology—is not simply a biological category. It is rather a mode of being a person.

Human designates, in its most significant meaning, a type of being whose nature it is to be a person. A person is a being who has the basic inherent capacity to function as a person, regardless of how developed this capacity is, or whether or not it is blocked, as in severe senility. We respect and value human beings, not because they are a certain biological species, but because they are persons; because it is the nature of a human being to be a person. All human beings are persons, even if they can no longer function as persons (severe senility), or cannot yet function as persons (small babies), or cannot now function as persons (sound asleep or under anesthesia or in a coma).

The theory is correct when it says that it is persons who are of moral significance; and that persons need not be human persons (they may be martians or angels). The error is to fail to recognize that humans are persons. Being human is a mode of existence of persons. So we should respect human beings—all human beings, regardless of race, degree of intelligence, degree of bodily health, degree of development as functioning persons—because they are persons.

"Do unto others as you would have them do unto you." Surely the class of others is not limited to functioning persons. It includes all human beings; perhaps others as well, but at least all human beings. "Do unto others" must include, very specifically, the lame, the retarded, the weak. It must include those no longer able to fuction as persons, as well as those not yet able to do so.

When we love another person, it is the *total human being* that we love, not just his or her rationality, or that which makes him or her capable of functioning as a person. We love their individual mode of being, expressed in many ways, such as gestures, facial features, tone of voice, expressions in the eyes, etc. These are, of course, in one respect, bodily features. This does not render them merely biological in the sense dismissed by Singer, Tooley, and others. They are dimensions of the total human person.

The present immediate capacity to function as a person is not essential to this fundamental reality, the total human being. When a loved one is under anesthesia, he is still fully that person, that total human being. More than that, part of the beauty, the charm, the lovableness of a small child is that he is *only a child*, not yet matured, not yet (fully) capable of functioning as a person. The total human being in such a case does not even require the present capacity to function as a person.

Warren, Tooley, and Singer fall into the trap of seeing "human" as a mere biological category because of an earlier, and more fundamental, error: confusing person and functioning person (present or past), indeed, grouping the two together. For if it is assumed that "person" equals "functioning person," and if a small child is not a (fully) functioning person, it follows that the child is not a person. If the child is not a human *person*, "human" can then refer only to a biological species. Once one strips the child of his status as a person (on the grounds that he cannot now function as a person), what is there left except his being a member of a biological species? Separated from the notion of person, the notion of "human" is indeed only a biological species, and as such morally irrelevant.

The fallacy is, then, the separation of human and person, the failure to see that humans are precisely *human persons*. Humans are human persons, where "persons" includes nonfunctioning persons as well as functioning persons.

The Notion of Potential Person

In arguing for his thesis that abortion is morally right, Tooley goes to great lengths to show that potential persons do not have a serious right to life. "There appears to be little hope of defending a conservative view [i.e., that abortion is wrong] unless it can be shown that the destruction of potential persons is intrinsically wrong, and seriously so."[23]

On the contrary, abortion is wrong because it destroys an actual person. The assumption that the being in the womb is merely a potential person is typical of the functioning-person theory. Thus Warren speaks of the "fetus" as a "potential person";[24] and of "its potential for becoming a person."[25] She denies that the latter "provides any basis whatever for the claims that it has any significant right to life."[26]

What is potential about the child in the womb is not her *being* as a person, but rather her *functioning* as a person. That functioning is potential in the sense that she now has only a latent capacity to function, and not yet a present immediate capacity, because her basic inherent capacity has not yet had a chance to develop sufficiently.

The child in the womb is not, as the functioning-person theory maintains, a potential person, but rather a *potentially functioning actual person.* To be a potentially functioning person already ensures that the baby is a person, an actual, real, full person, for a potentially functioning person must necessarily be a person.

In the words of Joyce, "a one celled person at conception is not a potential person, but an actual person with great potential for development and self-expression. That single-celled individual is just as actually a person as you and I."[27]

I submit that there is no such thing as a potential person. The ovum and the sperm are preparations for a new person. Each of them is not that person in potential form, because it is not that person at all. There is a radical break between sperm/ovum and the new person in the zygotic state. The transition from "potential x" to "actual x" always involves a continuity. Thus a medical student is recognized as a potential doctor because when the student *becomes* a doctor this will have happened within a continuity involving the same person. In contrast, as Joyce puts it, "sperm and ovum. . . do not, even together, become a new human life, because they do not survive beyond conception."[28]

"The sperm and the ovum," Joyce says, "are not potential [personal] life; rather they are potential *causes* of individual human life."[29]

The Achievement View

The *functioning-person theory* implies a certain elitism, something that may be called the *achievement view,* namely, that only human beings who have achieved a certain degree of development of the present immediate capacity to function as persons count as real persons.[30] Thus Mary Ann Warren, Michael Tooley, and Peter Singer dismiss infants as nonpersons simply on the grounds that they have not yet achieved the status of functioning persons. But why hold that against them? That they have not achieved this status is perfectly normal, and could not be otherwise; for they have not yet reached that stage in their development over time when such a capacity is normal. The achievement view is a clear example of discrimination: "You don't count as a real person, for you have not yet achieved the degree of development necessary for the present immediate capacity to function as a person."

The functioning-person theory is presented as if it were the product of careful, rational, philosophical analysis, a contribution to clear thinking. It gains this appearance largely from the element of truth it contains: that the concepts of "person" and "human being" are not identical, for there could be nonhuman persons. This hides its true nature, that it is in fact a form of elitism, leading to discrimination of the worst sort. For the theory implies that only some persons count: those who have achieved the status of functioning persons.

"At what point in its development does a fetus become a person?" (Or, when does it become human, meaning a person, since it is obviously human in the biological sense all along.) This whole question is misplaced. For there is a person, a human being, all along. It is only a matter of degree of development of the basic inherent capacity to function as a person. What we can now see, with new clarity, is that this question assumes the achievement view, indeed expresses it, and would collapse without it. Translated, the question reads: "How much must a human being achieve in the way of attaining the capability of functioning as a person in order to count as a person, that is, a being whose life we must respect?" The answer is clear: nothing. No achievement is necessary, and to demand it is elitism and discrimination. What is required is *being*, not achievement: being a person, having the nature of a person, regardless of how far along the achievement scale one has progressed.

It is wrong for a white to demand that real persons be white in order to count as persons. Blacks are equally persons, though they are "different." So too, it is wrong for a functioning person to demand that real persons be capable of functioning as persons. Small babies, incapable of this—or less capable—are equally persons, though they are "different." Being white is not a special achievement that blacks have failed to reach. Having the capability of functioning as a person, while it is an achievement, is equally irrelevant, morally. To demand it as a condition for membership in the class of persons is equally unjust and discriminatory.

It is wrong to discriminate against anyone who has not yet achieved the status of a functioning person. It is equally wrong to discriminate against anyone who is *no longer* capable of functioning because of severe senility. Likewise, it is wrong to discriminate against anyone who cannot now function, whether or not he ever could function in the past and whether or not he will be able to function in the future.

In the present context, in which we are analyzing a theory that raises—as a serious issue—the question of which human beings may be killed and which may not, it is not a matter of discrimination in merely a general sense, but something very specific, and particularly odious: It is a discrimination that takes advantage of a person's inability to function as a person and uses that against them as a pretext for killing them. The effect of adopting the functioning-person theory would be to legitimize this taking advantage of a person's lack of ability. This is sheer "might over right," power and ability over frailty and (natural) disability. Those who have power and ability exercise it over those who do not—infants whom their theory can rule out as non-persons. I submit that, quite generally, it is wrong for those who have the advantage of power and ability to take advantage of it over those who do not and to discriminate against them on the basis of this advantage. Let me express this in terms of the following moral principle:

> It is always wrong for persons who have power and ability to take advantage of their status by discriminating against persons who are powerless, especially in order to kill them.

And, as a corollary: it is always wrong to take advantage of anyone's inability to function as a person by acts of discrimination that would deny that individual the full respect that is due to every person.

This principle and its corollary apply not only to actions but also to rules and theories that would legitimatize such actions. Any theory that calls for or allows such discrimination is itself an immoral theory. (This is not a moral judgment on those who propose the theory, but strictly a judgment on the theory itself, in terms of its content and its logical consequences.) The functioning-person theory legitimizes the deliberate killing of small babies merely because they have not reached a sufficient level of development as predetermined by the theory. This is immoral.

Multiple Definitions of Functioning Person

The functioning-person theory wants to divide humanity into two separate categories: "persons" and "mere human beings," who are nonpersons. I have argued that this is a false division, that all human beings are persons, and that "person" does not mean "functioning person" but includes those with a merely latent capacity to function.

The falsity of the view that "person" means "functioning person" can also be shown in another way—that is, by carefully examining the notion of functioning person with respect to the definition provided by the advocates of the functioning-person theory. What is this definition? What characteristics must a being have in order to be classified as a person? A survey of the current literature on this topic reveals a bewildering array of suggestions, some brief, some detailed, some at variance with others.[31] Let us look at some examples:

Mary Ann Warren proposes consciousness, reasoning, self-motivated activity, the capacity to communicate, the presence of self-concepts and self-awareness as the characteristics of a person.

Peter Singer offers a definition of "person" that "selects two crucial characteristics . . . as the core of the concept": rationality and self-consciousness.[32]

Joseph Fletcher proposes "a list of criteria or indicators" of "human-ness" (by which he means personhood). They include minimum intelli-gence ("Any individual of the species *homo sapiens* who falls below an I.Q. grade of 40 . . . is questionably a person; below the mark of 20, not a person. . . . The *ratio*. . . is what makes a person of the *vita* [life]."), self-awareness, self-control, a sense of time, the capacity to relate to others, and curiosity.[33]

Michael Tooley, in his 1973 paper, "A Defense of Abortion and Infanticide," offers this list: (1) The capacity to envisage a future for oneself, and to have desires about one's future states. (2) The capacity to have a concept of a self, the concept of a continuing subject of experiences and other mental states. (3) Being a self. (4) Self-consciousness. (5) The capacity for self-consciousness.[34]

In his book, *Abortion and Infanticide*, Tooley observes, "There is very general agreement [among writers on this topic] that something is not a person unless it is, in some sense, capable of consciousness."[35] Further, that "many people . . . feel that mere consciousness is not itself sufficient to make something a person, and several proposals have been advanced as to what additional properties are required."[36] He then gives a list of some of "the more important suggestions" for these additional properties. Fifteen are mentioned, many of them similar to those listed above. Among the others are: (1) The capacity to experience pleasure and/or pain. (2) The capacity to have desires. (3) The capacity to use language.[37]

Tooley devotes a major portion of his book to his own proposal for defining a person. His perspective is that of "a right to continued existence." His thesis is, "An individual cannot have a right to continued existence unless there is at least one time at which it possesses the concept of a continuing self or mental substance."[38]

A few pages later he says "that some *psychological continuity* is required" for one to be a person; and that "there must also be *recognition of the continuity* by the enduring mental substance in question [the per-son]."[39] Putting them together, it seems that Tooley's criteria for being a person (as listed in his book) are: (1) being conscious, (2) possessing the concept of a continuing self or mental substance (at least at one time), (3) recognition of one's psychological continuity over time.[40]

Which of these definitions, or sets of indicators or criteria, or combinations of them, is the correct one for the concept of a person? Which features are necessary for being a person? Which ones are sufficient? Which ones are both necessary and sufficient? This problem is further complicated by the fact that the authors cited here offer conflicting views about the features to be used in defining the concept of person. Thus, *rationality* is affirmed by Warren and Singer, and denied by Tooley in his book.[41] It seems to be affirmed by Fletcher ("minimum intelligence"). *Self-conciousness* is affirmed by Warren, Singer, and Fletcher, and by Tooley in three of his articles.[42] It is later denied by Tooley in his book.[43] *Being an agent* or having self-control is affirmed by Fletcher ("control of existence"), denied by Tooley.[44]

Which criteria are to be employed is one problem. But there is another, equally serious problem. Given a criterion or feature that is to be employed in defining the concept of person, how much of it is necessary? How much is sufficient? Mary Ann Warren, for example, in listing reasoning as one of the features, says it must be "the *developed* capacity to solve new and relatively complex problems." That seems to be a tall order! Why wouldn't reasoning as the capacity to solve elementary problems be sufficient? In any case, how complex must the problems be? Or, more generally, what kinds of reasoning are to be required? And how extensive must the ability to reason be?

All, or virtually all, of these characteristics exist in degrees. Some people have more self-control, others less. Self-consciousness awakens gradually in a child. If it is to be counted as part of the definition of a person, how developed must it be? Parallel questions apply to the rest of the items on these lists.

There is still a further problem. Even if we knew which features were essential to being a person, and also how much development was necessary, even then we would have the problem of measuring the features and their degree of development. Given a small born baby, how do we know how much self consciousness the baby has? And suppose a child has a given feature but cannot display it? How are we to exclude such a possibility, so that we don't label the child a nonperson who is, in fact, a person? In a lengthy section of his book, Tooley tries to grapple with the problem of measurement, by examining a complexity of scientific evidence about "neurophysical development."[45] But such evidence, even if it were adequate, could only be indirect, in that it measures the physical requirements for functioning as a person and not the functioning itself, for example, having self-consciousness. Needless to say, Tooley does not solve the problem.

The conclusion to be drawn from this is the following: There is no one correct definition of "person," in the sense of functioning person. It is not that there is a correct definition but no one has yet found it. There are many definitions, and a given being will be a person under one of them, and not under another. It is similar to the term *capable*. Is a given person capable? Yes, for some things, or to a certain degree; no, for other things, or to a greater degree. There are many definitions of capable, and the attempt to find the one true definition would obviously be misguided. If "person" is to be defined in terms of "capable of functioning," the same thing applies. There can be no one correct definition of person as functioning person, because "functioning person" means precisely: one who has the present immediate capacity to function. And functioning as a person means a wide variety of things, each to varying degrees, as the above sample of proposals amply demonstrates.

This wide variety, representing the plurality and complexity of what it means to function as a person, involves two fundamental dimensions.

One is *gradual development*. The attainment of the status of functioning as a person is something that a human being develops gradually. During growth and development, both in the womb and after birth, the child gradually acquires more and more of the features discussed here, and each of them to greater and greater degrees. There is no one moment, or even a short period of time (such as a week), where one could draw a line and say, "Before that there is no functioning person, after that, there is." Thus even if we had an adequate definition, consisting of features A through Z, that makes someone a functioning person, it would still be impossible to divide humanity into two groups: human persons and human nonpersons. Whatever definition there is, a human being grows into the features that comprise it.

Consider self-consciousness: A human being is somewhat self-conscious at an early stage in life, a bit more later, still more at a later stage, and so on. The point is not that we do not know when these stages occur, or just what degree of self-consciousness is involved during each of them. The point is that self-consciousness is itself a matter of degree. And so a set of defining characteristics of the person, even if we had one, would have to be in terms of more or less. "Person" (in this context) means "functioning person," and a being that exemplifies more of A through Z, or exemplifies them to a greater degree, would have more capabilities of functioning as a person. There can be no definition of person that picks out certain beings and excludes others; there can only be various features (such as self-consciousness) that different human beings exemplify to varying degrees.

The plurality and complexity of what it means to function as a person involves a second dimension, *relativity to context;* that is, how we construe the term person when it is used to designate "functioning person" varies from case to case. Suppose, for example, that in order to be legally binding, a document must be signed with two persons present as witnesses. Here a degree of functioning as a person is required that far exceeds the level attained by, say, a child of three. A three-year-old would hardly be an appropriate witness for the signing of a will. So the degree of attainment of present capacity to function as a person that we have in mind, and require, for someone to be called a person varies according to the situation, and is determined by our needs and interests.

There is no such thing as *the* definition of the term *functioning person* because the features that constitute any definition vary across the spectrum of gradual development, and the spectrum of context. Hence, the definition itself varies: there is no one meaning of functioning person. This shows that the whole attempt, by Warren, Singer, Fletcher, Tooley, and others, to define the person is fundamentally misguided.

In her paper, "Abortion and the Concept of a Person," Jane English reaches what is in part the same conclusion; in part, because she fails to distinguish between being a person and functioning as person. Her thesis is that there is no such thing as the correct definition of a person. She offers a refutation of the view that "the concept of a person can be captured in a straitjacket of necessary and/or sufficient conditions,"[46] which is what would be required for an adequate definition of a person. "Rather," she claims, "'person' is a cluster of features, of which rationality, having a self-concept . . . are only part."[47] Thus, "People typically exhibit rationality . . . but someone who was irrational would not thereby fail to qualify as a person."[48] Her conclusion, in the first part of her paper, is that "our concept of a person is not sharp or decisive enough to bear the weight of a solution to the abortion controversy. To use it to solve that problem is to clarify *obscurum per obscurius* [the obscure by the more obscure]."[49]

When this is applied to the concept of functioning person, it is valid and of great significance. When, as in her paper, it is applied to the concept of being a person—and used as a reason for justifying some abortions—it is a serious mistake. The analysis offered by English is excellent, but she draws the wrong conclusion. What her analysis shows is that *functioning person* cannot be adequately defined. Nothing follows from this regarding *being a person*, especially not the conclusion that the being in the womb is not a person.

Practical Consequences

Consider again the fact that the meaning of *functioning person* is relative to context. When occasions such as validly witnessing the signing of legal documents arise, then a division of humanity into two groups is justified. Here the requirement of a particular level of achievement for functioning as a person is appropriate. But when it is a matter of deciding who will be respected as a real person, and who will be dismissed as a nonperson and treated as a being who may be killed, the requirement of a particular level of achievement for functioning as a person is another matter entirely. Specifically, if it is in the interests of some people to kill a certain class of human beings, they can simply define them as nonpersons, on the grounds that they have not attained (or no longer retain) a particular level of achievement as functioning persons. Abortion is an obvious example. When there is a strong predisposition on the part of some people to destroy a child, there is an interest that can obviously be used to draw a line in the scale of gradual development of the capacity to function as a person, designed specifically to exclude the child that one wants to get rid of. That line may come at birth, or it may come after birth, as in Tooley's analysis, which would justify infanticide as well.[50]

Since there is no one correct definition of person when that term designates "functioning person"; and since functioning as a person is something that develops gradually, any division of human beings into two classes, persons (who are to be respected) and nonpersons (who may be killed), must be based on a decision.[51] This will be a decision based on interests, and where the interest is "getting rid of," any person falling into that unlucky class can be labeled a nonperson and killed with impunity.

Preborn children are a striking example of this, but they are not alone. Parents who decide that their newborn child does not have a meaningful life because of a handicap, or who do not want to be burdened with the extra care that a child needs, can turn to the functioning-person theory, and use the achievement view inherent in it, to define their baby as a nonperson, in order to justify killing him.

When it is personal interests, utilizing the theory of the achievement view, rather than a person's inherent nature, that determines the morality of killing human beings, then ultimately no one is safe. For the functioning-person theory that underlies the achievement view can easily be formulated as excluding not only those who have not yet achieved functioning as a person (as in Tooley), but also those who no longer can function as persons in a particular, specified way. Thus if a person were to suffer a terrible accident that left him in a severely debilitated state, he could be classified as a nonperson and killed by those who wanted to get rid of him.

Ultimately, it would be a matter of power. Those in power could decide the level of achievement necessary for being counted as a person, and whether it would be only a matter of "not yet" or also a matter of "no longer." This is, of course, what we see in the case of abortion. Doctors kill babies, and not the other way around, because doctors have power, babies do not. This applies in an immediate and obvious way to the physical level. In general, the physically strong have the power to crush the physically weak. That is nothing new. What is new is the attempt to legitimize this by a theory: the functioning-person theory with its attendant achievement view. The effect of this is that those in power can decide who will, and who will not, count as a person, depending on whether or not the human being in question had attained (or retained) the requisite achievement.

"Might over right" is truly frightening. When it is raw physical might, with no pretense to moral legitimacy, it is frightening enough. When a claim to moral legitimacy is added, it becomes even more frightening. Murder is perpetrated without even being recognized as murder. The results of the functioning-person theory and achievement view is that, if adopted, they would provide precisely such a pretense of moral legitimacy to murder.

The Dignity of the Human Person

The true alternative to might over right is reverence for the dignity of each person as a person; because he or she has the being of a person.[52]

The important reality of the dignity of the human person can be seen, and taken seriously, in many ways, especially when that dignity is denied or under attack.[53] Slavery, child abuse, sexual molestation, and rape are among some of the more striking examples. Or, a person with a physical handicap is severely beaten by someone who takes advantage of that handicap. Another is the wrongness of taking advantage of a person's inability to function as a person, either because he is not now capable of doing so, or no longer capable, or not yet capable. This is perfectly parallel to the injustice of taking advantage of a person's physical inabilities. Persons are persons, they have the dignity of a person, whether they have these abilities or not. To take advantage of a person's inabilities is to affront his dignity. It is an antithesis to the reverence due to his dignity as a person.

It is wrong to kill a child in the womb, or a newborn baby, on the grounds that he has not yet reached a sufficient degree of functioning as a person. The same applies to a severely retarded child who probably never will achieve a certain normal level of functioning as a person. He has the same human nature, he is equally a person, he has the same dignity as a person fortunate enough to be normal. As always, it is his being as a person that counts, not his capabilities for functioning as a person.

It is the achievement view that constitutes the principal denial of this. In one case (the normal child), it denies his personhood, his dignity, because he has not yet achieved the required level of functioning as a person. In another case (the severely retarded child), it denies his personhood, his dignity, because he will never achieve the required level of functioning. But who says he must? Nobody has the right to set such standards, and impose them on others, especially at the price of their lives.

The normal person deserves our reverence, our respect for his dignity, not because he is normal, not because of actual or potential achievements in functioning as a person, but simply because he is a person. And the non-normal person is equally a person, and deserves equal reverence. If you were to become a victim of a disease or accident that left you severely retarded, incapacitated, you would want your dignity respected just as before. You would still be yourself, the same person, hence a person, hence a being with the dignity of a person. Exactly the same applies to the severely retarded child, and to the preborn child, who is in many respects similar in his capabilities.

Reverence is the most fundamental response due to another person in his dignity; it is not the whole of it. Love is the fulfillment and the highest form of this response. Each in its own way is an antithesis to using a person as a mere means, as in rape, enslavement, and other ways, and to the attitude of "get rid of it" so often displayed in the context of abortion. Each is also an antithesis to the achievement view and its odious discrimination between those who have achieved, and therefore count, and those who have not achieved, and therefore don't count, and thus may be destroyed.

The reality of love as the deepest response to another in his dignity manifests itself in the attitude and work of Mother Theresa of Calcutta. The story is told of a man whom she found abandoned in the gutter of a street. She picked him up, brought him to her home, cared for him in love for the few remaining days (or hours) of his life. He responded by saying, "I have lived like an animal in the street, but I will die like an angel, loved and cared for."[54]

8

A Woman's Right over Her Body?

Does a woman's right over her body give her the right to have an abortion? "After all, it is my body. Do I not have a right to control it? A right to determine what happens in it? Do I not have a right to reproductive freedom, to decide whether or not, or when, to become a mother? I may even grant that the fetus is a person, a small child. If there is a child in my body, and I do not want him there, do I not have the right to remove him? If he stays in me, he draws his sustenance from me. Does he have a right to do this? Do I have a duty to sustain him? Can I not expel him from my womb? Is this not what an abortion amounts to? If I perceive him as an intruder, can I not expel him? If he is a threat to my life or well-being, can I not defend myself by expelling him? In short, I have a right over my body, and if I have an unwanted pregnancy, I can terminate it by having an abortion."

There are three distinct claims here. (1) A woman has no duty to sustain the child; (2) she may expel the child as an intruder; and (3) she may defend herself against him if he is a threat to her life or well-being. The first two claims pertain directly to the general thesis that a woman has a right to an abortion because she has a right over her body. I will examine these two claims in turn. The third claim is more specific. Since it is limited to cases of threats to the life or well-being of the woman, it cannot be used as a ground for the general claim to a right to abortion based on a right over one's body. It belongs in the context of the question of abortion for the life of the woman, which I will pursue in chapter 10.

113

The "No Duty to Sustain" Argument

The core of this argument is the claim that "The woman has no duty to sustain the life of the child. Abortion is the exercise of the right to withdraw the support that the child is not entitled to." This argument has been proposed by Judith Jarvis Thomson[1] and Martha Brandt Bolton.[2] Bolton argues for the right to abortion, and against the view that abortion is immoral:

> To see the incoherence in the anti-abortionists' argument, we need to look at the gaps in their account of what is at stake in an abortion. They emphasize the fetus's alleged right to life. They do not emphasize a matter that is equally important. This is that if a pregnant woman is obligated not to kill a fetus, then she is obligated to do a great deal more than that. She can meet the alleged obligation not to kill only if she takes on the various obligations involved in bearing and having a child. At the least, she must nurture the fetus, carry it to term, and give it birth; she must then care for the infant or make alternative arrangements for its care . . .
>
> It is relatively easy to live without deliberately killing someone; but it may require an indefinitely large commitment of time, energy, emotion, and physical resources to nurture and care for a child.[3]

Thomson argues in the same way. She asks us to imagine the following case. You wake up one morning and find that another person, a famous violinist, is "plugged in" to you so that he can stay alive. You are attached to him, thereby sustaining his life. You did not agree to this; it was forced on you. But if you unplug yourself from him, he will die. It would not be proper to argue, Thomson says, in the following way: "All persons have a right to life, this violinist is a person, therefore he has a right to life, and so you may not detach yourself from him." You have no duty to sustain him, and therefore you may detach yourself from him. You have the right to do this; the violinist has no right to be sustained by you.

Most arguments for abortion try to show that the fetus is not a person, at least not in the same sense as a born person. In contrast, Thomson proposes "that we grant that the fetus is a person from the moment of conception."[4] She then tries to show that abortion is justified nonetheless by appealing to the analogy between being pregnant and having a violinist plugged into you. Being pregnant means the child is plugged into the woman, his life sustained by her. Thomson's basic argument is that, just as anyone may detach himself from the violinist, so too the woman may detach herself from the child. Abortion is such a detachment.

In refuting the "no duty to sustain argument," I shall focus on Thomson's formulation of it, and I shall assume, for the sake of argument, that Thomson is correct when she holds, as one of her basic premises, that the person plugged into the violinist has no duty to sustain him, but may indeed unplug himself from him. (That might be questioned too, but I shall not enter upon it here.) I want to argue that the two cases—the violinist plugged into the person and the child plugged into his mother—are radically and essentially different, that the alleged parallel does not hold; and this for three different reasons.

The First Refutation of This Argument

There are times when we may detach ourselves from another person, even though this results in his death. So far, Thomson has a valid point. Imagine a lifeguard trying to breathe life into a swimmer struggling between life and death. He does this for a long time, but the victim does not respond, nor does he die. He remains on the edge. At some point the lifeguard gives up—he cannot continue indefinitely. And the victim dies. Suppose that the lifeguard kept up his efforts for a reasonable length of time, and that he is then morally justified in giving up. Suppose also that his efforts sustained the victim's life, though he was just barely alive. When we say that the lifeguard was morally justified in giving up, we are saying that, at that point, he did not have (i.e., no longer had) a duty to sustain the life of the victim. It was morally right for him to withhold his support.

So too, it would be right, at least under most conditions, for Thomson to unplug herself from the violinist: she may withhold her support for his life, she need not sustain him. She may sever the link and thus act to withhold life support.

Thomson may withhold support from the violinist, and the lifeguard may withhold support from the drowning victim. They may withhold life sustaining measures—they may not kill the other person. This is the crucial distinction here. Thomson's argument tries to justify abortion as an act of withholding support. But it is also primarily an act of killing. So, even if it were justified under the heading of "withholding," it is not justified because it also falls under the heading of "killing."

Killing refers to actions where (A) the intention is the death of another person, or (B) the intention is something else, but what is actually done is in fact killing. Thus, (A) a killer shoots someone out of hatred because he wants him dead. For (B), imagine that you are trapped in a cave because someone is stuck in the entrance of the cave.[5] (He is there through no fault of his own, and he is not about to die.) You have some dynamite. If you blow him up so that you can get out, you may be said to intend his removal rather than his death, but the act of dynamiting him is of course killing, and murder. Thus killing, the deliberate bringing about of the death of an innocent person occurs, (A) when the agent acts because he wants the person dead, or (B) when it is something else he wants, which is obtained by an action that is in fact killing.

For *withholding*, as the term is used here, two conditions are necessary. The first refers to the intention: it can only be not to sustain, or not save the other person; it cannot be to cause her death. The lifeguard withholds support because he is exhausted, not because he wants the person dead. To withhold support because you want the person dead does not fall under withholding as understood here.

The second necessary condition refers to the mode of implementation. Withholding can obviously take the form of an omission, as when the lifeguard ceases further support for the drowning victim; or you do not give a lifesaving medication to one person because you have decided to give it to another who needs it just as much. It can also take the form of an action, as when Thomson cuts the link connecting her to the violinist. But that action can only be the cutting of the link or something essentially similar. It cannot be an action that is in fact killing, even though the intention is only the severing of a link, i.e., the cessation of support. Thus if the withholding takes the form of an action, it cannot be an action that is in fact killing.

This is where Thomson's argument for abortion clearly fails. Assume that the woman has no duty to sustain the child. This means only that she has the right to withhold her support from him. It does not give her the right to kill the child, which is what abortion is. If Thomson's argument seems to have a plausibility, it is because it views abortion only as an act of withholding support. But this is to overlook what abortion really is: killing the child, by dismembering him or poisoning-burning. Thomson seizes on the withholding of support aspect of abortion, suppressing the deliberate killing aspect. The fact that an act may be right when viewed under one description does not mean that the act itself is right. For example, to describe an act as driving one's car on a public street is to offer a description of it, under which it is perfectly all right. But if, in a particular case, that act includes running over a group of children who are playing there, then the act is quite obviously not right. What is clear from this example is that the latter description completely overrides the former one. Thus the act is clearly wrong because it is an act of killing, even if someone manages to find a description of it under which it is right. So, too, abortion is clearly wrong, even if Thomson manages to find a description of it under which it is, or might be, right.

Put another way, even if the child does not have the positive right to receive sustenance from her mother, she still has the negative right not to be killed. A beggar may not have the positive right to be fed and housed by me; I may withhold that. But he surely has the negative right not to be murdered by me. The same applies to the child.

"But," Thomson might argue, "if the only way I can exercise my right to withhold support for the child within me is by removing him, may I not do so? Even if this causes his death?"

Consider a parallel case. I find a stranger in my house. He will die unless I take care of him. Assume I have no duty to do this, that I may rightly withhold support. Then I may do just that. I cannot throw him out if this means throwing him off a cliff or into a pond where he will drown. That I throw him out in the name of withholding support does not mean that I don't also do something else: kill him. That the woman "throws the child out" in the name of withholding support does not mean that she does not also do something else: kill him. In both cases, the fact that the act is one of killing (murder) makes it wrong, the other description (withholding support) notwithstanding.

Quite generally, if I can exercise a right I have, such as the right to drive my car, to remove an impediment from the mouth of a cave where I'm trapped, to free myself from another person with whom I'm involved, if I can exercise such a right only by killing an innocent person, I may not do so.

Specifically, if the only way I can exercise my right to withhold support is to kill another person, I may not do it. My duty not to kill an innocent person takes precedence over the exercise of my right to withhold support.

Therefore, the "no duty to sustain" argument fails. The wrongness of abortion is that it is the deliberate killing of a person, even if the intention is the withholding of support. The woman's duty not to destroy the child, not to murder him, takes absolute precedence over any right she may have to withhold support.

The Second Refutation of This Argument

The alleged parallel between the person plugged into the violinist and the woman with child fails in a second, also very significant, way.[6] To see this let us put Thomson's argument aside for a moment and look at something else. We all recognize the obligation of parents to take care of their children: to provide shelter and protection, to feed them, to clothe them, to love them, and support them emotionally. They have this obligation even when it costs them a great deal of effort and sacrifice, when it places great burdens on them. The reality and significance of this obligation becomes clear when considering its denial: child neglect.

The parents of a particular child have this obligation to him, and not someone else, because they are his biological parents; because they, and not someone else, begot and conceived the child. It is the biological bond that creates the obligation of parents to take care of their children, and also the rights that accompany this obligation.

This obligation came into existence at conception-fertilization, when the event that grounds the obligation occurred. In begetting and conceiving the child, the parents brought him into existence; they also brought into existence, by the same act, their obligation to nourish and protect him.

Parents have rights over their child, which other persons do not have; for example, the right to discipline him. Rights and duties with regard to children go hand in hand. Parents have these rights because they first have the duties.

Both the rights and the duties of natural parents toward their children come clearly into focus when the process of adoption is considered. Adoption is a legal transfer of rights and obligations to a new party. Only the natural mother can do this (or possibly the father). And she can do this because she is the mother. One can only give over what one already has. What is given over in the adoption process is precisely the relationship of obligations to the child (and the rights corresponding to them) stemming from the fact of conceiving the child. The woman can give her child up for adoption because it is her child: her responsibility to sustain.

Thomson's "violinist argument" fails because the two cases are not parallel. The person hooked up to the violinist (we are assuming) has no duty to sustain him, for he is a total stranger, standing in a relation to the person that is most unnatural. This is exactly the opposite of the mother-child relation, which is most natural and proper. We do not have the obligation to sustain strangers artificially hooked up to us, but we do have the obligation to sustain our own children. So, the very thing that makes it plausible to say that the person in bed with the violinist has no duty to sustain him; namely, that he is a stranger unnaturally hooked up to him, is precisely what is absent in the case of the mother and her child. She does have an obligation to take care of her child, to sustain her, to protect her, and especially, to let her live in the only place where she can now be protected, nourished, and allowed to grow, namely the womb. If she ejects her from her womb, it is like a mother throwing her child out of her home, into the cold, refusing to take care of her. The preborn child must be viewed, and treated, just like the born child; even Thomson admits as much when she structures her argument on the assumption "that the fetus is a person from the moment of conception."

If the mother has the duty to sustain the child, she may not "unplug" herself from him. Therefore, abortion merely as unplugging is morally wrong. So the "no duty to sustain" argument is false at its very core: the woman does have a duty to sustain her child, because it is her child. The person plugged into the violinist does not, correspondingly, have the duty to sustain him, for he is not his.

Suppose the woman has been raped. She still has a duty to sustain the life of the child. Despite the absolute horror of rape, the terrible injustice and violence of this most despicable act, the reality of the child must be kept in mind; he is absolutely innocent. The father is guilty of a terrible crime; the child is not. The child conceived in rape is a reminder to the woman of the horrible event that led to the child's coming into being. That is certainly a powerful psychological reality. It does not mean that the child partakes of the moral evil of this event. The child is real, and innocent, and she has the same preciousness and dignity as the rest of us, and the same right to life. That is, the same right not to be killed, and also, the same right to be sustained. She is still the child of her mother. What was noted above, that a parent has the obligation to take care of her own child, because she is her child, is something quite universal. It applies to all parents and children. It does not cease to be true because the act of intercourse that led to the conception of the child was violent and forced upon the woman. The biological relation of mother to child is still there, unaffected by the circumstance of the rape.

It is interesting to note that Thomson herself does not press the rape argument for abortion in this context. She says, "Surely the question whether you have a right to life at all, or how much of it you have, shouldn't [doesn't?] turn on the question of whether or not you are the product of a rape."[7] Excellent point!

The Special Relation between a Woman and Her Child

Defenders of abortion, agreeing that killing an innocent person is wrong, argue that the case of abortion is different. According to Bolton, "It is relatively easy to live without deliberately killing someone; but it may require an indefinitely large commitment of time, energy, emotion, and physical resources to nurture and care for a child."

Is it really evident (as Bolton's argument seems to assume) that when such a commitment is necessary for the life of one person, the other person is released from the obligation to make it? And that she may exercise this option by killing the dependent person?

The relation between woman and child is a relation of two persons, A and B, where B is dependent on A for his sustenance and protection. The pro-abortion claim in Bolton's argument can be tested by reversing the roles. Suppose the woman, B, were dependent on another person, A, for her sustenance and protection. Would it be right for A to kill the woman in order to exercise his option of not sustaining her? Clearly not. Defenders of abortion, who appeal to the special relation between woman and child, would certainly not defend the right of A to kill B when B is the woman. It is no different when A is the woman and B is the child.

Another aspect of this relation is that A has absolute power over B, the power to destroy B. Abortion is the exercise of this power. To see the wrongness of abortion, let us again imagine the roles reversed, with the woman in the position of B, at the mercy of some person A who has the power to destroy her. Those who advocate a right to terminate the child by abortion because she is dependent upon, and at the mercy of the woman and her doctor, would be horrified if someone advocated a right to terminate the woman because she was dependent upon, and at the mercy of others. The child is a victim because she is helpless, because people do not identify with her as a real person.

There is indeed a special relation between woman and child: the child is entrusted to her, as she was entrusted to her mother when she was a child in the womb. The "no duty to sustain" argument arises out of a denial of this deep relationship of being entrusted, or a refusal to accept it.

The claim to a right over one's body (as a slogan for abortion) is not a genuine claim to a right, as when a member of one group of persons claims the same rights as the members of another group. It is rather a refusal to acknowledge the relationship of being entrusted. It is the expression of a determination to live one's own life even at the expense of utterly crushing that of another.

Abortion is a double evil: the killing of a helpless small child, in a most cruel way; and the denial of the special, profound relationship of entrustment. The woman who has an abortion destroys a child who is especially entrusted to her.

The Third Refutation of This Argument

Assume that being tied to the violinist represents only a light burden. The case for abortion based on this analogy is then significantly weakened if not destroyed altogether. Thomson herself admits as much:

> Suppose you learn that what the violinist needs is only one hour: all you need do to save his life is to spend one hour in that bed with him. Suppose also that letting him use your kidneys for that one hour would not affect your health in the slightest. Admittedly you were kidnapped. Admittedly you did not give anyone permission to plug him into you. Nevertheless it seems to me plain you *ought* to allow him to use your kidneys for that hour—it would be indecent to refuse.[8]

Assume then that being tied to the violinist represents an extreme hardship and burden, in order to give Thomson one fairly strong premise: since having the violinist plugged into you represents an extreme burden and hardship for you, you may unplug yourself from him. But the very strength of this premise is also the collapse of the argument for abortion based on it. For that argument (if otherwise successful) would justify abortions only when they represented an extreme hardship for the woman. If it is the extreme hardship that constitutes the justification for severing the link, then of course the absence of such an extreme hardship would mean that severing the link is wrong; hence that abortion as the severing of this link is wrong. What defenders of abortion want of course is a general, universal right to an abortion, especially when they stress a woman's right over her body. Thus the analogy to the violinist, when the connection to him represents an extreme hardship, will simply not provide. Hence the argument fails.

This refutation of Thomson does not, like the previous refutation, appeal to the special obligation of a mother to sustain her child. It is quite general. Except in cases of extreme hardships or sufferings, we do have the obligation to not let others die, hence to sustain them if they need our help. This applies to strangers as well as our own family and friends. If I see a person dying in the wilderness, I have a duty to try to save her, and not leave her to die. I have this duty even if it represents a considerable sacrifice for me. I am released from it only if it represents an extreme hardship or suffering such as permanent paralysis or blindness. How severe the hardship or suffering must be before I am released from my general obligation to save the life of another is hard to say. One rule that one might follow is to put oneself in the position of the victim, and ask how much of a burden one could reasonably expect from another to save one's life. "Do unto others as you would have them do unto you."

Thus even if we prescind from the specific obligation of a mother to care for her own child, there is the very important general obligation we all have to each other, to sustain one another when in need. A woman would have the duty to sustain the child even if she were a stranger, unless it were an extreme hardship or burden, one which very few pregnancies involve. Even then, she would have only the right to not sustain, not the right to kill.

The Child As Intruder Argument

The second claim for a right to an abortion based on a woman's right over her body concerns the child as an intruder. Thomson argues that the child is an intruder in the woman's body, like a burglar in one's home, or an innocent person who blunders in.[9] Just as the owner of the home has the right to remove the intruder, even if she is partly responsible for his getting in, so too a woman has the right to remove the child from her body even if she is partly responsible for his getting in: voluntary sexual intercourse with contraceptive failure. Let me offer two replies to this argument.

First, the child is not an intruder. He is precisely where he should be, in the place appropriate to the first phase of his life. That an argument comparing a woman's own child to a burglar or other intruder is even put forward is significant for what it reveals about the mentality of its proponents. That a woman looks upon her own child as a burglar or an intruder is already an evil, even if she then refrains from killing her. Imagine the mother of a born child looking upon her as an intruder in her house, being in the way, restricting her freedom. We would perceive this as a terrible selfishness. It is the same thing when the child is smaller, and in "her house" in another, more intimate sense, her own body.

What is forgotten in this mentality is the great gift and privilege of being a mother, the gift of being allowed to nurture a new human person. Also forgotten is the deep responsibility we have to each other, as members of the human community. This applies not only to helping a neighbor in need, and other obligations we have to born persons; it also involves our obligation to our own children. The woman who now looks upon her child, in her own womb, as an intruder, was once herself such a child in the womb. She would not have wanted to be looked upon as an intruder by her mother. "Do unto others as you would have them do unto you."

The woman has the right to be on this earth, in a place appropriate for her. In exactly the same way, the child in her womb has the right to be on this earth, in a place appropriate for her, for her protection, nourishment and development. So, contrary to Thomson, the child does have a right to be in the womb, as Thomson herself had this right when she was in the preborn stage of her existence. Thus the analogy to a burglar, or stumbling intruder, breaks down; and with it any argument that tries to justify expelling the child from the womb as if she were an intruder.[10]

Second, even if the child were an intruder, that would justify only her removal from the woman, not killing her. As already noted, I cannot throw an intruder out if this means killing him by throwing him off a cliff. And that is of course what abortion is: killing the child. Abortion is wrong because it is so much more than a mere removal. It means cutting the child to pieces, burning her skin, etc. Who would do such a thing to a born person who was an intruder?

Similar to the "intruder" argument, it is sometimes said that the relation of child to woman is parasitic: the child is a parasite living off the body of the woman.[11] This is a total distortion of the real relation between the child and her mother. A parasite is essentially an alien being; the child is clearly not an alien, but the mother's own child, whom she conceived, her own flesh and blood. A parasite can be understood as a being who should not be there; the child, in contrast, is in her proper place, exactly where she should be. A baby kangaroo is surely not a parasite when she is in her mother's pouch; a human infant in the womb is no different. A child at her mother's breast takes her nourishment from her, as does a parasite, but this relationship can hardly be called parasitic. The child in the womb is very much like the child at her mother's breast. The relationship is then less close, since the child is then more independent, but in both cases, the child is properly related to her mother, i.e., just the opposite of a parasite.

The Child's Right Over His Body

If there is a right over one's body then two very significant features pertain to it. One, it is a right everyone has; and two, it includes the right not to have one's body destroyed (e.g., by dismemberment), the right not to be killed. On both these counts, the appeal to a woman's right over her body as a justification for abortion backfires, and provides an argument against abortion. Thus if a woman has a right over her body, then the child has that right too. "For after all *the child's body is the child's body, not the woman's*. . . . The child, like his mother, has a 'just prior claim to his own body,' and abortion involves laying hands on, manipulating, that body."[12]

Summary

I have argued that a woman's right over her body does not justify the claim to a right to abortion. The major argument for this claim is the "no duty to sustain" argument. That argument fails on three counts:

1. Abortion is not a mere withholding of support, not a mere "unplugging," but a deliberate killing, even if the intention is the withholding of support.

2. The woman is not justified in withholding support from the child. The child is her own, entrusted to her, and so she has the obligation to take care of her. Failure to do so is child neglect. Hence "unplugging" is wrong already on the level of intending to withhold support.

3. The woman is not justified in withholding support from the child, even if the child were not her own, but a stranger. For we have a general obligation to save others' lives, to sustain them if they need us to live, unless this represents an extreme hardship.

4. The child as an intruder argument (with the analogy to a burglar) fails because the child is not an intruder, but in her natural place. Even if she were an intruder, she could not be ejected by being killed.

5. The argument of the right over one's body proves the wrongness of abortion: the child has the right not to have her body destroyed.

9

A Complex Issue or a Horror?

"There are no simple answers to the agonizing, complex issue of abortion."
How many times have you heard that? Most people take for granted the
complexity of abortion. And in some sense (to be explained shortly) it
really is complex. But in another sense it is not complex at all. Abortion,
on the deepest moral level, is painfully, brutally simple. Study these
pictures. Consider what abortion did to these children, what it does to any
children.

Pictures of the Results of Abortion

Some readers may object to the inclusion of the gruesome pictures that
follow. The theme of this chapter is the true nature of abortion. If these
pictures help us understand what this is, and to respond accordingly,
then they will have served their purpose. If it is painful to look at them,
then we will have participated, in a small way, in the pain that an abortion
is. If we find them sickening, if we are outraged, this is because abortion
is truly sickening, a terrible outrage, a horror.

These pictures are presented so that we may face the reality of what
an abortion is, what it does to the child. What is gruesome is not each
picture, but the reality it conveys: abortion itself is gruesome and
horrifying.

Many people support the right of a woman to choose abortion
without realizing what this really means. The pictures tell us. Many
people are indifferent to abortion. Others are opposed but not outraged.
If these pictures shake our complacency, they will have served a good
purpose.

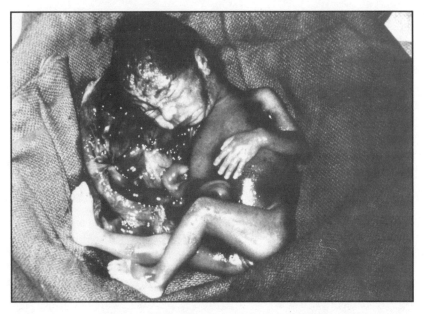

Salt poisoning abortion at nineteen weeks.

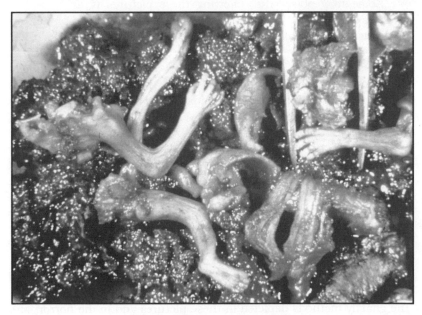

Suction abortion at ten weeks.

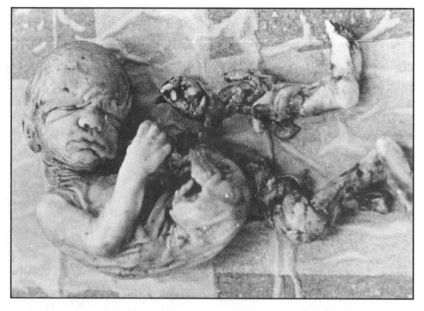

Dismemberment abortion, 27-29 weeks, Los Angeles 1982.

Some may object that showing these pictures is an appeal to emotion. Indeed it is. When we show pictures of the results of the Nazi Holocaust while exclaiming "Never again!" we are appealing to emotion. When we argue for a policy aimed at reducing the horror of mass starvation, and include pictures of starving people, we are appealing to emotion. And rightly so. We grasp truths not only with our intellects but with our hearts as well. And we should respond not only with our minds and our wills, but with our hearts as well. This applies to many things, including truths about massive horrors. What we should avoid are false appeals to emotion, and emotional appeals offered instead of reasons. These pictures parallel the arguments of this book that abortion kills a real human person; they are as true as those arguments, and supplement them.

Part of the message of these pictures is this: before you decide your position on abortion, know what abortion does! If you decide to support the pro-choice position, you should know that this is what you are in favor of allowing women to choose, and doctors to execute.

Even if abortion were neat and clean, quick and painless, it would still be a horror, for any killing of an innocent human being is a horror. The ghastly methods depicted in these pictures add to the horror; and contemplating the results of abortions helps us to grasp the horror of any abortion.

Judging Actions and Judging Persons

The theme of this chapter is the true nature of abortion as a moral horror. In addressing this, I am concerned only with judging the action of abortion, not with judging the persons involved in it. The question is, what kind of an action is abortion? Not, are abortionists and women who choose abortion guilty? The whole question of personal guilt lies outside the scope of this book, and varies from case to case.

Evidence indicates that in many cases women are the second victims of abortion.[1] In one sense they choose, but in a deeper and more significant sense, they succumb, because they see no realistic alternative. They feel coerced, their situation presents itself to them as leaving no other choice, they experience an absence of choice. Women can be victims of abortion in other ways. For example, the horror they experience when they realize what it means to have had their own child killed.[2]

The Abortion Holocaust

The pictures tell us what abortion does to an individual child. Another dimension of the horror of abortion is that this is happening on a mass scale, about 1.6 million per year in the United States, many millions more worldwide. That 1.6 million means well over 4,000 each day, or about one every 10 seconds.

The most apt description of the killing of innocent persons on such a mass scale is that of William Brennan, in *The Abortion Holocaust: Today's Final Solution*.[3] He notes many striking similarities between the massive killing of unwanted persons in Nazi Germany and unwanted persons today.

Atrocities Past and Present

In the Eastern territories special killing units . . . followed upon the heels of the German Army in a systematic search-and-destroy mission bent on eradicating Jews, Gypsies, the insane, and the handicapped. The victims were shot in cold blood in front of huge ditches. Their bodies toppled into the gaping holes of massive graves. Many expired from their wounds. Others were buried alive and suffocated to death.

Vacuum aspiration abortion, the most common method of destroying unborn children in the first trimester of pregnancy, is an especially brutal procedure. The child's tiny body—including arms, legs, head, and torso—is torn away from the walls of the uterus, ripped apart, and reduced to smithereens by the force of a suction machine many times more powerful than a vacuum cleaner. Little wonder that some nurses have referred to the aspirator as "the murder machine." The obliterated remains are sucked out of the womb through a transparent tube into a collecting bottle. They are examined and then incinerated or flushed into the sewer. . . .

Destruction inside the gas chambers of concentration camps was a painful and extended process in which the victims desperately gasped for breath and life. The hardiest inmates sometimes trampled upon women, children, and the elderly in their futile efforts to escape the deadly fumes. Body-disposal squads developed "special hook-tipped poles," thrust deep into the flesh of the newly exterminated, to facilitate the task of removing entangled, bloated, and deformed corpses with blood oozing from their noses and mouths.

A prime example of contemporary scientific butchery, D & E (dilation and extraction) abortion, involves the use of curettes to mutilate victims beyond the first trimester of pregnancy, and forceps to extract their slaughtered remains from the womb piece by piece. "The sensations of dismemberment," according to veteran D & E abortionist Dr. Warren M. Hern, "flow through the forceps like an electric current." The solid, well-formed heads of the victims must frequently be crushed before removal. Then the butchered body parts are assembled to ensure that the uterus has been completely emptied.

During the height of the killing season at Auchwitz living children were tossed directly into the fires of crematorium furnaces or flaming pits. Their screams could be heard throughout the camp compound. . . .

The injection of concentrated salt solutions into the amniotic fluid surrounding the unborn child is another example of the sheer barbarism with which human lives are done away with in the mid-trimester of gestation. The corrosive saline often burns away the outer layer of skin, exposing the raw, red under-surface. The effect is similar to that of napalm on innocent war victims. For the victims the dying process is agonizing and prolonged, lasting from one to several hours. . . .

During the 12 years of the Third Reich the holocaust consumed some 6 million Jews, 5 million non-Jews, 275,000 handicapped Germans in euthanasia hospitals, a quarter of a million Gypsies, and countless numbers of unborn expendables.

Since the 1973 Supreme Court decision which sanctified abortion on demand, well over 10 million [now 20 million] unborn lives have been extinguished by heinous acts of medical extermination not even legally permitted against animals, birds, or fish. The uterus, which once had been a private sanctuary exquisitely suited for growth and development, has been transformed into a deadly environment polluted beyond belief by the invasion of lethal instruments and poisonous substances that defy the most fundamental laws of ecology and humanity![4]

Goals

The goals of both concentration camps and abortion clinics are identical: the destruction of unwanted human lives.

Concentration camps specialized in exterminating Jews, Gypsies, Poles, asocials, and the unborn children of female slave laborers.

Abortion clinics are devoted to the task of destroying unborn children in the first trimester of pregnancy. Many abortoriums have even expanded their destructive operations to consume victims in the later stages of pregnancy.[5]

Psychic Numbing

This involves a loss of capacity to feel on the part of the perpetrator and a pervasive brutalization. "What happens is that the aggressor cuts the other person off emotionally, and 'freezes' him," concluded Erich Fromm. "The other person ceases to be experienced as human, and becomes a 'thing—over there.'"[6]

Non-Visibility of the Victims

Bureaucratic destruction works best when the technology employed keeps the victims out of sight. If they can be rendered nonvisible, a claim can be made that they do not exist. This in turn eliminates the emotionally-repulsive elements associated with killing visible victims and helps reduce destruction to the trivial level of a technical procedure.

Most Nazi victims were first removed from public view and then killed in concentration camps located in remote sections of Poland.

Although most unborn children are destroyed in large metropolitan areas, their massacre is hidden inside special facilities camouflaged as clinics.[7]

Language

"Many people underestimate the power of language to transform harsh realities into pleasant or emotionally-neutral phenomena."[8] In Nazi Germany, when people were gassed to death, "this destructive process was characterized as 'selection'." "Just as the Nazis claimed *the right to select* who would expire in gas chambers, today's perpetrators insist upon *the right to choose* who will perish in abortion chambers!"[9]

This is a perversion of the first order because it exploits the language of rights as a pretext for taking away the most fundamental right of all: the right to life. It is an arrogant, elitist assumption of the awesome power to destroy those who cannot defend themselves, an extreme manifestation of the strong victimizing the helpless. The catch words "selection" and "choice" represent a blatant sham because the individuals most drastically affected, the victims, are the very ones who are denied the right to choose. Someone else determines their fate— death by someone else's selection. This is not freedom, but the worst kind of oppression![10]

The Lack of Perception

Given that abortion is a horror, why is it tolerated in a civilized society? We "accept something as ghastly as the dismemberment of babies identical in size to preemies"[11] because we do not perceive it as a horror. Instead, we perceive it as a complex issue. This lack of perception (and its replacement by the "complex issue" approach) has many sources. They include:

1. *Lack of awareness.* Many people do not realize, fully and clearly, that the being in the womb is a small person; that at seven weeks (before most abortions), she is a well proportioned small-scale baby. Some are aware of the reality of the child for the later stages of pregnancy but unclear about the earlier stages, and the precise beginning of a person's existence at conception. "Perhaps it is just a 'cluster of cells' then." They feel uncertain as to when it becomes a real person. So it becomes a complex issue, one with no clear or definite right answer. This effectively closes the door to perceiving abortion as the horror that it is.

Most people are unaware of the methods, such as dismemberment. Most do not realize what a saline does to the child. Someone has said that "if the media were to show aborted children every evening for two weeks, legal abortion would be finished."[12]

2. *The veil of language.* Abortion is called a woman's choice; it is defended as an example of reproductive rights. These high-sounding terms obscure the ghastly reality of abortion as the destruction of a helpless child. No one wants to be against a woman's right to choose. It is impossible to see something both as an expression of someone's right and also as a horror. The language of rights and choice effectively obscures the reality of abortion as killing. "It can't be a killing if a woman has a right to choose it." And so it is the "termination of pregnancy," another example of the veil of language.

3. *Sympathy for women.* Many women say they need abortions, want them, have had them. It is difficult to have sympathy for the person, and at the same time recognize the action she is involved in as a moral horror. The result is that sympathy for the woman has the effect of obscuring one's vision of the horror of the action.

4. *Single aspect approach.* A person may be gripped by one aspect of the abortion question, especially women's rights. If this is seen as the all-important issue, then anything else that is viewed as interfering with it becomes obscured, even denied. It seems that one first decides that the right to abortion is necessary, and then concludes that abortion can't be wrong, and can't be a horror. From this stems the notion that the fetus is not a real child. "He can't be, else we could not have him killed." Being emotionally gripped leads to rationalization, which leads to blindness.

5. *The division of opinion.* People are divided over whether abortion is right or wrong, including questions about exceptions. So, abortion is seen as controversial. "If it is controversial, it must be complex; there are no easy answers." It is impossible to say this and also to recognize the horror of abortion, of each abortion for the individual child, and of mass abortion as a holocaust. And so the perceived complexity of abortion makes it impossible to perceive its true nature as a horror.

6. *Exceptions.* Even many people who are strongly opposed to abortion allow for, or seriously consider, certain exceptions, such as rape and incest. But granting one exception leads to the consideration of another, and soon the issue is perceived as complex and controversial, thus obscuring its horror.

No one can face the horror of the Nazi Holocaust and then say that a practice of this kind, while wrong, can be justified for certain exceptions. Perceiving a horror for what it is, and granting exceptions, are psychologically incompatible.

7. *The climate of opinion.* Given that most people do not perceive abortion as a horror, any one person's perceptions and moral judgments are influenced by what others see, by the general climate of opinion. "If most people don't see it, it's probably not there"—a plausible but often tragically false assumption. Or: "How can abortion be murder, a terrible moral evil, when so many respectable people approve it? When so many prominent organizations like the American Medical Association and various religious organizations approve it?" Part of the answer to this objection is what I shall call "the circle of mutual support." Some respectable people approve abortion because they see that others do. These others, in turn, approve it because they see that others do, including members of the first group. And so there is a complete circle: abortion is accepted by group A because it is seen as accepted by group

B, and it is accepted by group B because it is seen as accepted by group A. Each psychologically supports the other. This circle is virtually contained in the objection itself. A given person does not condemn abortion as a horror precisely because he sees so many others whom he respects approving it. And they in turn approve it because they see it approved by others.

"It can't be murder because it is so widely approved." On the contrary, it is widely approved because it is not seen as murder. And it is not seen as murder because it is, instead, seen as widely approved.

What we have in this objection is a classic example of the fallacy of shifting attention from the object (abortion itself) to people's attitudes towards it. What matters is abortion itself, its nature as an action, the reasons for and against holding it to be a moral evil; not what people think about it. The latter can never determine the moral rightness or wrongness of an action. And so it is never appropriate to argue that an action cannot be wrong because people do not recognize it to be such, because people approve it. If people approve something, the crucial question is, *should* they approve it?

The circle of mutual support gains a further hold on people, and further force as a psychological factor when the actual practice of abortion is added. "Abortion can't be murder, it can't be a terrible evil, because Miss Smith had one, and she's a respectable, nice person." But perhaps she had the abortion (in part) because she saw it approved by others ("therefore it can't be a moral horror"), and practiced by others. And so the circle continues: abortion is accepted because it continues to be practiced, and it continues to be practiced because it is accepted. The approval of abortion and its practice thus feed on each other.

The circle phenomenon is part of a larger picture, the general social climate of moral opinion. Many people adopt as their own opinion what is in fact the common or widely prevailing opinion in their society. They join the stream of popular thinking. They take it for granted, rather than challenging it or questioning it. Such a stream may be the dominant, almost universally accepted opinion in a society; or it may be one of two or more opinions, as in the case of abortion today. Either way, the opinions of many individuals are formed by the opinions of others. It is not simply that they imitate the prevailing opinions. It is, even more significantly, that they do not think of challenging them, or do not dare challenge them, because they are the dominant, prevailing opinions. There is a reluctance to criticize so many people; especially so many respectable people. And so the phenomenon we are examining here arises: People say abortion is not murder, it is not a moral horror but a complex issue, because others see it this way. But in fact it is murder, it is a horror;

and people could come to see it for what it is, if they would only look at it, rather than at what others say about it, or what other people do.

Two Types of Complexity: The Example of Slavery

Some moral matters are complex in the sense that they involve questions for which there really are no easy answers. A psychiatrist learns something from his patient that represents a potential danger to a third party. Should he reveal it to the proper authorities? Yes, to protect the third party. No, because breaking the doctor-client seal of confidentiality is wrong and also leads to bad consequences. Perhaps it depends on the seriousness of the danger and its likelihood. In such a case, either position could be reasonably defended, with objectively valid arguments; and the different, and mutually opposed, positions all deserve respect. I shall call this *objective moral complexity*. There are many questions that fall into this category. They are characterized in general by the pull of opposing values. Fidelity to promises and the protection of trust versus other values such as protecting life, the rights of the individual versus the good of society, and the allocation of scarce resources, are some common examples.

Objective moral complexity stands in contrast to things that are clearly wrong, and especially to moral horrors such as slavery and holocausts. Here, of course, there is no pull of opposing values. Slavery is a terrible evil, an absolute horror; there is nothing pulling in the opposite direction to mitigate its evil or to render it complex in the above sense.

And yet slavery was a controversial issue in America for many years. It was a complex issue for many people. I shall call this *psychological complexity*. This term is intended to include sociological factors as well. Recall the items listed above under "The Lack of Perception": a lack of awareness of the child and of what abortion does to her, the veil of language, sympathy for the woman, being gripped by one aspect, the problem of possible exceptions, and others. All of these factors help explain why abortion is perceived as complex instead of a horror, why it is (psychologically) complex for many people. Similar factors help explain why slavery was perceived as complex instead of a horror. The climate of opinion makes it understandable why people do not perceive the true horror of a massive evil, be it slavery or abortion. They perceive it as complex instead. But it is only complex for them, psychologically complex, not an objective moral complexity. The circle of mutual support appears again. "It can't be a horror because it's complex." On the contrary, it is not seen as a horror because it is considered complex.

The fallacy in this reasoning turns on the confusion between the two types of complexity. "It can't be a horror because it's complex." To make this true, or at least plausible, *complex* must mean moral complexity. But in fact abortion is only psychologically complex, and when that meaning is applied, the statement is false. What is psychologically complex may well be a moral horror, as in the case of slavery. People rightly see the psychological complexity of abortion—that it can be an agonizing decision, that opinion is divided, etc. They wrongly interpret this complexity as a moral complexity, and thus fail to grasp the horror of abortion.

A brief comparison between mass abortion and slavery is useful at this point. [13] Both slavery and mass abortion singled out a whole class of human beings and deprived them of their most basic human rights. In both instances the victims were treated as things, to be used or disposed of. Both were massive violations of human dignity. Both continued because of the sheer might of those in power. Both caused unspeakable suffering, and represented cruelty and injustice on a massive scale. Both continued because of public approval or apathy or insufficient opposition.

A further crucial point: In seeing the horror of slavery, we clearly see that no other good could ever justify it as a means to its achievement. Imagine saying, "Slavery is bad, but we need it for ____" (referring to some recognized good). But that is exactly what is being said today. "Abortion is bad, but we need it for the benefit of women and their right to choose." If slavery cannot be justified on the grounds that it benefits people, neither can abortion.

Slavery and mass abortion: Both are objective moral horrors, in contrast to objective moral complexities. Both are, or have been, experienced as cases of psychological complexity. What we see clearly in the case of slavery—that psychological complexity does not imply moral complexity—applies equally to abortion. For both, being psychologically complex does not mean being morally complex.

How could we have tolerated the horror of slavery, its physical cruelty, the disruption of families, the affront to human dignity? How could we have been so blind? As we look back at slavery, approved and tolerated in our country and practiced on a vast scale by respectable people, what can we say?

> What will the Toynbees, the Gibbons, the Spenglers of the future say about the American Holocaust? How could a nation which as recently as the late 1950s embraced what Langdon Jones has called the "Procreative Ethic" change in less than a generation into a giant human abattoir in which every third baby conceived is knived, poisoned, starved, choked or dismembered? [14]

The Undeserved Respectability of the Pro-Choice Position

The abortion issue is generally seen as having two sides, each representing a morally plausible position. They are somehow seen as roughly equal, sometimes in regard to the strength of their moral position, and almost always in regard to their respectability. Apart from the sincerity that defenders of "pro-choice" may have, the pro-choice (pro-abortion) position is itself an immoral one, for it is the attempt to defend, and promote as respectable, the option of killing babies, and doing this on a massive scale. It involves various attempts to camouflage this horror by the use of deceptive language, such as the "right to choose" (really, the "right to choose to kill a child"), and "product of conception" (for a small human person). That the "pro-death" side succeeds in presenting itself as respectable, as an alternate moral viewpoint, only adds to the psychological complexity of abortion and makes it difficult to perceive it as the horror that it is. "It's not a horror because its defense is a respectable position, one of two sides of a complex issue." On the contrary, it is not seen as the horror that it is because it is perceived, instead, as but one side of a complex issue.

Furthermore, people hesitate to condemn abortion as a horror out of an understandable reluctance to condemn those who defend it. "It's their opinion. How can I judge that they are not sincere?" Here the distinction between judging *persons* and judging *actions* is crucial. Granted, we should not judge persons (and their sincerity). This does not say anything, however, about the nature of the action at hand. If we keep this distinction clearly in mind, we can open our eyes to the horror of abortion as an action, and respond accordingly. One reason we should not make moral judgments about persons is precisely because of the psychological complexity surrounding abortion today. A complexity that in no way involves a moral complexity, and thus we can judge abortion as the horror that it is.

A Woman's' Choice?

The theme of this chapter is the three-fold character of abortion: (1) that it is perceived as a morally complex issue, and therefore tolerated, its defense accepted as a respectable position. (2) that it is a psychologically complex issue, individually and socially. (3) and that is a moral horror, the massive killing of small babies to get them out of the way, a holocaust.

How can a holocaust be tolerated in a society that views itself as basically moral, concerned for the poor and the downtrodden? How can it be that we have become "a giant human abattoir in which every third baby conceived is knived, poisoned, . . . choked or dismembered"?

One reason is lack of perception. Another is that abortion is seen as a woman's choice. This is the center and substance of the defense of abortion. People defend it as a woman's choice; they tolerate it for fear of violating a woman's "right to choose."

What is the role of choice in the abortion question? Does it have any moral or logical efficacy? If not, why does it nonetheless play such a prominent role? Does it contribute to the psychological complexity of abortion?

1. A woman does not have the right to choose to have her child killed. She does not have this right morally; she should not have it legally. This is absolutely clear from what has been established here. It must be emphasized, so that it is not forgotten or obscured.

2. The appeal to choice is not even an argument for justifying abortion, let alone a valid argument. It is a slogan, an appeal, the expression of a desire. Nothing in the notion of choice supports the contention that one has a right to a certain choice. A racist can use the same slogan and say that he should have a choice in hiring, specifically the right to refuse employment to a qualified black applicant. He wants a choice; this in no way shows that he is entitled to one. It will be said that the stakes are higher for a woman seeking a choice regarding abortion, than an employer seeking choice in hiring. Very true; and the stakes are higher for the victim of an abortion as well: the black applicant loses his livelihood and suffers an affront to his dignity, the child loses her life.

Choice has absolutely no substance either as a moral reality or as an argument for supporting abortion. What it has is a psychological force, and this in a number of ways. For example:

3. "Choice" has enough plausibility to function as an effective screen, hiding the true horror of abortion. Those who defend abortion have cleverly seized on the idea of choice as an ingenious device to promote their cause, by which they are in fact promoting the massive killing of small babies. To the extent that they succeed in bringing the killings under the mantle of something so respectable and positive as choice, they succeed in obscuring its horror. Who wants to be against choice? "Do you want to deny a woman a choice about something so intimate and private?" The success of this strategy stems from a number of factors, such as (A) the fact that choice as such is a positive thing. (But it is not the final word. The choice to kill, or to do any evil, is not a positive thing.) (B) The fact that, in one very important sense, a woman has a choice, namely, the choice between keeping or killing her baby. (But having such a choice says nothing about the rightness or wrongness of one or the other of the

options that constitute that choice.) (C) The fact that in today's climate of women's rights, it is not easy to take a stand against something that is advocated as a fundamental right of women. Not everyone is prepared, psychologically and logically, to offer the appropriate distinctions: legitimate women's rights, yes; the alleged right to have her baby killed, no.

4. "I'm personally opposed to abortion, but I do not want to impose this on others." Some who say this are not really opposed to abortion, but, on the contrary, are perfectly willing to see it continue. The phrase "personally opposed" is merely a shield. But there are others who say this with some measure of sincerity. They really do see the wrongness of abortion, but they are victims of the psychological power of the pro-choice slogan. Somehow the force of this slogan overcomes their vision of the horror of abortion, and it weakens their determination to stand up and be counted as opposed to this evil. As one of my students put it, "Although I am opposed to abortion, I feel that I do not have the right to choose for others. Therefore, I remain pro-choice." This was the conclusion of a paper presenting reasons why abortion is wrong, even a horrible wrong.

Imagine someone saying, "I'm personally opposed to beating small children to death, but I do not want to impose this on others." Why does this sound so absurd, whereas the same thing said for a preborn child, does not sound so absurd? Why is the latter so readily accepted? Because of the psychological force of one word: choice. A simple reply to this reasoning is that no one should choose to impose death on the child. Especially not such a cruel death, as by a one- to two-hour saline poisoning or by dismemberment.

5. In a presidential debate with George Bush on October 13, 1988, Michael Dukakis said that abortion is an agonizing, difficult choice. A choice that must be left up to the woman; that she must decide according to her own conscience, her values, her religious beliefs. That it is impossible to say in general who should live and who should not. He was speaking for many people when he said this. It sounds so lofty and compassionate, with the focus on the difficult situation that the woman is in. It evokes sympathy for her. Isn't this good? Yes and no. Yes, we should empathize with the woman, support her, but not by sacrificing her child to an agonizing death.

It is difficult to criticize this position, it sounds so noble. No one wants to deny, or make light of, an agonizing decision. And yet we must ask what this position is really saying. It is saying that a woman should have a choice, where one option is the killing of a small child (in an agonizing way). The very difficulty one experiences in holding this position up to the light of day, as legitimizing the option to murder a child, stems from the psychological power of the idea of choice. At the heart of this powerful appeal is the thesis that a woman should have a choice.

This appeal is defused when one realizes that its power is only psychological, not moral. Morally, what is being asked for is a horror, the option to murder a child. The decision may be psychologically complex for the woman. Morally it is not complex at all, it is a clear-cut terrible evil.

When blacks are mistreated in a certain society, we do not spin a tale about complex, agonizing decisions for the whites in power, when one of the options they may choose (according to their conscience, etc.) is treating blacks as less than full persons. We condemn the evil of racism; we do not condone choice. It is no different when the minority group in question is the preborn. What is presented as a lofty appeal to respect conscience is, in fact, a license to kill. Such is the appeal of choice.

6. Many people urge a "balanced view" that avoids the extremes of allowing all abortions or banning all abortions. The person most intimately involved, the woman, decides which ones.

It sounds attractive—until we realize that it means that some human beings are abandoned to the power of others to choose their deaths. And (especially) to choose to carry this out by dismemberment, poisoning and burning for one to two hours. Some things must indeed be balanced against others, but not the killing of innocent babies.

Racial justice demands that we respect all members of every minority in every essential way, above all, in regard to their life. The same is true for that neglected minority, preborn children. Who could plausibly urge a "balanced view" for racial justice? Why then is it urged for preborn persons? It sounds plausible, even attractive, for the latter because of the psychological power of choice.

7. Implicit in much of the defense of the pro-abortion position is the idea that being wanted is what makes something a human person. If the talk is about saving the being in the womb, she is called a child, or a baby. "We saved the baby." If it is about abortion, she is called a fetus. "We removed the fetus." The idea that being wanted is what makes something a person is absurd on the level of rational thought. Clearly, he or she is a person, whether wanted or not wanted. The metaphysical status of a being, whether "it" is a person or not, cannot possibly be determined by whether or not "it" is wanted. This is so obvious—how could anyone possibly hold the view that being wanted is necessary to being a person?

The answer, once again, is choice. The idea that a person is human only if he is wanted is an expression of a woman's right to choose. Her choosing to have the child makes him a real child. Her choosing to have the abortion makes him a non-person. Choice is supreme; actual metaphysical status and consequent ethical demands are swept aside.

This defense of abortion is not a genuine moral argument. It is not, "Abortion is morally right, therefore, a woman has a right to choose it." Rather: "A woman has a right to choose. Therefore, abortion is right if she so chooses." And, "Since it is wrong to kill persons, the being in the womb cannot be a person if the woman chooses to abort him. He is a person only if he is wanted. If he is unwanted, he is a non-person (perhaps a mass of tissue), who may be killed."

Here is the core difference between the two movements. Pro-life asks, "Is it a person? Does abortion kill a person?" Looking at the evidence, it becomes clear that the answer to both questions is yes. Therefore, abortion is morally wrong. It is a horror, especially if we add how it is done, and that it is carried out on a massive scale.

Pro-choice starts with the woman's right to choose. It is this which determines everything else. If her choice is to have the baby, then her wanting him makes him a person. If her choice is abortion, then her not wanting him reduces him to a non-person. The questions, whether the being really is a person, and whether abortion means killing, interfere with the promotion of choice. Their urgency is denied; choice is the supreme principle.

8. "I think women should have a choice because if I ever got pregnant, I would want a choice." Part of the movement for choice is, "I want it, therefore it should be." A moral guideline is derived from a desire. The right to choose is presented as if it were a genuine moral right; in fact, it is only the expression of a strong desire. But the presentation of this desire as a moral right gives it great psychological power and helps make abortion socially acceptable, hence tolerated, leading to its widespread practice.

9. "If women are not given a choice, they will resort to back-alley abortions, or self-induced abortions, as by coat hangers. Many will be maimed, many will die. The results will be horrible."

The present state is horrible! Every third child cut to pieces, burned and poisoned, or crushed to death. The very horror that this argument appeals to is repeated in *every abortion.* One can hardly be against horrible mutilation and death for one group of people, while condoning it for others. If back-alley abortions are also devastating to women, then that is an additional reason for not choosing them. No abortions should be chosen, neither socially and legally approved ones, nor disapproved ones. What this argument shows is only that some abortions are still worse than others, namely, those that also destroy women.

In addition, it must be stressed that the popular assumption that legal abortions are safe (for the woman; they are obviously deadly for the child) while illegal abortions are dangerous does not stand up against the facts. *Legal abortions kill women!* Reardon reports that "though the odds of any particular woman suffering ill effects from an abortion have dropped, the *total* number of women who suffer and die from abortion is far greater than ever before."[15] The myth of safe legal abortion persists largely because "the reported rate of deaths due to legal abortion is being deliberately kept low through selective underreporting."[16]

It must also be realized that the "back alley" argument is not really an argument for abortion. It does nothing to show that abortion is not the murder of a child (nor does it even attempt to). Its appeal is a psychologically powerful way of expressing the desire (or the demand) to have a choice. It is a kind of threat: "Give us choice, or else." It offers nothing to substantiate one's right to choose. It only points to a feared consequence of its denial. That the denial of something leads to bad consequences in no way establishes a right to it. A policy of equal treatment for blacks might lead to terrible riots. That hardly shows that blacks do not have equal rights, or that anyone has the right to deny them equal rights. So too, no one has the right to deny equal rights to preborn persons, regardless of the consequences.

The appeal to choice is a major factor making abortion psychologically complex. If a person does not clearly see the horror of abortion, if he nonetheless sees something wrong in taking human life; and if, on the other hand, the appeal to choice makes an impact on him, then it becomes very understandable that he perceives abortion as a conflict of values, an issue that is hard to sort out—in short, a complex issue.

But isn't abortion really complex (morally) in the case of pregnancy due to rape or incest? Or if the woman's life or health is threatened? Should she not have a choice in such cases? These questions will be pursued in the next chapter.

An Abortion Pill?

When an abortion pill is developed, will abortion still be the horror described here? Suppose it replaces the ghastly methods of cutting the child to pieces or burning her skin while poisoning her. Will this diminish the horror of abortion?

An abortion pill would be just as horrible, and in some respects, worse.

1. Abortion, by whatever means, at whatever age, with or without pain, is still murder.

2. The way in which an abortion pill brings about the death of the child could be just as ghastly as the current surgical methods. There is nothing in the nature of a pill to preclude this. It might, for example, slowly

crush the child to death by activating certain muscles. It might slowly choke her to death. We would then have exactly the same grim horror of abortion that we now have.

3. If the child's pain receptors are in place and functioning at the time that the pill works, then she would be subject to whatever pain the pill is capable of causing. Again, there is nothing in the nature of a pill to preclude this. Once more, we would see a repetition of the present horrible methods of abortion with respect to the terrible pain they cause the child.

4. The idea of a pill is to make abortion easier, more efficient, and private. It will not require a trip to the "clinic"; it can be taken at home like an aspirin. This will, of course, increase the number of abortion killings. The present holocaust will get worse as more babies are murdered. Each gain in ease means an increase in the quantitative dimension of the abortion horror.

A recent article compared the transition from surgical abortion to a pill to the leap from conventional warfare to nuclear warfare.[17] Killing would become easy: just take a pill. And with this, our reluctance to kill will diminish. That represents a quantum leap in horror, the advent of "nuclear war" on the unborn in terms of the massive scale on which they will be killed, and the ease with which we kill them.

Though largely hidden from public view today, the horror of surgical abortion can still be made manifest by describing the methods and showing the pictures. That will be much more difficult if not impossible with the pill. Abortion will be cloaked in a mantle of privacy. Preborn children will be still less protected, and many more of them will be murdered.

5. What does killing represent for the person who does the killing? A terrible evil, a heavy burden on one's conscience when one realizes the horror of killing. For aborting women, the effect of taking the pill will be no less than requesting a surgical abortion. In some ways, it will be worse. With the pill, the woman herself becomes the agent of death. And with the ease of the pill, many more women will become agents of death, and so the evil and the burden of having killed another human being will fall on many more women.

At this writing, the new RU-486 abortion pill is in the news. The woman takes it and waits anxiously.[18] If the pill succeeds (as it does about 80% of the time), a dead, bloody baby will be washed out. If not, she must repeat. She takes three pills, waits two days while the child dies, then takes prostaglandin and waits five to eight days for the bloody remains of the child to flow out. In about five percent of the cases she is not successful even then, and a surgical abortion is needed to complete the job of killing. The anxious wait, the uncertainty, the length of time cannot but heighten the agonizing drama of this experience. This is no "get it over and done with" method of killing the child. The woman is drawn into the death process at a time when she is particularly sensitive and susceptible to psychological stress and trauma.

Conclusion

Some of the dimensions of the horror of abortion include:

1. The horror for each child. Recall the methods, the pictures.

2. The horror of the abortion holocaust. "The legalized execution of sixteen million unborn children bears powerful witness to the infinite capacity of the human heart for cruelty and self-deception. As a culture, we have broken our moorings and set sail on the bloody seas of mass extermination."[19]

3. Any murder is a terrible thing, but when a person is deprived of his whole future life, a new dimension of horror is added.

4. Abortion is perpetrated on a mass scale, by the most horrible methods. It is being carried out and defended as a practice that is largely accepted by the society, its defenders enjoying a respected position. It is being done because those who carry out the abortions have absolute power over their victims. The preborn child is destroyed through the sheer might of the doctor, who simply takes advantage of his superior power, and the absolute helplessness of the child. She cannot cry out for help, she cannot defend herself, she cannot escape. She is trapped in a death chamber—a chamber that should have protected and nurtured her. We are horrified when we see a strong person brutally killing a small child by means of his superior power. This is a picture of an abortion.

Suppose, in the encounter between doctor and child, the child won half of the time, and killed the doctor in self-defense—something he would have every right to do. Very few doctors would still perform abortions. They perform them now only because of their absolute power over a small fragile, helpless victim.

5. Then there is abortion as sex selection. Pro-abortion is presented as pro-choice. Sometimes this choice is exercised in choosing the sex of the child: a baby boy is wanted, a baby girl is unwanted and therefore killed. Many people are horrified. But it is perfectly consistent with the logic of choice: "Abortion is a difficult decision; it is up to the woman to choose." So some women choose to kill their daughters in the womb. "Tens of thousands of fetuses, perhaps hundreds of thousands, have already been destroyed in Third World countries for the offense of being female."[20] And in the United States, "The *New York Times* reported a new

poll [December 1988] showing that nearly 20 per cent of . . . geneticists now approve the practice [of abortion for sex selection].[21]

6. To stop the abortion holocaust, we must first come to see it as a holocaust.

> The prevailing view of abortion in contemporary society is that of a minor surgical procedure carried out by upstanding physicians in the antiseptic settings of clinics and hospitals. It is this highly positive image—concocted by members of the medical establishment, legitimized by the legal structure, buttressed by linguistic technicians, implemented by advanced technologies, and disseminated by a media elite—which helps sustain the assembly-line massacre of over one and one-half million unborn children annually in America alone.
>
> The present-day carnage directed against the unwanted unborn will not begin to cease until a much larger segment of the public becomes aware of an entirely different perception of abortion as a horrendous holocaust comparable to the enormous destruction perpetrated on the unwanted of the Third Reich.[22]

In the end, the issue is not just about preborn babies; it is about all of us.

> The battle for life is not between pro-lifers and pro-abortionists, traditionalists and feminists, but rather between justice and injustice. Our opponents and their allies in the media know this deep down in their hearts, which is why they denounce us so bitterly. The battlelines are clear: Either life is for everyone, or the right to life is doled out at the whim of the powerful. Abortion represents in miniature a struggle that ultimately must result in the total victory of one answer to this question or the other, for the principles at stake are absolutely irreconcilable.
>
> If the partisans of "choice" win, what remains of our tattered sanctity of life ethic will be dismantled, piece by bloody piece. Because it is based on the right of the more powerful to oppress the less powerful, the pro-abortion position is at war with the core principles of our nation.
>
> So blinded are they by their own rhetoric, they hold "choice" to their bosoms as if it represented a kind of philosopher's stone that magically turns cruelty into kindness, selfishness into altruism. But barbarism with a human face is still barbarism.[23]

10

Abortion in Cases of Rape, Incest, or the Health and Life of the Woman?

Is abortion justified in the name of helping a woman who has been the victim of rape or incest? Or whose health or life is threatened by the continuation of the pregnancy? In answering these questions, we should be guided by two principal considerations. First, full and equal concern for all persons involved, the woman and the child, identifying with each. Second, adherence to the principle that we may never do wrong to one person in order to benefit another.

Abortion for Rape: The Destruction of the Child

1. The child conceived in rape is one of us, merely smaller and less developed and more dependent, and not in full view, but equally a person. Killing her is wrong, just as killing any child is wrong. We must remember that the child is absolutely innocent of the crime of her father. She is not a part of her mother's body, and she is not a part of her father's character. She inherits character traits from both her parents, but in her individual being as a person, she is absolutely distinct from both of them. Even the character traits that are received from a parent are now her own traits. The child is totally her own person. She is not responsible for the crime that led to her conception, and she is untainted by it.[1] Seeing her in these negative ways is sheer prejudice, not based on reality, but at odds with it.

2. Rape is horrible beyond words. So is abortion. Abortion means killing a child in ghastly ways that probably cause terrible pain. Abortion for rape is wrong because it adds a second horror to the first: the murder of an innocent child.

145

3. If abortion for a child conceived in loving intercourse is murder, it is still murder when the child is conceived in other forms of intercourse, as in rape. The form of intercourse, whether voluntary or forced, has no bearing on the dignity and preciousness of the child conceived. And it has no bearing on the question of whether abortion is murder. Abortion is murder because of what it does to its victim, the innocent child, regardless of how she was conceived.

4. We all identify with the woman. We must do the same for the child. We must identify with her, picture her in our minds and have compassion for her. We will then say, "Do not kill this child! Spare her the agonizing death of dismemberment or burning of her skin."

5. We may never do evil to achieve good. Denying a woman an abortion for rape is not a denial of the woman and of concern for her. It is a refusal to do evil. We could never kill the woman in attempting to benefit someone else in a way that is comparable to the alleged benefit for the woman expected of an abortion. If we cannot kill the woman to achieve an expected good, we cannot kill the child for a similar purpose either. There must be full and equal concern for both woman and child.

6. A specific application of this principle is that we may never kill innocent person B to save person A. We cannot kill John by removing a vital organ in order to save Mary, who needs it. This is not a lack of compassion for Mary; it is the refusal to commit murder, even for a good cause. John has a right not to be killed to benefit Mary, even to save her life. Mary has the same right. We could not kill the woman to benefit the child. Equally, we cannot kill the child to benefit the woman.

7. As a general principle, it is wrong to force a person to do something he has no duty to do.[2] The wrongness of kidnapping is, in part, that person A forces person B to come with him, something which B has no duty to do. A slaveowner forces a slave to work for him, something that the latter has no duty to do. In contrast, a motorist has a duty to stop when so ordered by a police officer, who therefore does no wrong in ordering him to do so.

An especially important application of this principle, which we may call the No Duty-Non Forcing Principle, is this: You have no duty to lay down your life to save another, still less to benefit her in some lesser way. Therefore, it would be wrong for anyone to force you to do so. Exactly the same applies to the child in the womb. She too has no duty to give up her life for another, including her mother. Therefore, it would be wrong to force her to do so by killing her. That she was conceived in violent intercourse changes nothing with regard to her being as a person, and her rights as a person—including her right not to be forced to die to benefit someone else.

Our two principles—full and equal concern for both mother and child, and that we may not do wrong to one in order to benefit the other—lead to some further points.

8. The moral judgment called for here—that abortion is wrong because it is wrong to commit murder to alleviate suffering—is basically a positive one for the child, not a negative one against the woman. It is made to protect the child, that she not be the victim of a second violence. It is not made to restrict the woman; it merely expresses the obligation to respect the child as a person.

9. The question of abortion is often presented as a conflict of rights: Whose rights are to prevail, mother's or child's? The real question is not *whose* rights are to prevail, but *which* rights: the right of the woman to try to alleviate her pain, or the right of the child to live? Clearly the latter. So, it is not that one person is an adult and another is a child. It is that, in general, the right to alleviate the pain of one person cannot be exercised by denying the right of another person to live.

10. Refusal to allow abortion for rape cases is not a failure of compassion. On the contrary, allowing abortion is a lack of compassion for preborn children. It is approving their murder, the violation of their most fundamental right, the right to live. Saying no to the woman is not a lack of compassion for her, but simply calling attention to what abortion really is: murder. Refusal to sanction murder is not a lack of compassion.

The Claim that Rape is Different

Many people who otherwise oppose abortion feel that the case of rape is different, and that the elements that make up this difference are sufficient to justify abortion.

First, "The woman was not given a choice. Had she freely engaged in the sexual act, she should now bear the responsibility for its consequence. But since it was forced on her, she should not be forced to continue the resulting pregnancy." In reply, if I am unjustly denied a choice, does that give me the right to kill an innocent person? I may not kill the person who denied me the choice (after the fact, as a way of trying to compensate for the denial of choice), nor may I kill a person totally innocent of unjustly denying me a choice. This is the child in the womb.

Second, "A woman should not have to endure a forced pregnancy." We must have the greatest compassion and sympathy for a woman who finds herself with an unwanted pregnancy that was forced upon her. We must support and encourage her, not destroy her innocent child. We sometimes find ourselves in situations where we are forced to do something difficult because the only alternative is to do a moral evil. A person in a concentration camp may have the opportunity to become an informer, which means a better life for him. But it also means betraying his friends and causing them additional suffering. Morally, he is forced to remain in his present, pitiable state, rather than do a moral evil, namely betraying his friends, perhaps causing their deaths. If a woman is forced to continue a pregnancy, the case is similar in this respect, that she too is forced to remain in a pitiable state because the alternative is a moral evil, the killing of an innocent child.

Third, "It was wrong for the woman to have been raped. It is wrong that she have this child. Therefore, she can now get rid of it through an abortion. She is justified in righting this wrong by removing the result of it." It certainly was wrong that the woman was raped. And this carries over in a certain way to the presence of the child. But the conclusion, that she can now get rid of it, does not follow. The child is *her* child; this remains true even when the child is conceived in violent intercourse and forced on her. The reality of the child as a person, and as entrusted to the woman as her mother, remains fully intact. The woman may not get rid of the child if this means child neglect, still less if it means killing, as in abortion.

Two wrongs do not make a right: they remain two wrongs. If you are wronged by person A, you cannot turn around and do wrong to person B as a way of undoing the first wrong. For example, if you are kidnapped by A, you cannot escape by killing innocent person B. The woman has been wronged by the rapist, A. She cannot now try to undo this wrong or its effects by doing wrong to her baby, B. Innocent person B has no duty to give up her life for another, either to benefit the other or to allow the other to right a wrong. Therefore, no one may force her to do so by killing her.

Fourth, "The child is a constant reminder of the horror of the rape experience. The woman should be allowed to get rid of this reminder."

To those who advance this point: Do you really mean to say that we can kill an innocent person on the grounds that she is a reminder of some horrible event? "But the child is a reminder inside her, so intimately involved with her." True, and this means a significant psychological difference from other cases. But it is not a morally relevant difference.

The child is a reminder of a horrible, violent act: rape. This by no means allows us to destroy her by another violent act: abortion.

Fifth, "A woman has the right to defend herself against the threat to her well-being posed by the child conceived in rape." A full analysis of killing in defense will be presented later in this chapter. It will be shown that three conditions must be met before a person has the right to kill another person in self-defense: (1) It must be an extremely serious threat, such as the threat of murder. (2) There must be no other alternative, such as running away or disarming the attacker. (3) The other must be an aggressor, an unjust attacker, and not merely someone who is in some unintended way causing the first person's death.

Does a pregnancy due to rape meet all these conditions? Most important, it fails condition 3 because the child is not an aggressor. She is absolutely innocent, in no way responsible for her coming into existence at this time and under these circumstances. It is only the rapist-father who is an unjust aggressor. Would it be right to kill him to prevent the rape? If not, then condition 1 is presumably not met. If it would be right, because this condition is met, it does not follow that it would also be right to kill the child. This is because (a) the rapist is an unjust aggressor while the child is not, and (b) because the killing would prevent the rape while the abortion would not. Finally, condition 2 is not met because there are alternatives to abortion in case of rape, which are even better for the woman, as will be shown.

Thus the appeal to self-defense cannot justify abortion for rape. Condition 3 is clearly not met—that is already sufficient. Condition 2 is also not met and 1 is doubtful.

Emotional Factors

There are valid emotional perceptions and responses, as when we feel compassion and sympathy for the woman and for the preborn child. There are also invalid emotional perceptions and responses: disgust at a child conceived in rape, and at the woman and her condition; denial and a desire to push it all aside.

If we come to recognize what these factors are, and that they are invalid, we will be able to view abortion for rape as what it really is: the unjustified killing of an innocent child, a terrible moral evil. Some of the invalid emotional factors are:

1. The desire to seek retribution against the rapist for the terrible thing he has done. As one cannot get at him directly, one tries to do so indirectly, at what is seen as "a part of him," his child. The child is attacked as a symbol of the rapist and his deed. But of course the child is not part of the rapist—no child is part of his father or mother. The association with the rapist father is completely unjust and unwarranted. The child of rape, like any other child, is completely his own person. The symbol is in the eye of the beholder—and should be removed.

2. The desire to get rid of the whole rape episode. However, abortion does not unrape a woman. In fact it adds more of the same: terrible violence against an innocent victim.

3. The desire to destroy the child because he is seen as an attacker.

4. The child is seen as "dirty" because of how he was conceived.

5. The child is "half the rapist's, therefore half evil."

Only the rapist is an attacker, only he has done something that makes it understandable that he would be considered dirty. Nothing of this logically transfers to the child. Every child is his or her own person. He certainly inherits physical and psychological traits from each of his parents, but not features such as being an aggressor or innocent, "dirty" or "clean," evil or good.

Seeing Rape Abortion for What It Really Is

Abortion for rape is, first of all, more of the same, a horrible violence against an innocent person, unable to ward off the brutal attack. Ellen McCormack gives us "a thought to ponder a minute":

> My attacker was tormented and sought peace. He didn't get it. In his attempt, however, he tore my life apart. Now I, in turn, am tormented and seek peace. Will I get it through abortion? In my desperate search, will I make the baby suffer, have his life torn apart as mine has been? Or will I do what nobody else in the world can do? Will I sustain and nourish this baby's life? Will I keep his heart beating? Will I give him a future?[3]

Second, abortion does not unrape a woman. The horrible event is past, done, and cannot be undone.

Third, what if the womb had a window, so you could actually see the child? Suppose the window could be opened, and you could actually hold her?[4] What if she could plead with you to spare her life? To spare her from the ordeal of an abortion killing? Wouldn't your heart go out to her? Isn't it morally irrelevant that she cannot be seen, or held, or that she cannot plead on her own behalf?

Fourth, what if there were a small, fully developed person inside the woman? It would not be right to kill her if she had been conceived in rape. Isn't it morally irrelevant that she is not yet fully developed?

Fifth, when the child conceived in rape is perceived as tainted, dirty, evil, etc., isn't this a prejudice? In reality, she is absolutely innocent, she is her own person, as precious as any other person. Isn't prejudice against such a child as irrational, and as morally evil, as any other prejudice?

Sixth, would you kill the born child of a rapist, if that was expected to provide a benefit similar to what is expected of abortion for rape? If not a born child, why a preborn child?

Seventh, if the idea is to destroy all vestiges of the horrible deed, one should kill the rapist who did it. If that is wrong, it is also wrong to kill a child totally innocent of the deed. Willke puts it well when he says, "Isn't it a twisted logic that would kill an innocent unborn baby for the crime of his father!"[5]

Eighth, the child is being sacrificed for the benefit of another. He has no duty to do this; it is not right to force him. Would those who favor abortion for rape volunteer their lives so that another may be benefited in a similar way? If not, is it right to force this on another person? If yes, at least they have the opportunity to make a choice; the child does not.

The Wedge

There are two fundamental reasons why we must be firm and hold steadfastly to the wrongness of abortion for rape. One is the injustice and suffering for the individual child; the other is the all-important matter of moral principle. If we say that abortion, though generally wrong, is justified for rape, we surrender the principle that one may never kill an innocent person to save or benefit another. Once this principle is abandoned by allowing an exception for rape cases, questions of other exceptions will naturally arise. "If abortion . . . [is] allowable in some cases, such as with rape, there . . . [is] no justifiable reason to 'arbitrarily' forbid abortion under other compelling circumstances."[6] And who will decide which circumstances are compelling? The woman, or the woman in consultation with her doctor? That means abortion on demand.

"Abortion only for rape" is a wedge that opens the door to all abortions. The sequence is quite logical. Once we accept the idea that abortion can be justified if the need is great enough, we accept the idea that an innocent person may be sacrificed for the sake of others. That idea underlies all abortions. With that idea in place, it becomes impossible to resist other abortions. "If she had an abortion because of her needs, why can't I?" Indeed, why not? If her child can be killed for her benefit, why not yours for your benefit?

Abortion is murder. Murder is never justified, even to alleviate great pain, and even if there was a prior injustice, such as the child being forced on the woman against her will.

It is sometimes said that pregnancy due to rape is extremely rare.[7] Rare or not, it is still an important topic because of the role it plays in people's thinking. Many oppose abortion except in this case. Their position is fundamentally flawed. It contains an inherent contradiction. If our commitment to the reality of the child and her right not to be killed for the sake of another person, is not firmly and consistently held, it will not be strong enough to defend the lives of other preborn children either. The position that abortion is wrong except in the case of rape cannot ultimately be maintained in the face of pro-abortion challenges.

If pregnancy due to rape is as rare as is generally maintained, the above position would lead to an unspeakable tragedy. For the sake of a (misguided) compassion in a few rare cases, a huge class of preborn children is surrendered to the choice of those who are ready to destroy them.

Objections and Replies

1. "A rape victim must not be punished by a forced pregnancy." Punishment is a response to a wrongdoer for the wrong he has done. The woman in being raped has obviously done no wrong. She is not being punished. She is only being asked to respect the life of another person, her own child; to do no violence to the child as was done to her. This burden is a suffering she must bear in order to avoid committing murder. Suffering as such is not punishment. The suffering we must bear in order not to do evil is clearly not punishment.

2. "The woman has suffered enough." Indeed. Any suffering of a rape victim is more than should be. She is not being asked to suffer more; she is being asked not to inflict death upon her child. That carrying the child is a further suffering for her means that the original act of violence inflicted this suffering on her too. Moreover, it is not at all clear that abortion represents a mitigation of her suffering; it may well cause additional suffering, greater suffering than carrying the child to term.

3. "Aren't there any exceptions to the rule against abortion? Don't all rules have exceptions? Isn't abortion for rape an obvious example? Rules should not be followed rigidly. A humane ethics allows for exceptions; it calls for a flexible application of moral rules, as opposed to a rigid legalism." To say yes to the mother in allowing her to have an abortion as an exception is to say no to the child in agreeing to have her killed. What is called a humane exception is actually a death warrant for the child.

Killing in defense against an unjust attacker is one exception to the rule against killing. There may or may not be others. The crucial point concerns what is not an exception: killing an innocent person to try to alleviate the pain of another person. That is what the exception to the rule against killing asks for in the case of abortion for rape.

Holding fast to the principle that we may not wrong B to help A is not an inflexible rigid legalism. It is simply faithfulness to moral principle.

This is clear when the principle is applied in other areas. We may not try to benefit society as a whole by denying black people their rights, or by denying women their rights. Saying no to abortion for rape is simply applying this principle consistently to the child.

Thus what may seem an inflexible or inhumane rule, the insistence that the child in the womb not be killed, that no exception be made, is actually something positive and supremely humane: the protection of an innocent person.

4. "To deny a woman an abortion even in the case of rape is an extreme position. Granted, abortion is wrong, but to go so far as to deny its legitimacy in the case of rape is going too far." The crucial question about a thesis or position is not whether it is extreme, but whether it is true. Should all innocent human persons be respected? Or only most people, almost all people, so that we do not adopt an extreme position? When it comes to respecting the civil rights of blacks, should it be most rights, of most blacks, most of the time? Or should it be *all* rights, of *all* blacks, *all* the time? Extreme or not, this is the only realistic moral position. The same applies to all people.

5. "Abortion is an evil but it is sometimes necessary. We must be realistic. And surely abortion for rape is a case where abortion is necessary." Realistically, to allow abortion for rape is not only to violate the right to life of the individual child involved, but also to open the door to all abortions. What is necessary is the recognition, and the putting into practice, of the two principles: equal concern for both persons, and never doing wrong to one to benefit the other.

6. "Isn't abortion a morally complex issue in the case of rape? Shouldn't the woman have a choice?" What was shown in chapter 9, that abortion is complex only in the psychological sense, that morally it is a horror, applies here as well. Abortion for rape is a clear-cut evil. This can be seen if the principle is kept in mind that the right of person B to live, not to be murdered, clearly overrides any right of person A to try to alleviate the pain and trauma of a horrible experience such as rape. Important as the degree of pain and truama is in itself, it does not affect this principle. It is not true that a very great pain may be alleviated by doing something that violates the right of another person to live. No pain justifies abortion. It is clear that we cannot kill the woman to alleviate the pain of another person, even a very great pain. The woman's right to live absolutely prevails. The child is no different. Her right to live absolutely prevails.

7. "If your daughter were pregnant due to rape, wouldn't you want her to have an abortion? Especially if she were very young, say twelve years old?" My personal response is no. No, I would not want her to

commit murder. That would be still worse, in itself and for her, than the anguish and pain of her situation. Is this answer heartless, lacking in compassion? Not at all. It is the answer of compassion: (a) for my daughter's child, that this child not be killed, that she not be the victim of a second violence; (b) for my daughter, that she not participate in a murder; and (c) for my daughter's own psychological and physical well-being, for reasons that I will show in the next section.

I would suffer with my daughter, I would support her, I would love her all the more, I would help her in whatever way I could. I would do anything I could do; there is much I cannot do. I cannot undo the past, I cannot undo the rape . And, I cannot undo the pregnancy; I cannot agree to the murder of the child. Undoing the past is physically impossible (actually, metaphysically[8]); undoing the pregnancy is morally imposs-ible. We should, by our free choice, abide by the second as much as we are necessitated to abide by the first.

Abortion for Rape: An Assault on the Woman

Abortion for rape is wrong because it destroys the innocent child. It is also wrong because it is an assault on the woman. It poses grave risks of harm to her, psychologically, physically, for possible future pregnancies, even for her life. Women are the second victims of abortion, in addition to their murdered babies. What is needed is a positive approach, of true under-standing, loving support, and counseling. Abortion is not a solution to the problem of rape—it destroys one person and poses grave dangers for another.

The case in favor of abortion following rape is based on the assump-tion that it would benefit the woman. It would not be justified even if it did. That it poses, on the contrary, a grave threat to her provides an additional reason why abortion for rape is wrong.

To illustrate the reality of what abortion can do to a woman, consider an actual case, the story of Holly (not her real name). Her story is entitled, "I Had an Abortion: The Agonizing Aftermath."

> I had an abortion 9-1/2 years ago, at the age of 16. Having an abortion has caused me great pain and I've always regretted not carrying my child to term. . . .
>
> The abortion itself was very traumatic emotionally. I was put in a room on the maternity ward, next to the labor and delivery room where I heard a woman give birth. When I was coming out of the

anesthetic, I dreamt that the doctor could put my baby back inside me and I cried out to him to please give my baby back to me.

I received no counseling afterwards and no one asked me any questions about my feelings. I left the hospital feeling very disoriented and confused.

I suffered greatly the next year and a half. Every time I saw a baby, I would mourn the one I lost and feel intense guilt.

Shortly after my abortion, I saw pictures of 10-week-old fetuses in Life magazine, and became absolutely horrified at what I had done. I would fantasize about running away to Hawaii, when I was pregnant, to escape the pressure on me to abort.

After I graduated from high school, I was hospitalized for a few days for minor surgery and saw a 15-year-old girl I knew who had just delivered a baby she gave up for adoption. I kept asking myself, "Why couldn't I have had my baby?" and almost had an emotional breakdown.

At that time, I told a priest my story and got some temporary relief from my guilt feelings. After that, I made a conscious effort to repress the whole experience and used any means I could, including drug abuse, to dull my pain.

This past year, when I became pregnant with my son and felt him move inside me, the whole experience came back to me. I was acutely conscious that I was carrying another person inside me and came to a full realization that I had allowed a child of mine to be killed inside my body.

I began to suffer horrible nightmares, insomnia, feelings of intense grief and guilt, and terror at what I had done.

I became clinically depressed, and my pain was so intense that I could hardly bear it. My depression worsened after the birth of my son, and I eventually sought psychiatric care.[9]

The story of Holly is typical of the devastating effects that an abortion can have on a woman. In discussing this topic, I shall refer principally to the work of David C. Reardon, *Aborted Women: Silent No More*, the most comprehensive book on the subject, to my knowledge. Reardon's basic thesis, that many women who have abortions suffer from them afterwards, is corroberated by numerous other works.[10] Reardon's book is based on extensive research, including a detailed survey of 252 women who have had abortions, and are now members of WEBA, Women Exploited by Abortion, an organization formed to serve "as a refuge and source of spiritual and emotional healing for women who have had abortions" and "to educate the general public, and young women in particular, about the physical, emotional, and psychological side effects of abortion."[11] One of Reardon's most significant findings is the following:

> If they had known where their lives would have been today, over 95 percent of those surveyed said they would not have chosen abortion. Asked if their lives now are better or worse because of their choice, 66 percent said that their lives are worse because of their abortions. [12]

The claim that abortion is harmful to women has recently been challenged. It has been claimed that most women do not suffer severe or long-term damage. Even if "most" do not, *some* do, and that is very significant! Perhaps forty percent suffer, while most do not. Perhaps only two percent suffer, in some categories. If 20 million women have had abortions, two percent is 400,000, a very significant number.

It is said that women feel a sense of relief after abortion. That is understandable. But the relief may mask deeper emotional scars (guilt, fear, anger, depression, feelings of loss). The feeling of relief may be maintained by denial, and it may not last. "Women . . . who suffer from abortion at a subconscious level are 'walking time-bombs,' waiting to explode over situations seemingly unrelated to their previous abortions."[13]

Another aspect is the failure to consider long-term damage:

> An abortion recorded as complication-free in a short-term study might in fact have caused long-term damage. . . . Short term studies of abortion complications reveal only the tip of the iceberg. . . . Women who may appear physically unaffected by an abortion after a one year follow-up may be found to be severely effected by the abortion as many as ten to fifteen years later.[14]

It is said that most women do not suffer lasting damage. Or, they are not hospitalized. But they may still suffer enormous pain at home. They may go through what Karen Sullivan describes:

> I had nightmares and recurring dreams about my baby. I couldn't work my job. I just laid in my bed and cried. Once, I wept so hard I sprained my ribs. . . . I was unable to walk on the beach because the playing children would make me cry. Even the Pampers commercials would set me into fits of uncontrollable crying.[15]

It is said that the data on the effects of abortion on women are insufficient. True. But that involves the frightening possibility that in some categories more woman may be suffering than reported. What we know may be the tip of the iceberg. There are a number of reasons for this:

Some women do not participate in surveys and studies because they are too deeply hurt. Leaving them out creates an unrealistically positive picture. Some of those who do participate want to focus on the good part, the relief; they do not focus on their deeper feelings, the anguish, the guilt. Some may be in denial of these deeper sufferings.

Some complications which are in fact caused by abortion are not recognized as such because of lack of follow up examinations, because women hide their identities or deny they have had abortions, or because examinations that do occur do not trace complications back to their real source, the abortion. This is especially true of long-term complications.

The data are insufficient because many women who suffer are never included in the statistics:

> Accurate statistics are scarce because the reporting of complications is almost entirely at the option of abortion providers. In other words, abortionists are in the privileged position of being able to hide any information which might damage their reputations or trade.[16]

The reason is a court mandated "Zone of Privacy":

> This prohibits any meaningful form of state or federal regulation other than broad "general requirements as to the maintaining of sanitary facilities. . . ." As a result, any laws which attempt to require that deaths and complications resulting from abortion be recorded, much less reported, are unconstitutional. Thus the only information available on abortion complications is the result of data which is *voluntarily* reported. Since abortionists want to hide their failures, underreporting of complications is the rule rather than the exception.[17]

What is unmistakably clear is that many women are hurting. What we do not know are the precise figures: How many? How severely? For how long? In what ways? We know that smoking is hazardous to health, even if precise statistics and accurate predictions in specific cases are not available. So it is with abortion. It is a terrible hazard to the well-being of women. To say that a particular woman has not suffered is to miss the point. Perhaps she has not yet suffered. Perhaps she is unaware of the root of her suffering in her abortion. Perhaps she is denying her suffering. Assume she has not suffered at all, and will not suffer. But many other women have suffered. That is the important point here, a point that Reardon's book makes abundantly clear. It is filled with facts and figures and their significance, and contains twenty-one stories of women devastated by their abortions, including that of Nancyjo Mann, founder of WEBA. These stories show that experiences like those of Holly are not isolated, but are tragedies repeated over and over again.

The conclusion is that abortion is a terrible risk for women. As we shall see, the risk is especially great for the "hard cases" such as rape. We have then another reason abortion for rape is wrong: it is a grave threat to the woman.

The following are some specific ways in which abortion may be destructive to women.

First, psychological harm. Reardon states:

> In a survey of available studies, the Royal College of Obstetricians and Gynecologists in England observed that, "The incidence of serious, permanent psychiatric aftermath [from abortion] is variously reported as between 9 and 59%." Naturally, the percentage is higher if one includes the "non-serious" and "non-permanent" aftermath. . . . A European study reported negative psychiatric manifestations following legal abortions in 55% of the women examined by the psychiatrists.[18]

Another study showed 40% suffering from nightmares and 20% from nervous breakdowns.[19]

Reardon reports on "one of the most detailed studies of post-abortion sequelae":

> "[The women] . . . were overwhelmed by negative feelings. Even those women who were strongly supportive of the right to abort reacted to their own abortions with regret, anger, embarrassment, fear of disapproval and even shame." In another paper, the same group of psychiatrists reported that when detailed interviews were performed, *every aborted woman, "without exception" experienced "feelings of guilt or profound regret.* . . . All the women felt that they had lost an important part of themselves."[20]

Abortion is intended to help and strengthen women. It may, in fact, do just the opposite. "Abortion often creates feelings of low self-esteem, feelings of having compromised values, having 'murdered my child,' and so on."[21]

Second, abortion may cause physical harm. In one study, fifty percent of the women suffered "from at least one type of physical complication" and eighteen percent "suffered permanent physical damage traceable to the procedure."[22]

About ninety percent of all abortions are by suction, also known as vacuum aspiration. "A major German study found that the total morbidity rate for vacuum aspiration abortions exceeded thirty-one percent."[23]

> Because the abortionist operates blindly, by sense of feel only, the cutting/suction device is potentially deadly. Perforation of the uterus is one of the most common complications. . . . Another common complication results from failure to extract all the "products of conception." . . . Third, as with all forms of abortion, suction curettage results in a high incidence of embolisms.[24]

Dilation and curettage (D & C) has complications similar to suction, but they are "approximately 20% more frequent."[25] For later abortions things get worse.

> Each year there are between 100,000 and 150,000 second and third trimester abortions. Most of these are saline abortions. The rate of "major" complications associated with saline abortion is reported to be about five times greater than for first trimester suction abortions. . . . In Japan, where abortion has been legalized since the 1940s, the saline abortion technique has been outlawed because it is "extraordinarily dangerous." Indeed in the United States saline abortion is second only to heart transplants as the elective surgery with the highest fatality rate. . . . Severe infections and hemorrhages are extremely common following saline abortions. In addition, seepage of the salt solution into the woman's blood system may result in life-threatening coagulation problems. . . . Furthermore, infections or uterine damage incurred during saline abortions frequently require removal of the uterus.[26]

Third, abortion may affect future pregnancies. Abortion kills the child now present. It threatens the woman. A third potential victim is a wanted child from a later pregnancy.

> Abortion poses a severe threat to the reproductive integrity of women. . . . Between 40 and 50 percent of all aborted women will suffer later reproductive problems. . . . It can be estimated that for every 100,000 previously aborted women who later attempt a wanted pregnancy, 14,329 will lose their babies. This is over four times the 3,320 losses which would be expected for a group of 100,000 non-aborted women. After subtracting out the "normal" fetal loss rate, it can be concluded that for every 100,000 pregnancies undertaken by previously aborted women, over 11,000 *wanted* babies will die as a direct result of latent abortion morbidity.[27]

This danger is especially great for teenagers.[28]

Fourth, legal abortions can lead to the woman's death. Contrary to the familiar slogan, "safe, legal abortion," which so many people assume to be true, "a woman's supposedly simple surgery can become an ordeal of nightmare proportions."[29]

> On June 14,1977, Barbaralee Davis underwent a routine suction abortion at the Hope Clinic for Women in Granite City, Illinois. After the customary period of observation in the clinic's recovery room, she complained of weakness and was sent home with instructions to rest. Alone in her bedroom, she slept and quietly bled to death. Her body was found less than twelve hours after the abortion After the incident was reported in the local press, Michael Grobsmith, chief of the Illinois Department of Public Health's Division of Hospitals and Clinics, commented on the death by saying: "It's unfortunate, but it's happening every day in Chicago, and you're just not hearing about it."
>
> One year later, during an investigation of only four Chicago-based clinics (in a state with over twenty abortion clinics), the *Chicago Sun-Times* uncovered twelve abortion deaths that had never been reported. Even when abortion-related deaths such as these are uncovered, they are generally not included in the "official" total since they were not reported as such on the original death certificates. If there are this many unreported abortion deaths in one city from only a few clinics, in a state with regulations as strict as any allowed by the courts, how many more are there across the country?[30]

The total number of deaths from legal abortion is unknown. It is enough to know that they are occurring, and that every abortion poses a terrible risk of death for the woman.

> What should be clear is that there is a major flaw in the mortality statistics for legal abortion. It is quite possible that only 5 to 10 percent of all deaths resulting from legal abortion are being reported as abortion-related. Even if 50 percent were being accurately reported, that extra margin of risk is far greater than women are being led to believe. Indeed, based on the *reported* abortion deaths alone, abortion is already the fifth leading cause of maternal death in the United States.[31]

There is another threat to the woman's life:

> For every 100,000 aborted women who later attempt a wanted pregnancy, 12 will die as a result of obstetric complications compared to a "normal" maternal mortality rate of 7.6 per 100,000 pregnancies.

Thus, previously aborted women face a 58 percent greater risk of dying during a later pregnancy than their non-aborted sisters.[32]

The evidence shows that abortion is not safer than childbirth. Abortion makes future childbearing more dangerous. It holds hazards for women: psychological, physical, even death. These examples should make it clear that abortion is not safer than childbirth. But let us look at some specific aspects of the comparison, both for complications following abortion and death from abortion:

> Compared to childbirth, the morbidity rate of abortion [i.e., the rate of complications following abortion] is astronomical. For childbirth, the overall maternal morbidity rate is approximately 2 percent. . . . The reported immediate complication rate, alone, of abortion is no less than 10 percent. In addition, studies of long-range complications show rates of no less than 17 percent and frequently report complication rates in the range of 25 to 40 percent. One public hospital has even reported an overall complication rate following abortion of 70 percent![33]

These figures are based on *reported* cases. Many cases go unreported, meaning that actual morbidity rates are higher, perhaps much higher. According to one report, "the risk of long-term complications following an abortion is ten to twenty times greater than the risk of *any* complications following childbirth."[34]

A careful study of the number of deaths resulting from childbirth and from abortion, was made by Thomas W. Hilgers, M.D. and Dennis O'Hare, and reported in "Abortion Related Maternal Morbidity: An In-Depth Analysis." They first note that "traditional comparisons have been seriously flawed by comparing incomparable data. In this study, adjustments have been made so that accurate reflections of the 'cases of pregnancy' can be made and compared."[35]

They concluded: "In comparing the relative risk of natural pregnancy versus that of legal abortion, *natural pregnancy was found to be safer in both the first and second 20 weeks of pregnancy.*"[36]

These studies indicate that childbirth is safer for the woman. When childbirth is dangerous, it is so because of an already present condition, while the dangers of abortion come from the abortion itself. In this sense it is hardly fair to compare the two cases:

> The overwhelming majority of women who die from a legal abortion are perfectly healthy before their lethal surgery; in carrying the pregnan-

cies to term few—if any—would die. But most maternal childbirth deaths occur within a very small group of high-risk patients. Those women who died in childbirth died from a disease process—an abnormality in the pregnancy/childbirth experience which for some reason could not be adequately treated. . . . The death of a healthy woman from a legal abortion is totally preventable simply by not aborting. . . . The death from childbearing of that woman with a disorder is mostly unpreventable because of medical inability to understand or control the disease process which takes her life.[37]

Therefore, even if more women who carry the child to term were to die than those who abort, this would not show that abortion is safer than childbirth. For the childbearing women who die do not die simply from childbearing but from already existing conditions in conjunction with their pregnancies. In contrast, since the vast majority of aborting woman are healthy, if they die, their deaths must be attributed to the abortion and its consequences.

Abortion can also make a future pregnancy more dangerous. Hence some of the existing conditions that can make childbearing dangerous actually come from abortion, though the death of the woman would be counted under the childbirth statistics rather than abortion statistics.

The Deep Connection

Abortion is wrong because it is the destruction of a child. It is wrong because it is an assault on a woman. There is a deep connection between these two. The woman and the child, though absolutely distinct as individual persons, are nonetheless intimately joined together, not only physically but in a meaningful personal way. The child is entrusted to her, sheltered and secured in her being. She carries the child in herself. Abortion is a violent attack on this intimate union. The child is forcibly ripped out, against his instinctive clinging to remain in his secure resting place. In this way, abortion is also an attack on the woman. Such an attack is bound to take its toll, physically and psychologically. That abortion is bad for women is what we should expect; it would be strange if it were not so. When it seems not to be, when women say they are better off having had an abortion, one wonders whether this optimism does not mask a deeper hidden wound. Sometimes they realize it later, as Nancyjo Mann did: "The abortion killed not only my daughter; it killed a part of me."[38]

A "Cure" That Aggravates the Disease

There is a risk for all women who abort, but especially for those who do so in the "hard" cases, such as rape. Reardon says such women "are much more likely to suffer from severe emotional and psychiatric stress after their abortion than are those who abort purely for reasons of convenience."[39] In general: *"The more difficult the circumstances prompting abortion, the more likely it is that the woman will suffer severe post-abortion sequelae."*[40] This is supported by an official statement from the World Health Organization that reads: "Thus the very women for whom legal abortion is considered justified on psychiatric grounds are the ones who have the highest risk of post-abortion psychiatric disorders."[41]

Reardon also notes, "Within all of the psychiatric literature available, there is not one psychiatric condition for which abortion is a recognized cure. Instead, the evidence overwhelmingly indicates that true psychological problems are generally complicated and aggravated by abortion rather than alleviated by it."[42]

The Real Problem and Its Solution

What we have just seen—that abortion for rape is especially threatening to women—makes it clear that abortion is the wrong solution to the problem of rape pregnancy. It is the wrong solution because the problem is misunderstood. The problem is not the child, carrying her to term. The problem is the effect on the woman of attitudes projected on her by others.

These attitudes are rooted in the valid response of abhorrence at the rape. But then they are extended to a kind of abhorrence of the woman herself, and her child. A stigma is attached, somewhat like that in Hawthorne's novel, *The Scarlet Letter*, where a woman was stigmatized by her society by having to wear a large "A" because of her sin of adultery.[43] The stigma in the case of rape pregnancy "is that the woman is somehow 'tainted' or 'dirtied' as a result of her tragic experience."[44] There is also an assumption that the woman was somehow responsible, that she must have provoked the attack and could have prevented it; that "nice women don't get raped."[45] The result is a strong desire to get rid of the whole thing, to push it out of sight. There is an obvious way to do this: get rid of the visible sign of rape; abort the child.

Mahkorn expresses the real problem. It is "that the attitudes projected by others and not the pregnancy itself pose the central problem for the pregnant victim."[46]

The absurdity and injustice of these attitudes and assumptions cannot be too strongly condemned. The woman must be seen only as an innocent victim. Just as a child who is a victim of child abuse is not tainted or dirtied by that despicable deed, so a woman is not affected in this way. By its very nature, rape is something forced on the woman, precluding her responsibility. Rape is rape, an unspeakable crime, regardless of what leads to it. And, nice women do get raped.

We should also note that part of the problem for a woman is the pressure to abort. This tends to aggravate her problems: "Because it is likely that the victim already harbors feelings of guilt as a result of the assault, medico-social pressures which encourage and result in abortion could compound the woman's feelings of guilt and self-blame."[47]

Another part of the problem is the suggestion that the woman needs an abortion. Such an attitude "can only serve to reaffirm the sense of helplessness and vulnerability that was so violently conveyed in the act of sexual assault itself. At a time when she is struggling to regain her sense of self-esteem, such a 'take charge' attitude can be especially damaging."[48]

What is needed is not the negative attempt to get rid of an embarrassment but a positive approach: support and encouragement for the woman, based on a total affirmation of her, in her present situation, with no shade of stigma, accusation, or condescension. An important part of this is encouraging her to face her situation realistically, and to talk about it. That is, we must "recognize that the victim . . . [has] a real need to discuss her feelings and fears with people who . . . [care] about her."[49]

The negative feelings projected by others may be transferred to the child, who is then seen as something that should be removed.[50] To understand the real problem allows us to become free from the impulse to remove the child, who is also an innocent victim of these negative feelings.

In a typical rape case, the woman is the first innocent victim, a victim of the attacker. Then she is an innocent victim a second time, a victim of the attitudes of others that stigmatize her. The child is also drawn in, and becomes another innocent victim in this tragic scenario. If an abortion is performed, the child is again an innocent victim. Abortion for rape does not help—it only adds another innocent victim.

The real problem is not the child but the social stigma unjustly suffered by the woman. This helps us to understand why abortion for rape is especially bad for women. The woman, already weakened and devastated by the assault of the rapist, now becomes subject to another assault on her body and spirit, the assault by the abortionist. If she is pressured to have an abortion the assault is compounded. She may feel that abortion is wrong, but that she must have one to please others or do what they insist is the right thing. In this way she is again a victim of something forced on her by outside forces. Already made to feel vulnerable by the rapist, she is now made to feel vulnerable by the pressure to abort:

> Abortion promises only to compound the trauma of rape with yet another experience of violence. In pursuing this course, the victim may assume to herself guilt for the entire episode. In an attempt to overcome the violation of her own person, she does violence to another, submitting to the added humiliation of abortion. This brings no peace of mind and no healing, only more pain and more regret.[51]

The negative social stigma also explains why there is such widespread support for abortion in cases of rape, and why it is so strong. Pro-abortion people consider it one of their strongest arguments, implying that any compassionate person must favor abortion in such cases. Many people (probably a majority) who oppose abortion as such, feel impelled to make an exception for rape. They mean to do well for the woman; tragically, what they advocate hurts not only the child but the woman as well.

The only positive alternative to abortion is support for the woman as she deals with the trauma of her experience, and as she carries the child to term. As Mahkorn puts it, "the central issue" is not abortion "but rather an exploration of the things we can change in ourselves and through community education to support such women through their pregnancies."[52]

Curt Young summarizes these points:

> The emotional trauma of rape is not mitigated by abortion. Regardless of what the woman does once she is pregnant, she must work through her rape experience and her feelings about it in order to resolve the trauma. This does not come easily and may involve professional counseling. There is no shortcut to coming to grips with the pain. From a counseling perspective, abortion is a simplistic and presumptuous suggestion. . . . In the course of choosing life and sacrificing for the child within them, women have regained their self-esteem and acquired a sense of their own worth they never before possessed. In the midst of their pain they have discovered a peace they never imagined was possible.[53]

Abortion for Incest

The first and basic moral argument against abortion for rape applies to cases of incest as well. If we realize that a child is present, if we identify with her, if we have full and equal concern for the mother and child, if we realize that we cannot kill one innocent person to try to benefit another, that we cannot do wrong to try to achieve good, then we will see clearly that abortion for incest is absolutely wrong; a clear-cut wrong, and not a legitimate exception.

The second major argument against abortion for rape—that abortion is an assault on the woman, that it is counterproductive, largely because it is based on a false picture of the actual problem—applies here as well. Reardon's argument is along these lines, and he adds certain features specific to incest pregnancies.

> As with rape, abortion proponents appealed to emotional abhorrence of incest to gain support for abortion while ignoring the real needs of the victims. Abortion was simply *presumed* to be the best answer—at least best for society if not for the women, girls or children. Through abortion, they suggested, we could cover up these embarrassing victims of our sick society; we could destroy the "unclean" offspring of our sexual perversions. But in fact, just as with rape, there is no psychiatric evidence, nor even any theory which argues that abortion of an incestuous pregnancy is therapeutic for the victim—it is only more convenient for everyone else.
>
> Setting aside the paternalistic attitudes with which society presumes that abortion is best for the incest victim, we must ask what do these girls themselves want? . . . Almost all incest victims actually desire to keep the baby, and the majority do! Those who do abort do so under pressure from the impregnating relative who is seeking to cover-up his crime, and even in these cases, the victims abort only with resentment.[54]
>
> Abortion of an incestuous pregnancy . . . not only adds to the girl's guilt and trauma, it also frustrates her plans for escape and attention. Abortion perpetuates the "conspiracy of silence" by covering up the incest, or at least its results, and continues the family pattern of denying reality.[55]
>
> The problem the pregnant incest victim faces is not the pregnancy, it is the psychological pain of incest. Again, as with rape, it is the discrimination and superstitions of those around her which make the pregnancy difficult, not the pregnancy itself.[56]

Dr. George Maloof speaks in the same vein:

> Whatever else we may be doing by an abortion of an incestuous pregnancy, we are promoting mental illness by not allowing the girl to accept the consequences of her own acts . . . Accepting the pregnancy can be the first step to accepting the incest and making the changes to alter the family pattern so that it can be more productive rather than withholding and destructive.[57]

The Health and Life of the Woman

Is abortion justified when it is deemed necessary for preserving the health or life of the woman? Cases where the woman's health or life is threatened by pregnancy are now extremely rare, perhaps so rare as to be virtually non-existent. For example:

> According to one obstetrician, "After many years' work in several large gynecological hospitals, I have never yet seen a woman's life in danger, necessitating abortion." In contrast, he adds, "I have seen two extremely sick women offered abortions because of serious heart-lung disease; both refused, and both delivered normal children, normally . . . Similarly, Dr. David Decker of the Mayo Clinic states that there are "few, if any, absolute medical indications for the therapeutic abortion in the present state of medicine."[56]

Despite the rarity of such cases, the question of abortion as it pertains to them is worth pursuing, as there are important principles involved. Such cases, though rare in practice, are not so rare in the discussion of the abortion issue. Hence, an understanding of the principles involved is of great importance.

To evaluate such cases, I suggest the following three principles. The first two have already been noted.

1. There must be full and equal concern for all persons involved, the woman and the child. Each is fully a person, each has the same dignity and preciousness of being a person; each has the same right to live as the other. What applies to one applies equally to the other. Just as we recognize the full reality of the woman, so too we must recognize the full reality of the child. Just as we identify with the woman, we must identify with the child.

2. We cannot kill innocent person B to save person A. Thus the fundamental point: We cannot kill the child to save the woman, any more than we could kill the woman to save the child. Parallel to the case of "abortion for rape," there are people who are fundamentally opposed to abortion, who recognize it as wrong, but who want to make an exception for "the life of the woman." But if abortion is murder, one cannot commit murder to save the life of another person.

3. Where complications arise, we must try to save both the woman and the child. Dr. Everett Koop describes this situation:

> When a woman is pregnant, her obstetrician takes on the care of two patients—the mother-to-be and the unborn baby. If, toward the end of the pregnancy, complications arise that threaten the mother's

health, he will take the child by inducing labor or performing a Caesarean section.

His intention is still to save the life of both the mother and the baby. The baby will be premature and perhaps immature depending on the length of gestation. Because it has suddenly been taken out of the protective womb, it may encounter threats to its survival. The baby is never willfully destroyed because the mother's life is in danger.[59]

What is crucial in such cases is that no one is killed. One person is saved, the other person would be saved if that were possible. Tragically, it is not. So, one saves one person and regretfully fails to save the other. The other is not killed. To apply a medical procedure to person A instead of to B—where both need it to survive but where it can be given only to one—is to save A, and to unwillingly withhold treatment from B. Unwillingly withholding treatment, in such a situation, differs sharply from doing something that kills. So, if it is the child who is to be saved, treatment is unwillingly withheld from the woman, but she is not killed. Conversely, if it is the woman who is to be saved, treatment is unwillingly withheld from the child, but he is not killed. No abortion is performed. To withhold treatment from the child—because it cannot be given both to him and to the woman, and the woman is selected instead—is not to abort the child.

If two people are bitten by a poisonous snake and I have an antidote serum for one but not for the other, I give it to one and withhold it from the other. I regretfully cannot save him but must let him die. I have not killed him. So too with the mother and child.

Difficult situations falling under these principles typically involve removal of the child. What kinds of "removal" are justified, and what kinds are not?

1. We may remove the child to save the woman, even if the child dies as a result. A typical case is the removal of the child in an ectopic pregnancy, where she begins to develop in the Fallopian tube instead of in the uterus. If nothing is done, both mother and child will die. Clearly it is right to remove the child in order to save the mother. What is intended is only her removal, not her death. And the method of removal is not one that actually constitutes killing, but is genuine removal. Death follows as a result of the moving, it is clearly not intended. A similar situation occurs when a child is removed from a cancerous womb in order to save the woman, even though the child's death is foreseen.

2. We may remove the child to save the child, if his death is otherwise certain, even if there is a risk to the mother. Just as we may remove the child to save the mother, if her death is otherwise certain, even if there is a risk to the child.

3. The primary kind of "removal" that is not justified is an action that is in fact the killing of the child but labeled "removal." Thus suction, where the child is torn to pieces, is a form of removal (as are all the other methods). The removal is accomplished by means of the suction. But the act of suctioning is itself the act of killing. Such acts of removal are really acts of murder. Abortion is that kind of act.

Removal, to be justified, must be genuine removal. It cannot be a de facto killing, which is then labeled "removal."

4. Another kind of removal that is not justified is the case in which it means the certain death of one person (as an unintended result), while it only increases the chance of life for another. We cannot remove a sick child to increase his chances of life if doing so would result in the certain death of the woman. So too, we cannot remove a child to increase the chance of life for his mother, if doing so would result in his certain death.

It is extremely important to be clear about these matters, specifically the three principles and the justified and unjustified forms of removal. The failure to be clear on these things accounts for the fact that a large majority of people who see the wrongness of abortion for all the reasons indicated here, nevertheless want to make an exception for the life of the woman. They fail to distinguish clearly between justified removals— where no one's death is intended—and abortion, which is intentional killing. Or they fail to see that not saving the child—because both cannot be saved, and one tries to save the woman—is radically different from killing the child by abortion. If one wants to save the woman (instead of the child), and one is not clear about these things, confusing them with abortion, one is likely to consider these procedures forms of abortion, and thus to favor abortion when necessary to save the life of the woman.

The view defended here is not, as so often charged, an extreme view. It is simply the result of a careful analysis of such cases by applying the two basic principles that all persons are to count equally, and that we may not kill one innocent person to save the life of another.

It is noteworthy that the United States Supreme Court, in the decision that legalized abortion (*Roe v. Wade*, January 22, 1973), recognized the inconsistency in saying that abortion is wrong as such, but right if necessary to save the life of the woman. The Court was considering a Texas law that prohibited abortion but included an exception for the life of the woman. The Texas law said "a fetus is entitled to Fourteenth Amendment protection as a person." The Court then noted: "But if the fetus is a person who is not to be deprived of life without due process of law, and if the mother's condition is the sole determinant, does not the Texas exception appear to be out of line with the Amendment's command?"[60]

One may not kill the child to save the woman when this benefit to her is a certainty; still less when it falls short of that, and even less when the abortion killing may actually be more dangerous for her. Reardon, speaking of "cases where the mother is suffering from other maladies, such as heart or kidney disease, which *may* worsen as the pregnancy progresses," and where the "death of the mother is only a possibility rather than a certainty," explains:

> The vast majority of these diseased women, if not aborted, will survive and carry their pregnancies successfully to term. Furthermore, since these women are already weakened by disease, they are also more susceptible to complications associated with abortion. Though child-birth poses extra risks for these women, so does abortion. In many such cases it has been found that "therapeutic" abortions are in fact far more dangerous than childbirth.[61]

The Appeal to Self Defense

Defenders of abortion sometimes appeal to the right to kill in self-defense in cases such as those in this chapter, especially when it is the life of the woman that is threatened. The child is viewed as an attacker who may be killed in defense of the woman. Judith Jarvis Thomson advances such an argument:

> Suppose you find yourself trapped in a tiny house with a growing child. I mean a very tiny house, and a rapidly growing child—you are already up against the wall of the house and in a few minutes you'll be crushed to death. The child on the other hand won't be crushed to death; if nothing is done to stop him from growing he'll be hurt, but in the end he'll simply burst open the house and walk out a free man. Now I could well understand it if a bystander were to say, "There's nothing we can do for you. We cannot choose between your life and his, we cannot be the ones who decide who is to live, we cannot intervene." But it cannot be concluded that you too can do nothing, that you cannot attack it to save your life. However innocent the child may be, you do not have to wait passively while it crushes you to death. Perhaps a pregnant woman is vaguely felt to have the status of house, to which we don't allow the right of self-defense. But if the woman houses the child, it should be remembered that she is a person who houses it.[62]

When does a person have a right to kill another person in self-defense? I submit there are three necessary conditions. There is a right to kill only: (1) In cases of extremely serious threat, such as the threat of murder. (2) If there is no other alternative. (3) Against an aggressor, an unjust attacker who is doing something to threaten me.

Regarding (1): I cannot, for example, kill a car thief in order to protect the possession of my car. There is a question about very serious threats short of life such as permanent paralysis or blindness or rape. They may or may not qualify, a difficult question we cannot pursue here.

Regarding (2): If I can escape, or distract my assailant, or temporarily disable him, or call the police, I must, of course, do so. Killing can only be a last resort.

Let us focus now on (3), the most significant of these necessary conditions, and the one most often overlooked. The crucial point is this. I cannot kill another person merely because he is in some way causing my death, or is a causal factor involved in my impending death. I cannot, so to speak, push people out of the way by killing them if they block the continuation of my life. I can kill them only if they are unjustly attacking me. To make this clear consider the following two cases:

Case A: A man attacks me, intending to kill me. I can save myself only by killing him. I kill him.

Case B: I'm fleeing for my life. An innocent man, not doing anything, blocks my way, without realizing it. I can get him out of the way only by killing him. If I do not kill him, I will be killed. Again: I can save myself only by killing him. I kill him.

I submit that I have no right to kill the innocent man in case B, while I do have the right to kill the unjust aggressor in case A. Why? Both are instances of "I can save myself only by killing him. I kill him." The crucial difference is that in case A, a person is attacking me unjustly and threatening my life, while in case B the other person involved is not an attacker, and his behavior is not unjust. I have a right to kill in self-defense against an unjust attacker, an aggressor, but not against someone who is merely a causal factor in my death. The fact that another person is, or is about to be, a causal factor in my death—perhaps even the main cause—is not sufficient to justify killing him in self-defense. The person who represents a threat to me must be more than a causal factor. He must be doing something to threaten my life, and he must be doing it unjustly. The injustice of his behavior is an essential element in the justification of killing in self-defense. The right to kill in self-defense is essentially a response to the injustice of what another is doing that threatens my life; not merely the fact that his behavior, or his presence, somehow contributes to, or causes my death.

We may have great compassion for the person in case B who kills someone to save his own life. We would not want to judge the person harshly, but this does not mean that his act was morally justified.

Suppose we deny this third necessary condition. It would mean that I have a right to kill you in self-defense in the following situations: (C) I need a life-sustaining machine, but you are using the only one available. I push you out of my way, since you are blocking my use of it, thereby killing you. (D) We are trapped in a wreck, I am under you, your weight (through no fault of your own) is suffocating me, I have a device that "pushes you out of my way," thereby killing you. (Note the similarity to Thomson's rapidly growing child.) (E) I am trapped in a cave where I will soon die, because you are blocking its entrance through no fault of your own. I "push you out of my way" by dynamiting you.

I submit that in all these cases I have no right to kill you to save myself. It is wrong to kill one innocent person to save another. Killing in defense in each of these cases would violate this important principle. *Innocent* in these instances means simply not unjustly attacking. In each of these cases, the person about to cause a death, or causally involved in such a process, is not unjustly attacking. He just happens to be in a position where his presence represents something that causes (or is a causal factor in) the death of another. It is not his fault, in contrast to the unjust attack of a real aggressor.

The no duty-nonforcing principle also makes the wrongness of killing in each of these cases clear. Since you have no duty to give up your life so that mine can be saved, no one can force you to give up your life. No one may kill you. Also, there is no duty that you are failing to live up to in any of these cases, a duty that might justify someone forcing you to live up to. This is precisely what is not true of the unjust attacker: Since he is failing to live up to his duty to respect my life, I may force him to do so by protecting myself against him, even if it means causing his death.

Abortion in the name of self-defense is not justified. The child is not an unjust attacker. He is not doing anything, especially not something unjust. He is simply in his natural place, developing and growing. If, in a particular situation, this has adverse causal effects on the woman, it is a terrible tragedy. But it is not an unjust attack, and so it does not justify killing in defense.

An important point that emerges especially from cases D and E is that the right to self-defense never applies when the cause of (or a causal factor in) my impending death is merely the body of another, and not that person as agent. The right to self-defense applies only when someone who threatens to do something to me acts as a personal agent, however irrationally. He may use his body, as when he threatens severe blows with his fists. But *he* is attacking me, not his body; though he attacks me by means of parts of his body. In contrast, where it is merely the body of another that becomes a cause of my death—as in the previous cases, or the child in the womb—I have no right to kill in self-defense.

Regarding Thomson's analogy, we can now see that she has no right to kill the growing child inside her, since that child is absolutely innocent. The same is true if the tables are turned. If a growth in the woman's body were about to crush the child, and he realized it, and could kill his mother to save himself, he would not be morally justified in doing so. For his mother is not an unjust aggressor.

Thomson will say that the two cases are not parallel; that, after all, the body is hers; the house in which the baby is crushing the woman is her house. But this does not alter the moral situation with regard to the right to kill in self-defense. I cannot kill you, an innocent person who is merely causing my death, even if this is taking place in my own house. A woman's right to her body, however far it may or may not extend, does not include the right to kill an innocent person.

Thomson's admission that she "could well understand it if a bystander were to say, 'there's nothing we can do for you. We cannot choose between your life and his, . . . we cannot intervene,'" is revealing. She is perfectly right. A bystander couldn't intervene because the child is innocent, a non-aggressor. If he weren't, the situation would be essentially different. In general, if A were an unjust aggressor threatening to kill B, then surely the bystander could, and should, intervene. He could kill A under the heading of the right to kill an aggressor in defense. That right applies both to the defense of another and oneself.

The fact that the bystander has no right to intervene to kill the child reflects the central point here: The child is innocent, he is not an aggressor, and so he may not be killed.

The bystander may not kill the child because he should not be killed, which of course means the woman may not kill him either. And Thomson's tiny house argument fails. A woman may not kill a growing child inside her (her house or her body) even to save her own life.

The self-defense argument for abortion fails. Virtually all pregnancies fail the first or second necessary condition, or both. (1) They are not life threatening, and those that are very serious are debatable in terms of their meeting the first condition. (2) Killing the child is not the only alternative. A woman can successfully carry her child to term; in fact, killing the child is sometimes more harmful for the woman, as the last quotation from Reardon indicates.

Most importantly, even if the first two conditions are met (something that virtually never occurs), the third condition is not met: the child is innocent.

11

Abortion for the Sake of the Child, or the Family, or Society?

Abortion is usually thought of as a procedure to benefit the woman. But it is also advocated in the name of benefiting the child and others, for the sake of benefiting the family and society. For the child, there are basically three arguments: (1) "Every child should be a wanted child. We should not bring an unwanted child into the world." (2) "Abortion is justified as a preventive measure against child abuse." (3) "We should not bring a defective child into the world."

Every Child a Wanted Child

It is argued: "Every child should be a wanted child. We should not bring an unwanted child into the world. It is not fair to him; he is better off if he is not born. He will have a miserable life, rejected by his parents, unloved. For his own sake, he should be spared such a life. Abortion, in such cases, is the merciful termination of a pregnancy that, if continued, will result in an unloved, miserably unhappy child. Abortion is the only humane thing to do in such a case."[1]

We must certainly have the greatest sympathy for a child who is unloved and rejected. We should do all in our power to alleviate her suffering. We should love her in a special way, and try, as far as possible, to make up for the love she has not received. These are the things we should do—not kill her by an abortion.

"We should not bring an unwanted child into the world." But the child in the womb is already in the world! The womb is part of the world. It is a part of the woman's body, and she is surely in the world. What is in the womb is just as much already in the world as the womb itself. Thus,

175

the child in the womb is as much here as her mother. She is merely not visible to us, and we cannot interact with her. And so we overlook her. But she is as real, and as present, as the rest of us.

As noted in the previous chapter, one cannot kill innocent person B for the sake of benefiting person A. The same is true when B is the supposed beneficiary. We cannot kill B for the sake of B. The obligation to not kill a person clearly overrides the obligation to benefit a person.

A child unwanted in his preborn phase may become wanted later. How many times have we heard of women with unplanned pregnancies, on the one hand considering abortions, on the other hand rejecting the idea of keeping the baby now and then giving him up for adoption after birth? The same child, unwanted as a baby in the womb, will then be very much wanted when he has emerged from the womb, when he can be seen and touched, when it is psychologically easier to identify with him. This is especially true when it is the pregnancy that is unwanted, and when the child is called "unwanted" because of this. There is evidence to suggest that "most women who are refused abortion will be glad that they carried the pregnancy to term."[2]

A child unwanted by his natural mother even after his birth may be wanted by others eager to adopt him. Thousands of couples would like to adopt babies. So few are available, and usually only after a very long waiting period. How tragic that at the same time a million and a half or more are slaughtered each year by abortion!

Can a disabled child be given up for adoption? There is a program called IMPACT, Innovative Matching of Parents And Children Together, which "places 'hard to place' children, many with multiple handicaps such as mobility impairments, hearing or vision loss, or mental retardation in adoptive or foster families."[3] These are parents who have "*chosen* to raise disabled children."[4] Marsha Saxton, meeting with these parents says, "What struck me was that the usual feeling of 'burden' seemed consistently to be replaced with a sense of challenge to find solutions. . . . To the IMPACT parents, their disabled children served as a source of enrichment, growth, challenge, joy."[5]

Suppose, despite this, that the child remains unwanted and unhappy. Even then the argument for abortion does not hold. For it says we should kill preborn children who will be unwanted or unhappy. Should we then not also kill other children who are unwanted? If, as the pro-abortion reasoning assumes, killing the preborn child who will be unwanted is doing him a favor by sparing him a life of misery, why not grant this favor also to other children? If preborn persons should be killed to save them from a life of misery, the same logic should apply also to post-born persons.

If there seems to be a difference between killing an unwanted born person and abortion, it is, I think, largely because of the assumption that we should not bring an unwanted child into the world. To regain our perspective we have only to remember that the child in the womb is already in the world!

Perhaps an unwanted child would not want to continue living. Perhaps he would decide that life in his particular condition is not worth living. It is one thing if he decides this for himself; it is quite another if we decide this for him, if we impose this awesome life and death decision on him. How dare we force such a decision on the child, the irreversible decision that a life in an unhappy state is a life not worth living!

The person recommending abortion in such cases should ask himself how he would feel if someone else forced such a decision on him. He would want his autonomy respected. He would claim the right to make such a decision himself. The child's autonomy should also be respected, as well as his right to decide. Why is he not allowed to live until he is capable of making his own decision?

Many persons who suffered through an unhappy childhood find happiness, meaning, and fulfillment later in life, through creativity, love, and many other things. The present argument for abortion assumes that an unwanted child will be an unhappy person. This is an unwarranted assumption, and when it is removed, the pro-abortion argument collapses.

The term *unwanted* seems to be an adjective modifying *child*. It is not. The child does not change her characteristics if she is first unwanted then wanted, or the reverse. We change. We should change from unwanting to wanting people.

So the whole problem of the unwanted child is our problem. There is nothing wrong with an unwanted child, no reason why she should be destroyed. There is very much of a problem with unwanting parents and an unwanting society. The changes that are called for to solve this problem are changes in us, not changes in the so-called unwanted child, from being alive to being destroyed.

There is no such thing as an unwanted child—there are only unwanting people among those who are born.[6]

Abortion and Child Abuse

It is argued: "Abortion is necessary to prevent, or at least to minimize, the terrible evil of child abuse. Anyone who has ever witnessed the absolute horror of child abuse cannot but wish that such a child had never been born."

As in the previous type of case, we must have the greatest sympathy for a child who is a victim of child abuse. We must do all we can to stop this abomination. But to kill the child before he is born?

First, abortion is not a solution for child abuse, because abortion is itself the ultimate child abuse! Recall what has been continually emphasized, the horror of the methods of abortion, such as saline burning of the skin for one to two hours or cutting the child to pieces, and the pain these methods cause to the child. Even by other "clean and painless" methods, abortion would still be child abuse because all murder is a form of abuse.

Second, abortion is not a solution for child abuse. It is simply false to assume that it is the unwanted child who will be abused while the wanted child will not. That is, abortion for this purpose, even if it were justified, would not be effective. "Many studies have demonstrated that the victim of child abuse is *not* the 'unwanted child.'"[7] It is the wanted child. In his study of child abuse, Edward F. Lenoski, M.D., found that "91% of the parents admitted they wanted the child they had abused. The mothers had also donned maternity clothing two months earlier than most expectant mothers."[8] Furthermore: "A higher percentage of the abused children were named after one of the parents,"[9] indicating that they were wanted.

Third, there is another compelling reason why abortion is not a solution for child abuse. "Instead of reducing the incidence of child abuse, the evidence shows that abortion actually *increases* child abuse."[10] There are a number of reasons for this:

1. The abused child is reduced to an object.

> The abortion mentality reinforces the attitude of treating children like objects, objects that can be wanted or unwanted according to whether or not "it" satisfies parental needs . . . What aborters and abusers have in common . . . is "the assumption that the rights, desires, and ideas of the adult take full precedence over those of the child, and that children are essentially the property of parents who have the right to deal with their offspring as they see fit, without interference."[11]

2. The abused child is a victim of the result of guilt. "Aborted women frequently feel guilt, and 'guilt is one of the major factors causing battering and infanticide.' This guilt results in 'intolerable feelings of self-hatred, which the parent takes out on the child.'"[12]

3. The abused child is a victim of the result of lowered self-esteem. "Child abusers almost invariably have a significant lack of self-

esteem. Since lowered self-esteem is a well-documented aftermath of abortion, the experience of abortion may help shape an emotional environment which is conducive to the battering of other or later children."[13]

Lenoski states that if the mother sees a resemblance of herself in her child, and if "the mother has very little self-esteem, she will see in the baby a reflection of the low self-esteem she feels toward herself,"[14] making the child a potential victim of the bad feelings the mother has for herself.

4. The abused child is a victim of the result of failures in bonding. Dr. Philip G. Ney, an authority on child abuse, explains:

> It would appear that those who abort their infants at any stage of pregnancy interrupt a very delicate mechanism and sever the developing bond that is critical for the infant's protection against the mother's carelessness or rage. It is hypothesized that, once bonding is interrupted in the primipara, there are long-lasting psychological changes which make it more difficult for the same bond to develop in subsequent pregnancies. For this reason, it is likely that abortion contributes to bonding failure, an important cause of child battering. Consequently, as rates of abortion increase, rates of battering will increase proportionately.[15]

5. The abused child is a victim of the results of marital stress.

> The marital stress caused by abortion increases family hostilities and thus heightens the possibility of violent outbreaks. If the father felt left out of the abortion decision or only resentfully agreed to the abortion, or if the woman felt pressured into the abortion by her mate, deep feelings of resentment and violation of trust might cause frequent eruption of emotions. In the heat of such parental disputes, children are likely to get caught in the crossfire, objects of release for the pent-up rage of adults.[16]

6. The abused child is a victim of the results of abortion, because, as Dr. Ney states:

> 1. Abortion decreases an individual's instinctual restraint against the occasional rage felt toward those dependent on his or her care.
> 2. Permissive abortion diminishes the social taboo against aggressing the defenseless.
> 3. Abortion increases the hostility between generations.
> 4. Abortion has devalued children, thus diminishing the value of caring for children.[17]

That abortion actually *increases* child abuse is tragically borne out by statistics.

> Since *Roe v. Wade*, child abuse has increased proportionately with the skyrocketing rate of legal abortions. The same pattern of increased child battery following legalization of abortion has also been observed in many other countries, including Canada, Britain, and Japan. During 1975 alone, the rate of child battery in New York increased 18 to 20 percent, leading to estimates that during the 1980s there would be 1.5 million battered children, resulting in 50,000 deaths and 300,000 permanent injuries.[18]

Other sources reveal a similar, or worse, picture of violence against children. Anne H. Cohn, executive director of the National Committee for the Prevention of Child Abuse, speaking at Brown University, March 8, 1989, told the audience that "about 2.25 million child abuse cases were reported last year, half of which required some form of treatment; 1,130 deaths were attributed to child abuse last year; the number of reported cases has risen 50 percent in the last 5 years."[19]

Abortion and child abuse go together. Each represents the loss of reverence for a human person, the willingness to use violence against him. Even when abortion and child abuse are not practiced by the same persons, they are manifestations of the same underlying attitude of loss of respect for human persons, and thus they tend to exist together. Again, abortion is not a solution to the terrible problem of child abuse; it is part of that problem.

Abortion and the "Defective" Child

The third of the three arguments for the sake of the child says, "We should not bring a defective child into the world. If we have reasonable grounds to believe that the child will be defective, and therefore handicapped, either physically deformed or mentally retarded, it is an act of mercy not to let such a child come into the world. He will have a miserable life, a life of anguish and suffering. We should spare him that. It is better for him that he not be born at all."

Abortion to prevent the birth of a "defective" child is not morally justified, for several reasons.

1. The verdict that a child in the womb will be born defective can easily be mistaken. It is hardly ever, if ever, a certain one. As a rule it is a mere probability, and not even a very high one. "There is some chance that your child will be born with a defect."

Since that is so, why not wait until birth? Why kill a child who might be defective? One may well be killing a child who is in fact perfectly healthy. So, if the reasoning is that a "defective" child should be terminated, why not wait until one knows with certainty whether she is in fact "defective." Why not wait until birth?

And kill her at birth? Does that sound horrible? But why is killing this same child before birth any different? Why is killing her at an earlier phase of her existence "all right," "an act of mercy," while killing her at a later phase such a horrible thing? The difference is purely psychological. One who favors killing before birth—called abortion—need not see the child, hear her cry, or look into her pleading eyes. The child is not seen, so she is psychologically not there as a real person with whom we identify. That says a lot about us; it says nothing of any significance about the child herself.

2. It is one thing if a severely handicapped person decides for himself that his life is not worth living; it is quite another if we impose such a decision on him. The same reasons, in terms of individual autonomy, that make it wrong to kill an unwanted child also make it wrong to kill a defective child.

3. Many handicapped people have happy lives. They find meaning and fulfillment in life through creativity and love. They are glad to be alive. The argument for aborting a defective child assumes that such a child will be unhappy. This is an unwarranted assumption, and when it is removed, the pro-abortion argument based on it collapses.

Eugene F. Diamond, M.D., speaks to this point, and to the previous one:

> There is no evidence that the handicapped child would rather not go on living. As a matter of fact, handicapped persons commit suicide far less often than normal persons. An interesting study was done at the Ana Stift in Hanover, Germany, a center where a large number of children with phocomelia, due to thalidomide, are cared for. Psychological testing on these children indicated that they do indeed value their lives, that they are glad that they were born and they look forward to the future with hope and pleasant anticipation.[20]

There are numerous case histories of handicapped persons leading productive, fulfilled, meaningful lives, glad that they are alive. Each of them is a refutation of the idea that a handicapped person cannot achieve a meaningful life; or that such a person is merely a "vegetable."

In a 1973 issue of *Newsweek* magazine, the medical section carried an article entitled "Shall This Child Die?" It reported on the work of

Drs. Raymond S. Duff and A. G. M. Campbell at the Yale-New Haven
Hospital. These men permit babies born with birth defects to die by
deliberately withholding vital medical treatments. The doctors are
convincing the parents that these children would be a financial
burden and that they had "little or no hope of achieving meaningful
'humanhood.'" The doctors understood that they were breaking the
law by doing away with what they called "vegetables," but they
believed the law should be changed to allow for such deaths.

Sondra Diamond, who is in private practice as a counseling psychologist and is currently completing her doctoral work, responded to
the article in a letter to the editor of *Newsweek.* . . .

"I'll wager . . . that you have never received a letter from a
vegetable before this one, but much as I resent the term, I must
confess that I fit the description of a 'vegetable' as defined in the article,
'Shall This Child Die?'

Due to severe brain damage incurred at birth, I am unable to
dress myself, toilet myself, or write; my secretary is typing this letter.
Many thousands of dollars had to be spent on my rehabilitation and
education in order for me to reach my present professional status as
a counseling psychologist. My parents were also told, 35 years ago,
that there was 'little or no hope of achieving meaningful humanhood'
for their daughter. Have I reached 'humanhood'? Compared with Drs.
Duff and Campbell I believe I have surpassed it!"[21]

The term "vegetable" is one of the greatest affronts to the dignity and
preciousness of each person; its use cannot be too strongly condemned.
No human beings are "vegetables," they are all persons. Some lack the
physical skills, mental abilities, or other capacities that we associate with
"normal" persons. This does not make them nonpersons, "vegetables." If
we use this term, we are failing, they are not. We fail in our response to
their being as persons, as full persons, with the same dignity and rights
as the rest of us.

Not all handicapped people can reach a level of achievement like that
of Sondra Diamond. Meaningful human life does not require this. My
father, Balduin Schwarz, told me of the moving experience he had long
ago in a home for the severely mentally retarded. Though very limited in
their activities, they showed by their facial expressions and gestures a
deep gratitude to those who took care of them. They were capable of
receiving and giving love. They appreciated what was done for them, they
responded from their hearts, and in this their lives had a deep meaning.

4. But suppose a handicapped person is not happy, even miserably
unhappy. Does that mean we should kill him? Should we kill all unhappy
born persons. Why try to kill all unhappy *preborn* persons?

I suggest that the argument for abortion for a "fetus" diagnosed as probably "defective" rests on the assumption that the "fetus" represents a merely potential person who is not yet there, and who may therefore be terminated before he actually arrives. Hence the phrase "let us not bring into the world a defective child," as though the child were not yet here. Once the fallacy of this assumption is recognized, and it is seen that the child is already here, then anyone who reverences human life, all human persons, whether normal or handicapped, will understand the absurdity of abortion in the name of "not bringing a 'defective' child into the world." (The same point applies to the "unwanted child.")

5. I noted above the inappropriateness of the term *unwanted* as applied to children: there are no unwanted children, only unwanting adults. Some such parallel applies to the term *defective*, as in "defective child." It is true that there are real differences among children, between those who have the capacity to walk and those who do not, between those who can see and those who are blind, and so on. These are important differences, and the negative in each case does imply a defect. But it is not a defect of the *person*; it is a defect in ability and bodily state. The term "defective child" is odious because it implies that it is the child himself who is defective, rather than something about his body.

"But many defective babies die naturally before birth, in the very early stages, or later by miscarriage. Nature 'takes care of them' by providing a merciful death. Where nature fails, should we not do the same: provide a merciful death? Should we not, therefore, abort defective babies?" No. There is a world of difference between natural death and murder! If a very sick person dies of his illness, that is a natural death; it is not a moral evil, it is not murder, since no one intentionally killed him. If he is deliberately killed, "mercy killing," that is murder. What is perfectly obvious for born persons applies equally to preborn persons.

Abortion for the Sake of the Family

Abortion is sometimes advocated for the sake of family welfare. "We cannot take care of another child. It would not be fair to the other children." These, and other similar reasons, may be valid for not bringing another child into existence. But once a child is there? We have only to remember that the child in the womb is already there, as much as any born child. She is just as real as a born child and should be treated in the same way.

The reply to this abortion argument is basically twofold. One: Abortion would not be right even if it did benefit the family. As I have been stressing, we cannot benefit people by murdering someone. We cannot kill B to benefit A, not even to save A's life, still less for other benefits.

Two: Abortion does not benefit a family. On the contrary, it has in general a disastrous effect on the family and its members in four specific ways.

First, in a society where abortion is accepted, children who survive to be born naturally wonder why they exist when many of their brothers and sisters were destroyed. Such children, Dr. Ney states, may suffer from guilt, from distrust regarding their future, and from carrying a heavy burden of expectation they may not be able to fill. "Since their fate once hung on their desirability, they tend to feel secure only when they are pleasing to their parents."[22] This is a heavy burden to carry; not all children succeed. In some cases it may lead to depression and suicide. Ney also explains that having abortions causes guilt leading to "antepartum depression that interferes with a mother's ability to bond."[23] Failure to achieve bonding with the child tends to lead to child abuse, problems with subsequent pregnancies, and aversion to touching a child born later. Children who are abortion survivors, since they feel they exist only because their mothers chose them, tend to feel deeply insecure. "Since their security rests in their wantedness, . . . [they] keep checking . . ., 'Do you really want me?'"[24]

Second, perhaps the deepest and most devastating effect of abortion on family life, and the other children especially, is that abortion cheapens life:

> Abortion diminishes the value of all people, particularly children. When the destruction of the unborn child is socially sanctioned and even applauded, the child can't have much value. More than anyone, children realize they are becoming worth less. Thus, the rate of suicide has increased correspondingly.[25]

"Every child a wanted child" sounds noble. When it is taken to imply the destruction of children who are unwanted, it becomes something frightening.

> If society adheres to the ethic that the unborn child only has value when he is wanted, that ethic can easily be applied to small children. . . . If the unborn has no value and it is all right to kill him, then it is defensible to kill children who have lost value because they are now unwanted.
>
> People do not harm what they highly value. As children decline in value, it becomes easier to neglect and dispose of them.[26]

A third dimension of abortion on the family is its destructive effect on the structure of the family. Under current American law, a woman can get an abortion without her husband's consent, even without his knowledge. The child conceived by the man and woman together is torn from the man and put at the mercy of the woman who has the power to have him destroyed. The union of father-mother-child is destroyed; the family structure is effectively destroyed. Or, if it survives, it does so in spite of the power, enshrined in law, of a woman to destroy her unborn child, a child that should be seen as belonging in a family rather than to an individual woman.[27]

The same applies to the right, under current American law, of a minor to have an abortion without her parents' consent or knowledge. A child who cannot have even minor surgery without parental consent may have an abortion! Recall the hazards for women from abortion, physical and psychological. These alone should mandate the necessity for parental consent. The preborn child may be torn from the young (minor) woman; and she may be torn from her parents in her decision to abort. In no other way could the family structure be more effectively destroyed.

Noonan puts it well when he observes that making abortion legal and readily available means that a "childbearing woman . . . became a solo entity unrelated to husband or boyfriend, father or mother, deciding for herself what to do with her child. She was conceived atomistically, cut off from the family structure."[28]

Finally, abortion can be devastating to the man, and to the relation between him and the woman. The man is often the forgotten figure in the abortion drama. "What many people don't realize is that men, too, suffer from the abortion process—especially fathers of aborted children. Whether they encouraged the abortion or opposed it, they endure feelings of guilt, depression, grief, and often describe the abortion experience as bewildering and painful beyond their coping abilities."[29]

Here is an exerpt from a pamphlet titled: "How Abortion Affects Men: They Cry Alone." Referring first to the woman, it says: "The evidence grows daily that she is, indeed, a causality—that she is a real victim, along with her unborn baby, of this most unnatural procedure. . . . The purpose of the pamphlet is to point out that much the same can be said of the aborted child's father."[30]

Dr. Vincent Rue expounds:

Sociologist Arthur Shostak observed in an article for *The Family Coordinator* that three out of four male respondents studied said they had a difficult time with the abortion experience and that a sizable minority reported persistent day and night dreams about the child that never was, and considerable guilt, remorse and sadness.

> For men and women alike, the feeling of emptiness may last a lifetime, for parents are parents forever, even of a dead child. Emotional resolution is nearly impossible because there is no visible conclusion—just a memory. Because the unborn child was denied humanity, he or she is denied a grave or marker. The grieving process is left unfinished. . . .
>
> Because of the basic inequality between the partners in the abortion decision, the capacity to develop trust, . . . intimacy, honesty and companionship is severely restricted. This same inequality has the potential to breed displaced male aggression via child abuse, spousal abuse or self-abuse.[31]

A woman's "right to choose" abortion, and the law that protects this, means that the father is denied any rights to protect the child. In many cases the father very much wants the child. To have his own child destroyed, at the request of the woman with whom he begot this child, is devastating.

Not all men want the child. Some in fact take just the opposite position. This too is harmful, for it is harmful to human relations. Speaking of men who support abortion, Walling says, "Now they can pursue their pleasures without a thought about the consequences. When told of a pregnancy, they say to the woman, 'That's your problem.' Other men do even worse—they apply great pressure on the woman, threatening to break off the relationship if she doesn't have the abortion. She must choose between the baby or the baby's father."[32]

Not surprisingly, abortion takes its toll on human relationships: "Researcher Emily Milling found that of more than 400 couples who went through the abortion experience, most of the relationships (70 percent) had failed within one month after the abortion."[33]

Abortion for the Sake of Society

It is argued: "What will we do with all those unwanted babies? Abortion is needed to control population growth in the face of the threat of overpopulation." And, "It is unrealistic to say that all abortions are immoral. If we lived in a perfect world, we would not need abortion; but we do not. Killing is never good, but it is sometimes necessary, as in war time."

First, abortion is bad for society because it is bad for people! Abortion is bad for the child. The child is already in the world. She should not be excluded from membership in our society merely because she is still in a secluded place, necessary for her so that she is nourished and protected during those first formative weeks of her life. Abortion is bad because it represents frightening hazards for women, physically and psychologically. It is bad because of its effects on other children. It is bad because of its effects on the family structure. It is bad because of its effects on men. Abortion is bad because of its effects on human relations.

Many other dimensions could be added: its effect on the medical profession when doctors, committed to healing and saving, become hired killers; its effect on nurses having to reassemble the broken pieces of a baby torn apart by the abortion knife; and its effect on the society that lives in the midst of a holocaust. Abortion is a deadly plague with many victims.

Second, "What will we do with all those unwanted babies?" Often it is the pregnancy that is unwanted. The child once born, and perhaps even before birth, is very much wanted. A child unwanted now may be very much wanted later. And if a child is at first wanted, then later unwanted, does the objection imply that she should later be killed, when she is born? Adoption, not abortion! While millions of babies are killed, so many couples who want to adopt cannot.

If there are still many babies "left over," we can make room for them. We can adjust our lifestyles to take care of them. If a boat full of poor, hungry refugees were to come to our shores, begging to be allowed in, would we turn them away to their deaths? Or would we open our hearts to them? Open our gates to let them in?

Abortion is, if anything, still worse than a closed door to refugees; that is more like withholding support, as discussed in chapter 8. Abortion should be compared to killing the refugees after they land on our shores. ("The child is already in the world.")

In the worst case scenario, we return to the original question, "What will we do with all those unwanted babies?" Mass extermination, as the Nazis did with "all those unwanted people" in their society? If it would be an atrocity to kill "all those unwanted babies" *after* birth, would it be any less of an atrocity to kill them *before* birth?

It is sometimes said that abortion is cheaper than welfare; that eliminating or sharply curtailing abortion means adding welfare costs later on. This is not evident when we consider the thousands of couples eager to adopt and take care of babies. But grant the premise for the sake of argument. "Abortion is cheaper than welfare." Of course. It is always cheaper to kill a child than to feed him and clothe him! The same applies to the aged, infirm, and to handicapped persons. What follows? That we should kill people to get them out of the way?

Third, "Abortion is needed to control population growth in the face of the threat of overpopulation." The question of overpopulation is broad and complex, far beyond the scope of this book. Let me suggest three significant points in reply to this objection.

1. There is evidence to suggest that population growth, far from being a threat, is actually healthy. One author who argues for this is P. T. Bauer. His thesis is that as population increases the standard of living increases.

> Since the 1950s rapid population increase in densely-populated Hong Kong and Singapore has been accompanied by large increases in real income and wages. The population of the Western world has more than quadrupled since the middle of the eighteenth century. Real income per head is estimated to have increased by a factor of five or more. Most of the increase in incomes took place when population increased as fast as, or faster than, in the contemporary less developed world. . . .
>
> In both the less developed world and in the West some of the most prosperous countries and regions are extremely densely populated. Hong Kong and Singapore are probably the most densely populated countries in the world, with originally very poor land. . . . In the advanced world Japan, West Germany, Belgium and Holland are examples of densely populated countries. Conversely, many millions of extremely backward people live in sparsely populated regions amidst cultivable land. Examples include the backward peoples in Sumatra, Borneo, Central Africa and the interior of South America. They have ready access to vast areas of land—for them land is a free good. In South Asia, generally regarded as a region suffering from over-population, there is much uncultivated land, land which could be cultivated at the level of technology prevailing in the region. . . .[34]

2. Evidence contradicts the idea that unchecked human reproduction will fill the earth because the sheer number of people will outdistance food resources, as Malthus warned. James A. Weber argues against Malthus (and contemporary Malthusians such as Paul Ehrlich):

> This Malthusian drama of despair has captured the imagination of generation after generation of population experts, including our present crop of doomsayers. However, there is one thing wrong with the scenario. It is exactly the opposite of what has happened in the past or what can be expected to happen in the future.
>
> Far from outdistancing material progress in the past, population growth has lagged far behind, as is evidenced by continuing rapid increase in per capita income that has occured in the United States and other advanced countries since Malthus formulated his population principle.[35]
>
> However, *based on broad trends of past and present world population growth*, it is possible to suggest that world population will return

to an extremely slow growth rate about the time it reaches the neighborhood of 10 billion people, which should be approximately the middle of the next century.[36]

Jacqueline R. Kasun argues that 10 billion people is not too many for the world to sustain:

> Colin Clark, former director of the Agricultural Economic Institute at Oxford University and noted author of many books on population-resource questions, classified world land types by their food-raising capabilities and found that if all farmers were to use the best methods now in use, enough food could be raised to provide an American-type diet for 35,100,000,000 people, almost 10 times as many as now exist! Since the American diet is a very rich one, Clark found that it would be possible to feed three times as many again—or 30 times as many people as now exist—at a Japanese standard of food intake. Nor would these high levels of food output require cropping of every inch of available land space. Clark's model assumed that nearly half of the earth's land area would remain conservation areas. The noted city planner, Constantin Doxiasis, arrived independently at a similar estimate of the world's ability to feed people and to provide conservation areas.[37]

Clearly there is plenty of room on this earth for 10 billion people. "We could put the entire world population [around 4 billion] in the state of Texas and each man, woman and child could be allotted 2,000 square feet [the average home ranges between 1,400 and 1,800 square feet] and the whole rest of the world would be empty."[38]

3. There is evidence to suggest that the problem, far from being a population explosion, is rather the opposite: a declining population, a population rate below replacement, leading to extinction:

> Ansley J. Coale, director of the Office of Population Research at Princeton University, states: "Of the 31 countries that are usually listed as highly developed, 21 now have birthrates below replacement." Coale points out that, in the U.S., "by the time the Zero Population Growth movement came along, fertility was in the midst of its steepest decline in history—50% in 16 years. We are below replacement now and are continuing to grow only because of the age distribution of the population. If the downtrend continues, we will begin to have a shrinking population not long after the end of the century." . . .
>
> Thus, there is no population explosion in the U.S. or in the other developed countries. Population scholars estimate that rates of growth are higher in the less-developed world, but also note evidence of

declining growth rates in a majority of the countries for which data are available.[39]

4. Suppose the worst, that there is a real danger from a population explosion. Are we simply going to kill off all the "extra people," a Nazi-type "final solution"? It is shocking even to mention this. The alternative is that all persons be respected, that no one be killed to get him out of the way. All persons means everyone, born or preborn.

Fourth, "Isn't an absolute ban on abortion unrealistic? We don't live in a perfect world. Killing in war is bad, but war is sometimes necessary. Isn't it the same with abortion?

We do not live in a perfect world. We live in the pervasive presence of moral evil. Abortion as the unjust killing of small, helpless, innocent children, especially on a mass scale that makes it a holocaust, is a frightening example of this. Far from being a solution, abortion killings make the world more imperfect. And much worse than imperfect.

The destructive effects of abortion—on women, on men, on other children, on the structure of the family, on society—make abortion hardly a realistic solution, but exactly the opposite. A realistic solution is something positive, not destructive like abortion.

The argument for abortion that compares it to war is not valid. If "going to war" is a way of trying to settle disputes, the comparison is indeed apt: Both are terrible moral evils. For both are assaults on innocent people, both cause horrible sufferings, both have terrible side effects; both are fundamentally destructive. If it is the question of defense against unjust attack, war becomes a complex subject, far beyond the scope of this book. Some defensive wars are indeed unjust, and some tactics in war are unjust. Intentionally killing an innocent person is always wrong, whether by a rifle, a bomb, a saline solution, or a knife.

Abortion is indeed a war, a war on the preborn, in which they cannot defend themselves, in which they are killed in extremely cruel ways. Saying that war is not a solution applies most aptly to the war on the preborn.

12

Should the Preborn Child Be Given Legal Protection?

Considering everything we have seen so far, the preborn child should definitely be given legal protection. The child in the womb is a person, one of us; he should be given the same legal protection we have. Killing him is murder, and all murder must be outlawed.

However, to give the child the same legal protection we have is to prohibit abortion, to make it illegal, a criminal offense. This evokes strong resentment and opposition, not only on the part of those who approve abortion, but even on the part of some who recognize it as a moral evil. What is needed, therefore, is a careful analysis of this question, one that examines the objections to making abortion illegal and offers replies, and, more fundamentally, provides a clear understanding of the question of the legal status of abortion.

This question is a moral question, a question of what, morally, should be done. It is a moral question about the legal order, what the law should say. Murder, theft, and rape are, first and primarily, moral evils. But it is also true that they should be illegal. It is a moral requirement that the state should protect people from these moral evils. Its failure to do so, by making these actions legal, would itself be a moral evil; a moral wrong in addition to the wrong these actions represent in themselves.

The Fundamental Argument That
Abortion Must Be Made Illlegal

If the reality of the child in the womb is kept clearly in mind, killing such a person is, morally, exactly like killing any other person. And so, if killing a born person is murder, a matter for state law, then killing a preborn person is murder and a matter for state law as well.

191

Recall the horrible methods of abortion. The child is dismembered or soaked in a saline solution that burns his skin for one to two hours. Abortion is a *public* moral evil, one that the state has the duty to forbid. If the state has the duty to protect born persons from such terrible evils, it has exactly the same duty to protect preborn persons from them.

Think also of how killing a person to get rid of him is a violation of human dignity. It is the duty of the state to uphold this dignity, to protect it from assault. This is perhaps the highest obligation of the state. Balduin Schwarz argues, *"The dignity of the human person is the highest legal good."*[1] And it is for this reason that the state exists, to protect this good.[2] It is an inalienable, absolute good, that cannot be compromised for expediency.[3] In fact, every law and legal code must be measured by this standard, whether or not it upholds and protects the dignity of the person, or accedes to the violation of this dignity, such as a law that allows slavery or the murder of born or preborn persons.[4]

Thus abortion must be made illegal. The prohibition of abortion is one of the duties and concerns of the state. Preborn human beings must be given the *same protection of law* that the rest of us are entitled to. If we fail to see abortion as murder, it is because its victim is unseen, and smaller, and the circumstances of the killing are somewhat different. These are morally irrelevant. The crucial thing is that an innocent person is killed to get him out of the way, as clear a case of murder as can be found. The respectability in which the act, and the doctor who performs it, is clothed must not hide its true reality: abortion is the murder of an innocent child. It must be labeled as such, and therefore outlawed.

Abortion is a *civil rights* issue, just like racial justice for blacks, or equal treatment of the handicapped, and of all minorities. In allowing abortion, the state is not being liberal, but on the contrary, repressive. It is denying the basic human right of a large segment of the population. The fundamental duty of the state is to protect the rights of its people. Legalized abortion, saying yes to abortion, means abandoning this most basic civil right, the right to live, of a whole class of human beings to the brutal power of those who would kill them. Nothing is a more flagrant contradiction to the basic reason for the existence of the state.

Making abortion illegal is necessary to guarantee preborn persons *equal rights,* the same rights you and I have. Legal abortion, saying it is wrong to kill born persons but acceptable to kill preborn persons, is an outrageous violation of the latter's right to equal protection under the law.

Allowing abortion is a form of *discrimination.* In allowing abortion, the state is saying to a class of persons: "You're too small, too dependent, not sufficiently developed. We can't see you; you're not in an environment like the rest of us. So you don't count. While it is a criminal offense to kill other persons, it is all right to kill you." Blacks were treated as nonpersons because they had the "wrong" skin color; the preborn are treated as nonpersons because they have the "wrong" size, location, level of development, etc. We move from one form of discrimination to another. In each case a human being is denied his civil rights because he is perceived as different. In each case the differences are morally irrelevant.

Legalized abortion is a form of *slavery*.[5] The essence of slavery is that a person is treated as a thing, in the sense of being "owned," as if he were a car or a house. He is looked upon as something to be used or disposed of at will. In the case of black slavery, slaves were used for work. In the case of abortion, the child is disposed of. But in each case there is the core idea of a right to treat a person as a thing, to determine his ultimate fate (use or disposal). That such a view is translated into practice in which a person is actually enslaved is horrible enough. But that the state allows this and puts its blessing on it by making it legal is an additional horror. Abortion is today's slavery. The child belongs to the woman—not in the noble sense of being entrusted to her, but in the ignoble sense of being a "thing" that may be disposed of. All with the blessing of the law.

Making Abortion Legal Is a Further Evil

It is often said that making abortions illegal will not stop them. Quite true. Making rape illegal does not stop it from occurring. But now imagine a government that made rape legal![6] That would be an outrage beyond words. Imagine a government that made the murder of adults legal. Or that made child abuse and child murder legal. It is terrible enough if people commit these crimes against the explicit laws of the state. But if the state says, "It's all right, you can do these things"—if it gives these crimes its blessing by allowing them—that is an unspeakable, and new evil.

It is said that making abortion illegal means "restrictive abortion laws," and that we should instead have "liberalized laws," namely those that allow abortions, in whole or in part. First, all laws that protect the innocent from attack (rape, murder, child abuse, etc.) are restrictive, for their whole purpose is to restrict the actions of all potential offenders in order to protect potential victims. Restrictive in this context is a good thing. It is only undue restrictions that are bad, especially those that preclude doing things one has a right to do. No one has the right to kill an innorcent person, born or preborn.

Second, and especially significant, liberal or liberalized abortion laws are the greatest imaginable misnomer. The true liberal spirit is freedom, especially the most basic freedom, the freedom to be. Laws allowing abortion are precisely a denial of this freedom to the preborn child. They are thus a direct antithesis to what is truly liberal. By calling laws liberal that allow the killing of innocent preborn children, one manages to veil their absolute anti-liberal character. Abortion seems acceptable, even respectable, because of the veil of language. Black is called white; suppression is called liberalism.

One can also say that the true liberal spirit is compassion and concern for others, especially the weak and the helpless, those who cannot fend for themselves. The opposite of this is oppression. Legalized abortion is enshrinement in the law of the worst sort of oppression: killing a child because he is helpless, unable to escape or defend himself.

As noted, a new evil comes into existence when the government fails to protect preborn babies, saying, in effect, "You may kill them if you like." A still greater evil comes into existence when a high level of government not only fails in its duty to protect preborn persons, but mandates that no one may protect them. This has been the situation in the United States since the Supreme Court decision *Roe v. Wade*. It claimed that a woman has a constitutional right to have an abortion, hence that all laws forbidding abortion are unconstitutional. Therefore, the states may not protect children in the womb.

What this means is that those who want to protect preborn persons are attempting something illegal. What they want is contrary to today's law.

The Practical Necessity of Making Abortion Illegal

Making illegal the crime of killing an innocent person, while it does not eradicate it, does make it far less frequent. Our government's power to protect people, while far from perfect, is still quite significant.

There are several important dimensions to this. One is the deterrent power of criminal penalties attached to laws that forbid attacks on innocent persons. If a person will not respect the integrity of another for moral reasons, let him at least do so for practical reasons, the avoidance of punishment. The important thing is that the potential victim be protected, whether it is protecting a woman from rape or a child from being killed.

Thus, doctors who are abortion killers must be subject to the same penalties as all other killers. The manufacture and distribution of child-killing drugs such as RU486 must be made illegal and subject to criminal penalties.

A second dimension concerns the protection of women. To a large extent, women do not really want abortions. Reardon emphasizes this fact again and again:

> As we have seen in story after story, women choose abortion because they feel there is "no other option." They abort because it is the "easy way out." They abort because they feel abandoned by their lovers, friends, and families. Without the support to do the right thing, they yield to doing the "easy thing." In today's society, it does not take courage to abort; it takes courage to stand up against all the pressures and inconveniences which push towards abortion.[7]

A law allowing abortion makes it much easier for the man, family members, and others to pressure a woman into an abortion she does not want. What the woman needs is protection against such pressures. A law forbidding abortion, and its penalties, provides that. Reardon explains:

> Legalization . . . has made abortion *too* easy to obtain. It has now become easier to coax, or even coerce, a woman uncertain about her pregnancy to accept abortion as the "easy out." Such women are made to believe that aborting is something they *should* do, if only for the male, or for their parents, or for their own vague "future" which friends and family hold in such high esteem. Before, these women were protected from being pressured into an abortion because they had ready reasons for refusal: "But abortion is illegal! What if we're caught? Isn't it dangerous?"[8]

A third, very important, dimension is the law as a teacher, as a guide to people's thinking. The law helps to create a certain climate of moral opinion. Making abortion legal conveys the message that it is morally acceptable. However incorrect it is to suppose that whatever the law allows is morally right, there is an element of truth in this idea; namely, the expectation that if something is a violation of the fundamental rights of persons, then the state will forbid it. That expectation is absolutely correct; the state should forbid such things. It should forbid all murder. In allowing abortion, the state fails people and their legitimate expectations.

This is yet another reason why abortion is seen as complex. Making it legal creates a climate of opinion in which many people see it, to one degree or another, as acceptable. Others see it as wrong, some as absolutely and clearly wrong, as the evil it really is. A division of opinion ensues and one concludes it is controversial; hence it must be complex. In fact, it is not complex but a clear-cut evil, the appearance of complexity stemming in part from the fact that it has been made legal.

Reardon explains the importance of the law:

> Laws against abortion may seem restrictive to those who want
> abortions, but they are also an encouragement to those who are
> tempted by abortion but know that it is wrong. For those women who
> struggle against the pressures that force them toward abortion, the
> law is a backstop that reminds them that their sacrifices are worth-
> while, that they are doing the right thing if not the convenient thing.
> Social acceptance of abortion, on the other hand, tells women that
> they are foolish not to abort an inconvenient pregnancy. . . .
>   Studies into the psychology of morality reveal that the law is
> truly a teacher. One of the most significant conclusions of these
> studies shows that existing laws and customs are *the most* important
> criteria for deciding what is right or wrong for most adults in a given
> culture. . . . Most people look to law for moral guidance. Right now the
> law is teaching that abortion is a moral and presumably effective
> solution to unplanned pregnancies. As a result, millions of unborn
> children are being destroyed, an equal number of women are being
> physically and emotionally violated, and society's compassion for
> both women and their children is being eroded.[9]

The statistics support this. Legalizing abortion means increasing
abortion:

> Before legalization there were only 100,000 to 200,000 illegal abor-
> tions per year—a range substantiated by both statistical evidence and
> the testimony of aborted women. But in 1983 there were approxi-
> mately 1.5 million legal abortions. This means that legalization has
> caused a *ten* to *fifteenfold increase* in the number of abortions
> performed.[10]

The law influences women's perceptions of abortion, and their
decisions whether or not to have them:

> Given their doubts about the morality of abortion, most aborting
> women are strongly influenced by the legal status of the abortion
> option. When asked "Did the knowledge that abortion was legal
> influence your opinion about the morality of choosing abortion?" 70
> percent said that the law had played a major role in their moral
> perception of abortion.[11]

Asked whether or not they would have sought an illegal abortion if
a legal abortion had not been available, 75 percent said they definitely
would not have sought an illegal abortion.[12]

13

Objections and Replies

The Appeal to Privacy

"The question of abortion is something very intimate, very private to a woman. Only she should decide whether to continue her pregnancy to term, or to end it by abortion. No one else, and certainly not the government, should tell a woman what to do. She alone should decide. Hence abortion should be legal."

There is certainly something very intimate in the relation between a woman and the child she is carrying. The child is hers, entrusted to her, residing in her, nourished by her, protected by her. And it is a terrible evil if someone comes from the outside to interfere with this relationship destructively. It is abortion, not the prohibition of it, that violates the intimate realm of a woman who is pregnant. It is abortion that intrudes into this beautiful sanctuary, where a small, innocent, defenseless child is nestled and protected. Abortion sunders the beautiful and natural relation that exists between woman and child by violently tearing the child out, brutally killing him in the process.

That the woman herself requests the abortion in no way nullifies this point. It is objectively a violent sundering of this natural, intimate relationship. By her abortion she becomes a part of this terrible evil, and often suffers from it as the second victim.

Yes, there is something private and intimate that we should protect: the child. Abortion is a violation of the child's privacy, an intrusion into what is intimate for him, his own person. The methods of abortion and the pain they cause are a violation of intimacy and privacy.

Thus the appeal to intimacy and privacy, insofar as it is valid and reasonable, means forbidding abortions. The child's right to live, not to be killed, especially by the painful methods of abortion, that right surely outweighs anyone's claim to a right to privacy. And the state must protect that right, just as it protects other civil rights.

Many of these objections rest on the idea that abortion is private to the woman, where no one else should interfere. It is not. It involves another human person, the child, who is killed by this act. It involves other people as well. The family structure, human relations, and other children may be adversely affected by abortion. Noonan outlines the many ways in which abortion affects society at large:

> Each act of abortion is, by declaration of the Supreme Court of the United States, a private decision. Yet each act of abortion bears on the structure of marriage and the family, the role and duties of parents, the limitations of the paternal part in procreation, and the virtues that characterize a mother. Each act of abortion bears on the orientation and responsibilities of the obstetrician, the nurse, the hospital administrator, and the hospital trustee. The acceptance of abortion affects the professor and student of medicine and the professor and student of law. In the United States, abortion on a large scale requires the participation of the federal and state governments.[1]

A Woman's Right over her Body

"A woman has a right over her body, to decide what happens in it, and to it. She should have the right to make her own decision regarding her pregnancy. Someone else cannot tell her what she may or may not do with her own body."

This objection has been discussed at length in chapter 8. In short, a woman's right over her body does not give her a right to an abortion. The child is not a part of her body, but a distinct individual, entrusted to her, to be sustained and protected by her. The woman has a right over her body, including the right not to be destroyed. The child has the same right not to be destroyed. Granting a woman a right to an abortion denies the child his most fundamental right.

Not Legislating Morality

"We should not legislate morality. Morality is a matter of private choice, not government legislation."

We legislate morality all the time, in many ways: laws against the murder of born persons, against rape, against other forms of assault, against theft, against libel and slander, and many more. These moral evils, as violations of the rights of persons, must be reflected in the law and made illegal.

It is true that certain parts of the moral domain should not be reflected in the law. For example, to be ungrateful is a moral wrong that should not be reflected in the law; indeed, it cannot be. There are other matters that are genuinely complex with regard to the question whether or not—and if so, to what extent—they should be reflected in the law. But surely the fundamental right to life, not to be killed, belongs within the domain of law. All civil rights should be protected by law.

> Some years ago many people opposed civil rights legislation, saying, "You cannot legislate morality." Dr. Martin Luther King responded, "It is true, the law cannot make a white man love me, but it can discourage him from lynching me."[2]

The distinction drawn here, between the command to love and the prohibition against lynching is a good example of the difference between the non-legal domain of morality (love) and the legal domain (killing).

Not Imposing Our Morality on Others

"We should not impose our morality on others. One group should not impose its beliefs on the rest of society. I'm personally opposed to abortion but I will not impose that belief on others."

Suppose someone said, "I'm personally opposed to rape, but I will not impose that belief on potential rapists." How absurd! This argument is as absurd in the case of abortion as it is in that of rape. The law must protect *all* innocent persons from assault: women from rape, babies from slaughter. The morality of not raping, and of not murdering, a fellow human being is not "my morality" or "our morality" but morality itself.

Perhaps some people who say they're personally opposed do so because they feel abortion is wrong but do not fully understand why; they are unable to articulate good moral reasons why it is wrong. Thus they think that others may feel differently about it, and they want to respect these differences of opinion or feeling. "That's the way I feel, but maybe you don't."[3] This attitude is psychologically understandable but morally disastrous, for the result is that a cruel death is imposed on the child. We must look at the evidence that abortion is wrong, that it is murder; we will then see that it is not merely a feeling, but the truth of the matter.

It is true that we should not impose on people. We should have compassion and concern for others, especially the weak, the oppressed, the poor, the downtrodden. We should protect the helpless, not step on them. Legalized abortion is the enshrinement in law of oppression, stepping on the weak and defenseless. Legalizing abortion is saying, "Abortionists may crush the little ones if they like." Precisely because we should not impose on others, we must not allow such an imposition, the crushing to death of innocent, helpless babies in the womb.

The term *impose* suggests that outlawing abortion is something bad because it imposes a burden or restriction on people. But all laws impose. Traffic laws impose on us certain obligations and restrictions. Laws making abortion illegal are nothing special in this regard. They are simply another instance of the general feature of all laws, to impose certain obligations and restrictions for the common good, and to respect other individuals as persons and not to hurt or kill them. Laws outlawing abortion merely apply this general feature to one class of persons, preborn babies.

Abortion a Controversial Matter

"Abortion is a controversial matter. Opinions are divided. The law should reflect this and be neutral, and let each person decide for himself."

The government cannot be neutral on this question. It either recognizes the child in the womb as a person, entitled to the same protection of law, or it doesn't. The first is a decision, the one being urged here. The second is equally a decision; it is the decision to surrender the child (or "the being in the womb") to the power of a woman and her doctor to destroy him. As William James points out: "*To say, . . . 'Do not decide but leave the question open,' is itself a . . . decision—just like deciding yes or no—and is attended with the same risk. . . .*"[4] For example, for the government to leave open the question of whether toxic wastes may be dumped into rivers, and to let each person decide for himself by legalizing such actions is clearly a decision, not neutrality. So too, legalizing abortion is a decision, the decision to allow abortions to take place legally. It is clearly not neutrality, but a definite stand: "Such actions are to be legally sanctioned."

The point being made here is independent of the question of which side is correct on the abortion issue; i.e., whether it is morally right or not, whether it should be allowed by law or not. The point is rather that allowing abortion is as much a public policy as not allowing it. The fact that abortion is controversial, that opinion is divided on the question, no more speaks for allowing it than for not allowing it.

Legalizing abortion means settling the issue in favor of those who claim that abortion is justified. Legalized abortion does not correspond to neutrality on this issue, it is a verdict against the pro-child position.

Saying that each person should decide for herself sounds reasonable and tolerant. In fact it represents a death verdict against millions of children. It means surrendering them to the power of those who would have them destroyed.

Abortion a Religious Issue

"Abortion is a religious issue. No group should impose its religious values and prohibitions on the rest of society. We live in a pluralistic society. Different groups of people have different moral beliefs. An individual religious group may oppose abortion as morally wrong, but it has no right to impose that belief on society as a whole."

The crucial thing is to understand that abortion is wrong because it is the killing of an innocent person, the violation of his most fundamental right, the right to be. This is not only a religious matter, but a basic ethical concern, accessible to all people. I have urged that we identify with the child and do to her what we would want done to us. These are universal ethical appeals, not sectarian religious ideas.

Abortion is a civil rights issue, one that parallels slavery and discrimination. To argue that preborn human beings be given the same rights and respect as the rest of us is no more a religious matter than to argue that blacks be given the same rights and respect as the rest of us.

There are two senses of the term "religious issue." One refers to what the objection is based upon, that is, questions and topics that are properly left to individual persons and groups, such as the nature and existence of God. The other refers to religious issues that are also matters of public concern, for example marriage, divorce, capital punishment, human equality, and discrimination. To say that something is a religious issue in this second sense does not preclude government involvement in it. On the contrary, the government cannot be neutral on these things; for example, it either allows no-fault divorce or it does not. Abortion is a religious issue in this second sense.

Questions and topics that are religious issues in the second sense are generally also philosophical issues; that is, questions that are to be answered by the use of reason, rather than appeal to religious faith. Thus, in showing that the being in the womb is a real child and that abortion means killing this child, I have made no appeal whatever to any religious

faith or theological principles. It has been a strictly philosophical argument, appealing to reason. In showing that a human person begins her
existence at conception, I used scientific data and philosophical arguments, especially the one showing that conception-fertilization is the
radical break. The two major philosophical arguments attempting to
justify abortion—Thomson's "no duty to sustain" argument and the
Tooley-Warren argument that the being in the womb is only biologically
human but not a person—were refuted by strictly philosophical arguments. Finally, given that the being in the womb is a small person, it
follows logically that he should be given the same legal standing as the
rest of us, that abortion must be made illegal just as any other killing of
innocent persons.

It is interesting to note that the preborn child was recognized as a
person in Roman Law, with the same rights as born persons. Thus, for
example, Julian, the classical Roman jurist, expresses this recognition in
Roman Law when he teaches that the child in his mother's womb is to be
treated as a member of human society in terms of legal rights. And the
jurist, Paulus, teaches that whoever is in his mother's womb is to be
protected as if he were already born; he is to be granted the same civil
rights and the same benefits accruing from them as anyone else.[5] Roman
Law was surely not a religious matter. What the Roman Law clearly
recognized, we too should recognize.

Furthermore, there are widely recognized secular codes of ethics that
explicitly condemn abortion and/or acknowledge the sanctity of human
life in the womb. Thus the *Hippocratic Oath* includes the promise: "I will
not give to a woman a pessary to cause abortion."[6] And *The World Medical
Association Declaration of Geneva* states, as part of the Physician's Oath,
"I will maintain the utmost respect for human life from the time of
conception. Even under threat, I will not use my medical knowledge
contrary to the laws of humanity."[7]

No Consensus to Make Abortion Illegal

"There is no consensus for making abortion illegal. Hence doing so would
mean unfairly imposing the beliefs of some people on the rest of society."

First, just as there is no consensus for making abortion illegal, there
is also no consensus on making it legal. Abortion is a controversial matter,
opinion is divided. The objection argues equally against the pro-abortion,
or pro-choice, side: "Abortion should not be legal because there is no
consensus for making it legal."

Second, we must examine the nature of abortion itself—whether or not the being in the womb who is killed is a real person—not what people think about abortion. If abortion is not the killing of a child, if it is something private, then it should be legal, consensus or not. If abortion is a woman's right, then she should have that right under the law, consensus or not. Those who campaign for women's rights, including "the right to abortion," believe that this is something right in itself, called for in justice, not something that should be enacted only if there is a consensus for it. This shows that consensus is not relevant in this kind of issue, where questions of fundamental human rights are at stake.

Third, when we examine the nature of abortion itself, carefully and objectively, we see that the being who is killed by it is a real person, one of us. With this we come to the core fallacy in the consensus objection, and the fundamental reply to it as an argument for legalizing abortion. What this argument really says is that a person is not to be given recognition under the law as a person, his right to live protected by the state, simply because he is a person, and entitled to this protection; but only because other persons have agreed to recognize him as a person. If that view is taken no one is safe. If your right to live, your right to equal protection under the law, depends on there being a consensus that the group you belong to should be protected, then your rights are fragile indeed.

In short, fundamental rights, above all the right of a person to be recognized and respected as a person, do not depend on the democratic voting procedures that are perfectly appropriate in other matters. The recognition of fundamental rights cannot be made subject to popular votes. Such rights are not granted by the people by majority votes; they cannot rightfully be taken away in this manner. They are above the level of democratic processes based on majority opinion.

Fourth, suppose there is a lack of consensus for outlawing abortion. Rather than wait for a consensus to enact laws to protect the rights of preborn persons, these laws should be enacted as a matter of justice, with the expectation that the laws will then help create the consensus. Rather than the consensus leading to the laws, the laws can lead to the consensus. This is what occurred in the case of civil rights laws to give equal treatment to blacks. If an oppression is legal (racist oppression of blacks, the killing of preborn babies), it tends to be widely practiced. This tends to make it respectable, which in turn tends to create a lack of consensus to outlaw the oppression. We must reverse this process. Our obligation is to respect persons, irrespective of the shifting tides of popular consensus.

No Simple Answers to Complex Questions

"We should avoid simplistic answers to complex problems. Abortion is a complex problem, and simply outlawing it is a simplistic solution."

First, abortion is only complex psychologically and socially, not morally, as was shown in chapter 9. The killing of an innocent child to get rid of him is as clear-cut an evil as one can find.

Is the outlawing of murder of born persons simplistic? In a way, yes: you simply cannot do that! The same must apply to preborn persons.

Second, if prohibiting all abortions is simplistic, allowing all abortions—which is the current state of affairs in America[8] and throughout much of the rest of the world—is no less simplistic. What, in the view of those who use this objection, would be the ideal or true solution? A law that forbade some abortions and allowed others? But then why should only some innocent preborn children be protected and not others? Because there are justifying factors in some cases, such as rape and incest? These factors do not justify murdering the child. An innocent person cannot be killed, or allowed to be killed, for the benefit of others.

What, after all, is wrong with a "simple" prohibition of murder? That is all that is being asked for, for preborn and born persons alike. Changing "simple" to "simplistic" is merely inserting a negative emotional overtone, to try to frighten people away from supporting what is demanded by "simple" justice: protection of innocent, defenseless small babies.

Individual Conscience Decisions

"Abortion decisions should be left up to individual conscience. Abortion is often an agonizing decision for the woman. We must leave her the freedom to make her own decision, in conscience, free from state interference."

These are noble sounding phrases, and it is understandable that people are impressed by them and brought to support a woman's right to make her own decision in conscience. They are psychologically plausible, but they are not logically and morally sound. The law that would *give* a woman this right to decide in conscience would thereby *take away* the child's legal right to equal protection under the law. The noble-sounding phrases veil the horror of the reality of abortion.

There are things that should be left up to individual conscience. There are other things that should not. Equal treatment of blacks in society is an obvious example. Equal treatment for preborn persons is another.

When it comes to questions of fundamental civil rights, laws that allow individual conscience to decide mean the surrender of some to the power of others to deprive them of these fundamental rights, including the power to destroy them.

Return to Back-alley Abortions?

"Do you want to return to the butchery of self-induced or back-alley abortions? Keep abortions safe and legal." "The right to legal abortion is crucial to the health and well-being of American women. This fundamental right is guaranteed by the U.S. Supreme Court decision of January 22, 1973, which: Affirms every woman's right to end an unwanted pregnancy safely and legally. Affirms that women need no longer be forced by desperation into the horror of underworld abortion."[9] "Desperate women will get abortions in any case. Let us keep them legal so that they are safe, so that women are not forced into the horrors of back-alley abortionists. Or to self-induced abortions by coat hangers!"

"Keep abortion safe and legal." First, legal abortion is not safe for the child! The idea of a "safe" abortion can arise only if the reality of the child is overlooked.

The force of this argument is its own destruction. It is the horror of death and mutilation for women at the hands of back-alley butchers. But this is precisely the horror that is repeated in every abortion! That is why every abortion, legal or illegal, must be prevented at all costs. The true response to back-alley abortions is to be outraged at *all* abortions, to condemn *all* abortions—not to propose one kind (legal) in place of another (illegal). The very evil that the argument appeals to is the essence of every abortion. And for this reason every abortion must be condemned, morally and by the law.

The "back-alley" argument for legal abortion is a contradiction. It is the argument, "We should allow abortion so that women are not killed." But, since abortion is itself killing, the argument reads: "We should allow killing so that there is no killing."

We cannot legalize murder. To appeal to terrible side effects for the person ordering the murder is not an argument. It does not justify the murder. Mary Ann Warren, who advocates the right to abortion, is clear on this point: "The fact that restricting access to abortion has tragic side effects [i.e., death due to illegal abortions] does not in itself show that the restrictions are unjustified, since murder is wrong regardless of the consequences of prohibiting it."[10]

The "back-alley" argument is not really an argument, either for the moral rightness of abortion or for its legalization, but merely a threat: "Give us legal abortions, or else." A law protecting preborn children is a just law. Everyone ought to obey it. Pointing to the hazards of disobeying the law is no more valid in this case than it would be in any other.

There is a second major reply to the appeal to "safe abortion": legal abortion is not safe for the woman. Reardon's research reveals a frightening fact: "Legalization has improved the odds that an individual will survive an abortion, but the astronomical increase in the number of abortions performed means that more women are dying. *The percentage chance of survival is improved, but the absolute number of those who suffer has increased!* "[11]

He goes on to add that this increase in suffering applies also to abortion complications and that one must also include "the deaths which are *indirectly* caused by abortion," namely future wanted babies: "Each year approximately 100,000 'wanted' pregnancies will end in the sorrow of a spontaneous miscarriage because of latent abortion morbidity."[12]

Keeping abortion illegal is better for women: "The number of women dying and suffering from physical complications alone far exceeds the number who would have suffered similarly if abortion had remained illegal. Rather than reducing the pain and suffering of women, legalization of abortion has increased it by exposing many more women to its inherent risks. The only difference is that now the pain and suffering can be antiseptically ignored because it is 'legal.'"[13]

These numbers are based on reported deaths, and, as I noted before, "the reported rate of deaths due to legal abortion is being deliberately kept low through selective underreporting."[14]

As an example, Reardon mentions a Los Angeles doctor, Lester Hibbard, who was "charged with keeping track of maternal deaths." While "four abortion-related deaths [were] officially reported as such," Dr. Hibbard said that "he *personally* knew of at least four other deaths which had followed legal abortions but had not been reported as such on the death certificates. Furthermore, he said he was certain that these unreported abortion deaths were only the tip of the iceberg."[15]

Reardon reports, "According to one estimate, less than 10% of deaths from legal abortion are reported as such."[16]

Women are suffering and dying from legal abortions partly because abortion is inherently unsafe for the woman, an assault on her, and partly because, in many cases, the staff at legal abortion centers can be as dangerous (or nearly so) to the woman's health as some of the infamous "back-alley" abortionists at illegal abortion centers. Reardon presents a frightening array of data:

Abortion clinics routinely hire low-cost, unskilled staff members to fulfill the quasi-medical tasks normally performed by physicians or nurses. . . . There are no educational or certification requirements for abortion clinic personnel. . . . The depth of knowledge which abortion staff members have, therefore, is generally far below the usual standards of the medical and nursing professions.[17]

In the typical abortion clinic, these staff members counsel the patients about the procedure, examine the patients, estimate gestation, perform any required tests (e.g., pregnancy tests and blood samples), record vital signs, prepare the patients for surgery, and assist patients through the recovery room. . . . By delegating responsibility and minimizing patient/doctor interaction, abortionists free themselves to work solely on performing the actual abortion in the least amount of time possible.[18]

As a result of cost-efficient measures, most clinics do not have transfusion supplies and blood type selections available, even though 2 to 12 percent of aborted women bleed enough to warrant a transfusion.[19]

"Keep abortion safe and legal." And, "Let us not return to the days of back-alley abortionists." How do these phrases square with the reality of legal abortion? Reardon explains: "To increase profits even further, abortionists try to work as fast as possible in order to handle as many patients per day as possible. Besides the obvious risks in hurrying a blind operation which involves sharp instruments and vacuum pressures capable of tearing out organs, the rush for efficiency often results in 'cutting corners' on normal sanitation standards."[20]

The *Chicago Sun-Times* series shocked readers with the fact that many abortions were being performed by "moonlighting residents, [and] general practitioners with little or no training in women's medicine." But once again this "revelation" was not unique to the four Chicago clinics which were investigated. Instead the use of such "untrained" abortionists is perfectly legal and commonplace.[21] Abortionists are essentially free of oversight by state and local governments or even by state medical boards. Even if an abortionist causes numerous complications or deaths, there is no mechanism to prevent him from continuing to perform abortions short of imprisonment for criminal neglect.[22]

Both illegal abortions and legal abortions are dangerous for women, legal abortions being somewhat safer. Most women wanting abortions are dissuaded from seeking them if they are illegal. ("75 percent said they definitely would not have sought an illegal abortion."[23]) What, then, is the actual implication of the appeal to keeping abortion legal for the sake of safety? It would mean increasing the safety margin for a small group of women—25% or so who would resort to it in defiance of the law—while at the same time opening the floodgates of massive destruction for millions of preborn children and an increase in suffering and death for women as a whole. Legalization improves the odds that an individual woman will survive an abortion, but the astronomical increase in the number of abortions performed means that more women are dying.

A word about self-induced abortions by coat hangers. Here too the force of the argument is its own destruction. The horror of a woman killed by a coat hanger is repeated in *every* abortion, with the child the victim of a horrible death. If the woman should not be killed by one instrument of death, a coat hanger, then neither should the child be killed by another. We cannot legalize murder in order to dissuade people from choosing particularly dangerous forms of carrying it out.

In addition, coat hangers will be a thing of the past, replaced by new "do-it-yourself" forms of abortion, such as an abortion pill.

Finally, "a return to illegal abortions" for those who choose to defy the law "does not mean that there would be a return to the death and complication rates of illegal abortion prior to 1973," when abortion was legalized throughout the United States. "Instead, the complication and death rates would be much lower" because of improvements in "medical care for abortion complications" and in "the abortion techniques used . . . Illegal abortionists would continue to use the suction curettage that is used in legal abortion clinics today." This means that "illegal abortions performed by physician/abortionists will be no more dangerous than legal abortions—they will only be far less common, and that alone will save lives and reduce complications."[24]

Fewer women proportionately are dying from abortions now than before, not because of legalization, but because of improvements in medicine. Dr. Willke tells us: "With penicillin, the number [of deaths] dropped sharply. . . . " The general decline in deaths "was clearly due to better antibiotics, the establishment of intensive care units, better surgical techniques, etc."[25]

The actual number of women who died from illegal abortions prior to legalization is far lower than is sometimes claimed by pro-abortion groups. Dr. Bernard Nathanson, in the past a leader in the effort to legalize abortion, and now a leading opponent of abortion, tells in *Aborting America* the story of his struggles and his profound change, and that the high figures were an outright lie.

> When we spoke of the [number of deaths from illegal abortions] it was always "5,000 to 10,000 deaths a year." I confess that I knew the

figures were totally false, and I suppose the others did too. . . . But in the "morality" of our revolution, it was a *useful* figure, widely accepted. . . . The overriding concern was to get the laws eliminated, and anything within reason that had to be done was permissible.[26]

Keeping in mind that not all abortion deaths are reported, it is still of some interest to see what the reported figures are: "In 1967, . . . the federal government listed only 160 deaths from illegal abortion. In the last year before . . . [abortion was legalized throughout the country], 1972, the total was only 39 deaths."[27]

Abortion Laws Unenforceable

"Laws prohibiting abortion are not enforceable. Desperate women, denied legal abortions, will find ways to obtain abortions in other ways. Trying to ban abortion is like trying to ban alcohol: it would be Prohibition all over again. The law would be flouted, creating disrespect for law in general."

It is simply not true that the prohibition of abortion is not enforceable. Abortion "clinics" could be shut down; hospitals now performing abortions could be prevented from doing so; doctors could be prosecuted, jailed, and barred from practicing. Those who counseled women to have abortions, and those who assisted at them, could be prosecuted. For most of our history, until very recently, abortion was illegal. Those who committed this crime were prosecuted. The child in the womb received legal protection in the past; what was unjustly taken away from him should now be restored to him.

Perhaps what the objection has in mind is that there would be widespread resistance to outlawing abortion. That should not be a factor in deciding law. "We will protect you as long as it is not too difficult to do so, as long as such a measure meets with popular approval." Imagine saying this to a minority suffering discrimination. Persons must be given equality before the law because it is demanded by justice, not because (or only if) it is easy.

The protection of certain rights is more difficult to enforce than that of others. It is easier to protect a person's right not to be beaten or killed in a public place than it is to protect the right of a child against child abuse at home. But the law must stand with equal clarity and firmness in both cases. The case of the child in the womb is similar to the child at home: both are more difficult to protect than an adult or child in a public place. But the essential point remains, that both should be protected, and protected equally.

"Desperate women will flout the law and try to have abortions anyway." In general, some people desperate to do something prohibited by law will try to do it anyway, and some of them will succeed. This is surely not a reason to have no law. Consider rape. Some desperate men will commit this crime anyway, even though it is illegal. Making rape illegal does not eliminate it. However different the psychology and motivation may be in the two cases, the effects on the victim are comparable: a violation of the intimacy and integrity of an innocent person. Such attacks on the person must be prohibited by law. That some people will disobey the law is tragic, but is not the point here.

Most women are not "desperate women [who] will flout the law." As was cited above, seventy-five percent of women seeking legal abortion "said they definitely would not have sought an illegal abortion." These are the women who are, to a large extent, "*protected* from being pressured into an abortion" by its illegality.[28]

"Trying to outlaw abortion is like bringing Prohibition back."[29] This is simply not true, for a number of reasons. First, the aim of Prohibition was to prohibit the consumption of alcoholic beverages. This is largely a private matter, where the state has no clear and evident right to interfere. In direct contrast to this, abortion is not a private matter, but the killing of one person by others.

Second, even if prohibition of alcohol were justified, it would not be required as a fundamental principle of law. Prohibiting murder, all murder, is required as a fundamental principle of law.

Third, a basic defect of Prohibition (of alcohol) was the confusion between a practice and its abuse. What Prohibition wanted to eliminate was the *abuse* of alcohol; what it actually prohibited was *alcohol itself*. No such confusion, or even distinction, exists in regard to abortion. It is abortion itself that is a terrible crime; there is no question of any abuse.

Finally, there is the charge that making abortion illegal would mean widespread flouting of the law, and a consequent loss of respect for the law. On the contrary, when the law fails to recognize a whole class of human beings as persons before the law, when it fails to protect their rights, it invites disrespect. The law must protect *all* fundamental human rights. It cannot hesitate in one area out of fear of disrespect.

Illegal Abortion Discriminates Against the Poor

"If abortion is made illegal, the rich will still be able to get an abortion, for example by traveling to another country where it is legal, while the poor will be unable to. This is unfair discrimination."

The first point to stress is that the difference involved here is not a matter of discrimination, of being unfair. That applies when the law itself discriminates. But when the law applies equally to all persons it is not discriminatory, even though compliance is unequal. Generally, the rich can often evade a law that the poor cannot evade (e.g., by hiring expensive lawyers who can find loopholes in the law). That is a defect in law enforcement, not in the content of the law. The issue here is the content of the law: should it recognize and protect all persons? That question is not answered by pointing to something quite general, namely, that, whatever the law says, whatever its content, the rich are often in a position to evade it in a way that the poor are not. This is an injustice perpetrated by the rich. It has nothing to do with the question of what the law should say, what it should allow or forbid. Sexual exploitation of children, for example, must be prohibited, as a matter of principle, because it violates their rights, rights the state is required to uphold and defend. That a rich person can evade the law prohibiting this in a way a poor person cannot is completely beside the point. *Neither* should be allowed to do it. If there is a discrepancy, the rich person should be brought to where the poor person is: prevented from committing such a crime. Not the other way around: allowing the poor person to do what the rich person already manages to do.

This is what applies to abortion. If abortion is the horrible crime that it has been shown to be, then neither rich nor poor women should be allowed to perpetrate it. They should be made equal, not by allowing the poor to kill their preborn babies but by more vigorous enforcement to prevent the rich from doing so.

Discrimination means the denial of a right that one really has. Poor women (and all women) have no right to kill their preborn babies. The real discrimination is against the child when killing him is allowed by law. This is the discrimination that must be prohibited—the discrimination that means the denial of his most fundamental right, the right to live.

Illegal Abortion Would Create Havoc

"Making abortion illegal would create havoc with existing laws and systems; e.g., the census, apportionment of legislatures or services based on population, tax law."[30]

This is simply not true. Many of these items would be unaffected by the enactment of a law recognizing preborn persons and upholding their right to live. An example is apportionment of legislatures, which can continue to be based on the number of born persons. Generally, we can legitimately make legal distinctions between born and preborn persons in some respects, without condemning preborn persons to the status of non-persons who may be legally destroyed. We legitimately distinguish between minors who cannot vote and adults who can, without declaring minors to be non-persons who may be legally destroyed. Precisely the same thing applies to a sub-class of minors: preborn babies.

Some of these, and possibly other similar items may be affected by enactment of the legal recognition that is due to preborn persons. So be it. If we owe them a service let us give it to them. Making the necessary adjustment would not creat havoc, but would be a requirement of justice.

Above all, the reciting of such a list should not obscure the elementary point, that we owe the child in the womb recognition as a person, and the equal protection of law that flows from it.

Legal Status of Unborn Would Limit Women's Freedom

"If the fetus is granted legal status equal to other persons, would pregnant women be forbidden to smoke, since that has a harmful effect on the fetus? Would they be forbidden to do other things that might have harmful side effects on the fetus? Such prohibitions are absurd, an invasion of a woman's privacy. In any case, they are impossible to enforce."

It is true, as the objection assumes, that it is morally wrong to do things like smoking that adversely affect the child. The child has a right that such things not be done to him. It is a new question whether this right can be, and should be, enshrined in the law. Perhaps it should not be, and cannot be, because of the privacy factor. If so, that hardly means that another right the child has should not be enshrined in law, namely the right to live, the right not to be murdered. From the unfeasibility of protecting the first right, nothing whatever follows regarding the second right. Not all rights can be given the protection of law, but some surely can, especially the right not to be murdered.

A born child has a right to good health care, proper diet, protection from harmful effects. To some extent this right can be enshrined in law, to a large extent it cannot. We cannot have police at the family dinner table ensuring that the child gets all the nourishing food and vitamins he needs. Nor can he be protected from all harmful effects in the home, parallel to the harmful effects for the preborn child from his mother's smoking. But surely the born child's right to live must be enshrined in the law, and given the same legal protection the rest of us enjoy. Exactly the same applies to that child before he is born.

It is interesting that this objection argues equally against the pro-abortion view that the being in the womb is only a potential person and not an actual person. For the harm done to the "fetus" by the pregnant woman's smoking will be manifest, and will be suffered, when that being is a person after birth. Even if he is not a person before birth, as this position holds, he is surely a person after birth, and suffers then because of the adverse effects of his mother's smoking before his birth. So the wrongness of smoking while pregnant is in no way removed, or even mitigated, by adopting the view that no person is present in the womb. Correspondingly, if smoking is already wrong on the assumption that the "fetus" is merely a potential person, nothing significant is changed or added when we come to realize that he is already a real person, an actual person. Hence the objection is not peculiar to the position defended here, that the being in the womb is a real person, entitled to the same legal status and protection as the rest of us.

Can a pregnant woman undergo medical treatment or take medication that is beneficial to her, but has a harmful side effect on the child? In some cases, yes, in some cases, no. I suggest three principles to help decide such cases: (A) The woman and her child must be treated equally as persons. (B) We must try to benefit both as much as possible. (C) Proportionality must be observed. A harmful side effect for one person must not be caused that is out of proportion to the good effect intended for the other person.

Illegal Abortion Would Make All Miscarriages Suspect

"If abortion were made illegal it would 'perhaps require women who had spontaneous abortions [miscarriages] (and their doctors) to undergo special scrutiny to prove that they were in no way induced.'"[31]

If there are reasonable grounds for suspecting that the spontaneous abortion was indeed deliberately induced, there should be a special scrutiny; for inducement of abortion means that a small child had been deliberately killed. Deliberately killing him should be treated just like deliberately killing any child. If there are no reasonable grounds for suspecting a deliberate killing, there would be no scrutiny. This is precisely the same situation as the death of a born baby from an accident at home. If there are reasonable grounds for suspecting that the accident was deliberately caused, there will be, and should be, an investigation. If not, there will not be.

Illegal Abortion Would Proscribe Certain Treatments

"If abortion were made illegal, it would mean that treatment for certain medical conditions would be proscribed if the treatment had an abortifacient side effect."[32]

The force of the objection assumes the pro-abortion position, that women have the right to bring about the death of the child within them. Once this assumption is removed, the objection collapses. A woman does not have the right to a treatment that benefits her while killing the child. One cannot benefit B by killing innocent person A, as has been noted so often already. The objection arises because one does not recognize the reality of the child. Imagine someone suggesting the converse of this: a treatment for certain medical conditions in the child that would have the side effect of killing the woman. The term *abortifacient side effect* does not sound so bad, until one realizes what it means: a human person is being killed.

The reply to this objection is simply that such medical treatments should be proscribed if they include the killing of the child, just as any treatment, or any action, should be proscribed if it includes the killing of an innocent person.

Illegal Abortion Would Prohibit Certain Contraceptives

"If abortion were made illegal, specifically, if it were declared that human life begins at conception-fertilization, that would make illegal certain kinds of contraception, such as the IUD and some oral contraceptives (such as the Morning After Pill)."

The first point to make is that this formulation of the objection (which is common) confuses two essentially different terms: *contraception*, which means preventing the coming to be of a new person, and *abortion*, including abortifacients, which means destroying an already existing person. Outlawing abortion would in no way affect what are really contraceptives. It would outlaw abortifacients such as the IUD and the Morning After Pill, which destroy a tiny human person.

The reply to the objection applying only to abortifacients is that making abortion illegal would indeed outlaw the IUD, the Morning After Pill, and other abortifacients. If the child is recognized as a person from the very beginning—despite his small size, lack of development, and inability to function as a person—his right to live, his right not to be killed should be recognized also. If our right to live is enshrined in law, his right should likewise be enshrined in law. It is very easy, and often very convenient, to kill a preborn child by an IUD, while it is generally difficult, especially psychologically, to kill an older person. That is hardly a morally relevant difference. It is unfair to take advantage of a person's small size and inability to defend himself in order to kill him. It is likewise unfair to deny a tiny child the legal protection we enjoy.

Protecting a child from death by IUD or the Morning After Pill is much more difficult than protecting him from death by D & C, saline, and other surgical killings. But the principle is the same: the child must be protected by the law. There must be a legal prohibition on the manufacture, transport, distribution, possession, and use of IUD's, Morning After Pills, and other death-dealing devices. That which has as its sole purpose the destruction of a small person cannot be legally tolerated. That enforcement of such a prohibition will be difficult is no argument against it. Protecting babies from child abuse in the home is also difficult in terms of enforcement, but is of course absolutely imperative.

14

Some Legal Dimensions

On the Question of Penalties

If abortion is made a criminal act under the law, should it be declared murder? Should the penalties be the same as for other cases of murder? How should they apply to the doctor? How should they apply to the woman?

1. Abortion is the deliberate killing of an innocent human being. It is a case of murder. It must be called by its proper name, both in the moral and legal order. Anything less is an injustice to the child. The seriousness of the charge of murder is a reflection of the seriousness with which we take the reality of the victim of the killing. Preborn babies are not lesser persons—they are our equals. Killing a child before birth is as much murder as killing that child, or anyone else, after birth. The law must reflect and express this. It must call abortion by its proper term: murder.

2. A doctor deliberately kills a sick five-year old child. A second doctor kills a newborn baby. A third doctor deliberately kills a preborn baby. Surely the first doctor commits murder. And the second? Of course. There is no morally relevant difference. And the third? Again it is murder, there is no morally relevant difference. The only difference between the three is that the child is a bit younger and smaller in each succeeding case, and in a different environment in the third case. But the horror of the deed, the gravity of the offense is the same in all three cases. The third has a different name, *abortion*, and perhaps a different psychological appearance, but it is of the same nature as the other two.

Doctors who perform abortions are hired killers, paid professional killers. They should be indicted for first-degree murder just as in all other cases of deliberate, premeditated murder. The penalties for doctors for killing preborn babies should be the same as the penalties for killing born persons. Only in this way do we grant the preborn child the equal treatment he or she deserves.

Does this judgment sound harsh? If so, is it because we do not seriously consider the child to be a person? If we do, does it still seem harsh? If we recognize that the doctor is deliberately killing a small child who cannot defend herself, who is ruthlessly crushed because the doctor has the power to destroy her, how can we say that the doctor's deed is anything but murder?

Recall the horror of abortion, how the child is cut to pieces, dismembered by suction, or subjected to being burned all over her body for one to two hours, and then ask: Where is the harshness? In the judgment on the doctor, or in what the doctor does to the child?

It goes without saying that any doctor who kills a preborn child should immediately be suspended from the medical community and barred from any further medical practice. He has violated his professional trust and obligation in the most fundamental way. Medicine exists to heal and save people, not to kill them. A greater contradiction to the spirit and essence of that noble profession can hardly be imagined.

A doctor who performs an abortion may see it as a service for the woman, an act on her behalf. This has to do with the motive of the agent; it does not affect the nature of the action. That action is still murder, and should be declared so under the law. A doctor who kills a handicapped newborn baby may also do it as a service to the parents, perhaps out of compassion. Whatever the status of his motive, his deed is clearly murder, the deliberate killing of a helpless infant. Abortion is no different.

3. Let us turn to the question of penalties for women. On the one hand, as I have shown, women are in various ways the second victims. They are often pressured; they turn to abortion because they are not supported and see no alternative. Far from being a genuine choice, abortion is often an act of desperation. Women are often devastated in many ways, by feelings of guilt, regret, depression, and by physical damage. Abortion is a terrible assault on the woman, psychologically and physically. One might easily say they have suffered enough. Moreover, women are often unaware of the full reality of the child, and how horrible abortion is for the child. All these are surely mitigating factors.

On the other hand, we must not retreat from the stand that abortion is murder, and, therefore, that the woman in choosing abortion participates in murder. Women themselves sometimes say, "I have murdered my baby," or something similar.

"But is it not an extreme and harsh view that would treat women who have abortions as murderers?" This is sometimes asked by defenders of abortion as an objection to making abortion illegal: "It would treat women as murderers." It is assumed that any sensible person will immediately see that this is absurd.

But is it? If we recall what a horrible act abortion is, as we have repeatedly stressed here, any apparent absurdity will quickly vanish. Abortion is murder, and therefore all those who are involved in it are involved in murder. It is not my judgment that makes the killing of an innocent human being murder, but the facts of the case itself. The alleged absurdity here comes from failing to see the reality of the child in the womb and the horror of deliberately killing her. Given this horror, how can abortion be anything but murder?

Part of this question/objection stems from the idea that we should have pity on the woman. Indeed we should. But to call such an action murder is not to contradict pity. If a desperate person kills an innocent person, we can have great pity on him; we do not judge him harshly, and yet we say his deed was murder. Pity is a response to the *person;* the question of murder pertains to the nature of the *action.* The action, if it is the deliberate killing of an innocent person, does not cease to be murder because we have pity on the person who committed it, or the person involved in it.

We should pity the woman who has an abortion. And the child! We should have the same concern for the child that we naturally have for the woman. If what is done to the child in abortion were done to the woman, we would be outraged. We would surely call it murder, regardless of who did it, or why that person did it. We must be equally outraged at what is actually done to the child, and we must call it murder as well.

4. At first the two aspects—calling abortion murder, recognizing that women who choose abortion are involved in murder; and having pity on women as second victims of abortion—may seem contradictory or opposed. I think that on a deeper level they unite. The law must recognize abortion in all its seriousness and apply penalties that reflect this. This is not only in response to the child as the primary victim, to protect him, but also in response to the woman, the second victim, to protect her. Paradoxical as it may seem, we can have pity on women by recognizing abortion as murder, with appropriate penalties. It is a way of conveying the message that abortion is a terrible thing, from which women must be protected. "Do not commit murder" is a powerful warning.

5. In all of this I have not spelled out what the penalties for abortion should be, for the doctor and for the woman. That is a topic beyond the scope of this book, belonging to other subjects, the ethics of punishment and criminology. I have argued for two main points: equal treatment for the preborn child, that killing her be treated as murder, just like the killing of a born child, or any other person; and protection for the woman. Whatever penalties are imposed must reflect this, as well as take into account any relevant mitigating factors, just as in all other cases of

murder. There are, however, several points that should be made in regard to the question just raised.

First, the severity of the penalty should reflect the seriousness of the crime. The gravity of the penalty is a measure of the seriousness with which we take the offense. If we value human life, we must impose a corresponding penalty on those who would deliberately destroy it.

Second, should we pity the criminal? A tension between pity and justice runs through the whole of the criminal justice system. The rapist who evokes our wrath may also evoke our pity if we look into his miserably unhappy childhood, and if we see him harshly punished. This tension is a very general one, not confined to any single type of crime. And it is not, I think, easily resolved. The pity/justice tension that we see in the case of abortion, pity for the woman, justice in response to the murder of the child, is part of this general tension. It should be seen as such, and not as something special. And neither element should completely over-shadow the other, as when pity for the woman leads to a denial that the abortion she requests is a case of murder.

Third, consistent with justice, the penalty for a crime should be severe enough to provide maximum deterrence against committing it. The principles here are the same as for the murder of born persons. Murder of the preborn must be punished in such a way as to afford the potential victims the maximum protection of the deterrent effect of law, consistent with justice. This is the kind of protection we owe the woman; and her preborn child.

Finally, as in all cases of killing, the severity of the penalty should also reflect all the relevant factors of the individual case. All the elements that make women the second victims of abortion enter here as mitigating factors. In some cases, similar considerations may also apply to the doctor. As a general rule, however, it seems to me that the penalties should be more severe for the doctor than for the woman. As noted, the doctor is a hired killer, and should be treated as such.

The question of penalties for women is an agonizing one. In trying to resolve it, I suggest we keep in mind the four points immediately above, paying special attention to the second: pity for the woman, but also a concern for justice.[1]

On the Question of Exceptions in the Law

Should the law prohibiting abortion allow for exceptions? Specifically, to save the life of the woman and in cases of pregnancy due to rape or incest? A law incorporating such exceptions is advocated either because its proponents feel that such exceptions are justified and called for, or because they believe no other law is possible, that a law that mandates an exceptionless prohibition stands no chance of passage. They then argue that it is better to have a law that bans almost all abortions, and saves many lives, than the present situation (in the United States, and in much of the rest of the world) in which there is, in effect, abortion on demand. "Better to save most babies and allow a few to be killed, than to allow the number of abortions we have today."

The motives of such people are noble. They want to save as many lives as possible. And surely it is better to save some than none at all. If a thousand innocent people are about to be exterminated by the Nazis, and we can rescue only some, we should, of course, do so: better to save some than none at all. But is an abortion prohibition with an exception clause parallel to this?

In analyzing the question of exceptions, I will begin with the rape/incest case, then discuss the "life of the mother" case, and finally the question of exceptions regarding the IUD and other abortifacients.

A law is enacted that says, in effect: Abortion is wrong; it is prohibited, except if the woman is pregnant due to rape or incest. Then abortion is permitted. What it says is that it is wrong to kill almost all babies in the womb, but all right to kill a few. For a child conceived in rape or incest, the law says, "You may kill this child for the benefit of his mother."

Even in the case of rape or incest, there is a child present, a real person, essentially like the rest of us. Abortion is murder, and remains murder when the victim is conceived in rape (or incest). The child is absolutely innocent, completely her own person, not a part of her father's character, just as she is not a part of her mother's body. Even assuming abortion benefits the woman, we cannot kill one innocent person to benefit another. The child has no duty to give up her life to try to benefit her mother, and we may therefore not force her to do so by killing her. If we do not kill the rapist for his crime, still less should we kill the child who has committed no crime. Abortion for rape is not a solution because it is an assault on the woman, a cure that aggravates the disease, and because it does not address the real problem of rape pregnancies (the social stigma against the woman and her child). And finally, abortion in the case of rape is more of the same: first a horrible violence against the woman, then a horrible violence against the child. For all these reasons, abortion in the case of rape (and incest) is not justified.

The child in the womb conceived in rape or incest has the same right to have her life protected by law as anyone else has. This means there can be no exception in the law for rape or incest. There are two fundamental reasons for this, one concerning the principle at stake, the other, the practical effects. The second follows naturally from the first.

First, the question of principle. A law that incorporates the rape/incest exception means that murder is given the blessing of law in certain cases. "Yes, go ahead, you can murder this child, since his conception was due to rape." The law can never allow murder. A law that does so is not only a gross injustice in itself but also a contradiction to the very meaning of law, the upholding of what is right and just in the public domain. That is, the whole law prohibiting abortion would be fatally flawed by this exception clause. Such a law could never be a genuine prohibition of murder of the child when it makes an about face and says, "Yes, you can murder this child." The exception clause would mean the breakdown of the entire law. It would no longer have a foundation to stand on. It would not be like the removal of one checker from a board of checkers, leaving the rest intact. It would be like removing the foundation of a building: the whole building would collapse. For the foundation of the law banning abortion is that abortion is murder. If the law allows murder, it has destroyed itself.

Such a law admits that abortion can be justified under certain circumstances, namely rape or incest. But if in these circumstances, why not also others? The question is surely a reasonable one. And with it we come to the second part: the practical effects of a law that allows the rape/incest exception. There are six specific points:

1) Such a law will be challenged. On what basis is abortion to be prohibited in all other cases? Is it because there is a child there, and abortion is murdering that child, and the law may not allow murder? But that applies equally to the child conceived in rape. If abortion in such a case is allowed, the reason just given can't be the basis of the prohibition. By allowing murder, the law defeats itself. It invites a challenge that is not only perfectly reasonable, but cannot be met by those who agree with the exception law.

That is, in proposing or agreeing to an exception law, we would surrender everything that is essential to protecting any infant in the womb. We would forfeit our chance to enact any legal protection for preborn infants. We would grant our opponents who favor allowing abortion the idea that the child may be killed for the benefit of another. Granted, we would be conceding this in only one area, but it would be the crack in the door.

2) If the exception for rape or incest is granted, should we then have another exception based upon pain and trauma from other causes? To deny such a request at this point would be impossible. If trauma and pain due to one cause are to serve as a reason for permitting abortion,

then the   similar trauma and pain for another cause must be given the same privilege.

There is a further, very serious problem. How much pain and trauma are to be counted as sufficient? How are they to be measured? Who is to decide? The decision will be left to a psychiatrist and other doctors. In practical terms, it will mean that a woman seeking an abortion has only to find a doctor willing to certify, in his professional judgment, that she needs an abortion for psychological reasons. When she does, no one will be able to dispute this doctor's claim. We will no longer be able to appeal to the state for protection for the innocent. We will have surrendered that element in the law that allows for exceptions.

The first of the two fundamental reasons for rejecting a law with exceptions, namely, that it violates principle, is no idle or stubborn clinging to the abstract, in disregard for practical consequences in the real world. On the contrary, the principle that *all* persons must be respected, that *all* murder must be condemned by state law, is needed for practical reasons. Abandoning the principle has disastrous consequences in the real world, consequences which flow directly from the surrender of the principle.

It may be claimed that abortion for rape is essentially different from all other abortions to benefit the woman, because in rape she was unjustly coerced. The presence of the child in her represents an injustice, and therefore she may remove him. Two wrongs, however, do not make a right; I cannot try to undo a wrong done against me by doing another wrong— especially murder—against another person. The woman cannot try to undo the wrong done by killing the rapist, or the innocent child. Allowing such killing in the name of undoing a wrong is a violation of the principle that all innocent persons must be respected and protected. Holding fast to this principle is not only important in itself but also essential for practical reasons.

3) Will a rape exception law require proof that the woman was actually raped? If the answer is yes, there are insuperable objections and difficulties. She may be unable to prove it for lack of witnesses. The rapist might not get caught; and even if he is, it is her word against his, with no proof. Forcing her to go through court proceedings is wrong and unrealistic. Even if it were expected, and the woman were forced to submit to it before she could get the abortion, it would take too long. The baby would be far along in development and suffer a late-term abortion. The proceedings might even take longer than the pregnancy itself, thus nullifying the whole intent of the law.

It is clear from this that no requirement for proof could be written into the exception law. This means that a woman could legally claim an abortion on the basis of rape without proof. The mere claim of rape would suffice. It is easy to predict what will happen. Women who feel they need an abortion could claim rape and get their abortions. Family members and others who feel the woman needs an abortion could pressure her into claiming rape. We would be back to where we are now: abortion on demand.

It may be charged that I take a cynical view here, saying that women will lie in order to get an abortion. Those women who claim abortion as a right will understandably see in the restriction to rape clause an unwarranted intrusion into their privacy, a provision in the law put there in order to appease those who want to forbid abortion. They will feel justified in trying to evade this restriction. "If a woman who has been raped can get an abortion, why can't I?" The same applies if it is others who pressure her into an abortion. If we surrender the principle that abortion must be prohibited as murder, that every child in the womb is entitled to the same protection of law that we are entitled to, we really have no answer to this question. In comparison with the horror of abortion itself, and the terrible violation of justice of allowing some preborn persons to be killed with the blessing of the law, a woman lying in order to obtain an abortion is very insignificant indeed.

4) We are now in a good position to see the essential difference between a geniune concern to save as many people as possible rather than none at all, and a law prohibiting abortion that allows exceptions for rape and incest. A thousand innocent people are condemned to die by the Nazis. We have several trucks, that together hold two hundred people. We can make only one trip. We take two hundred, saving them. We are unable to save the rest. But we do not compromise those eight hundred that we cannot save. We do not say to the Nazis, "It's all right, you can kill these people." But that is precisely what the exception clause in an abortion law would say. A law containing such a clause does not merely fail to save, as in the case of the shortage of trucks, it gives a positive sanction to killing. It enshrines it in the law. That is what is so objectionable, first as a violation of principle, then in its practical consequences, which are essentially the unfolding of the violation of the principle. The exception law must be rejected because written into it is the idea that some persons may be murdered.

It is sometimes said that a law need not, often cannot, include all that should be prohibited. Granted. But the crucial thing, in the present context, is that the law cannot incorporate an immoral principle, such as "You may kill the child if he was conceived under certain conditions." The very purpose and meaning of a law prohibiting abortion is to protect every child, to prohibit murder. An exception for rape is a contradiction to this, a negation of the very essence of the law.

5) An exception law delivers the message that it's all right to have an abortion under certain circumstances. With this the whole edifice of state protection for preborn persons collapses. "This must mean that abortion isn't really murder, else it wouldn't be allowed in some cases." These are the thoughts that will naturally suggest themselves to people if the law to protect preborn persons contains exceptions.

The practical effects of such a climate of opinion are easily predictable. An exception law will not be respected. It is a law that contains an inherent contradiction, for it is a law that both wants to prohibit murder (in most cases) and also to allow it (for rape and incest). And the exceptions will be widened. Why shouldn't they be, once the idea is accepted, and enshrined in the law, that a benefit for the woman can justify abortion? The exception law would not save most babies as its advocates expect. It would leave us where we are, with a legal system that sanctions murder.

6) "A law containing a rape and incest exception is all we can get. There seems to be a consensus for that, but not for an absolute prohibition on abortion. Most Americans oppose abortion on demand, but only a minority supports an absolute prohibition."

First, there is every reason to be confident that if the American people fully realize what an abortion is, they will demand an absolute prohibition on abortion, no exceptions. We must make clear the reality of the child in the womb. We must publicize pictures of the child that show he is one of us and may not be destroyed for any reason. We must publicize pictures of the results of abortion. The full impact of the horror of abortion should silence any thought of exceptions. How can one stare abortion in the face and still suggest exceptions?

Second, a law with exceptions is not only a violation of fundamental principles, it is also useless; its practical consequences will be abortion on demand. If we settle for an exception law, we may not get another chance to enact a real prohibition on abortion. We will have compromised ourselves to ultimate defeat. We cannot let this happen. Therefore an exception law is not only useless; much worse, it is something that may close the door to any real protection for preborn persons.

Should the law allow an exception to save the life of the mother? This question has, in effect, already been answered. Abortion is murder, and murder can never be sanctioned by the law. We cannot kill the woman to save the child. Equally, we cannot kill the child to save the woman. We may not be able to save both, we may have to withhold treatment from one if it cannot be given to both, but we may never deliberately kill the one to save the other.

The law should incorporate the three principles discussed earlier, in chapter 10. I propose it include the following section:

> If complications arise, all reasonable efforts must be made to save both the woman and the child. Each must be respected and treated equally as a person. Neither may be killed for the benefit of the other, or in an attempt to save the life of the other.

Let us turn finally to the question of exceptions regarding the IUD and other abortifacients. The same principle applies here too: there can be no exceptions, *all* preborn persons must be given legal protection.

Suppose, however, that a law prohibiting abortion that includes a ban on all abortifacients cannot be passed, that only a law prohibiting surgical abortions, including prostaglandins, can be enacted. Isn't it better to save most of the vast number of babies being killed by these methods, and forego legal protection for tiny infants who would be killed by abortifacients, than to have nothing at all? In addition, enforcement of a ban on abortifacients would pose great difficulties.

This is a difficult question. Let me suggest the following points:

1) Any law that is passed must be free from all the objectionable compromises discussed above in regard to exceptions for rape and incest. It cannot be a law that contains an expandable loophole.

2) Specifically, it cannot be a law that explicitly allows early abortions (abortifacients). It could only be a law that omits mention of abortifacients and focuses on outlawing the savagery of surgical abortions. It would have to be a law that represented a real parallel to the example above, of saving some potential victims of Nazi extermination while failing to save others because it is impossible to do so.

3) If such a limited law could be formulated and enacted, it would have to be seen as a temporary measure. We would have to work vigorously to extend its prohibition to all preborn persons.

4) We should not, however, assume too readily that a law including a ban on abortifacients cannot be enacted. We must make full use of all the arguments and evidence available to us, primarily all that which makes it clear that a person begins his existence at conception-fertilization, that the zygote-embryo-fetus is a person all the way through and does not become one gradually. We should supplement these arguments with the probability argument (If there is any significant chance that the zygote is a human being essentially like the rest of us—and surely there is—we may not destroy him.); as well as with the "no difference" argument (If the child is to be killed,

what difference does it make whether he is killed earlier or later? Either way he is deprived of his entire future life). All of these provide an abundance of reasons to help people realize that a tiny human being near the beginning of his existence is a person too, essentially like the rest of us, and therefore entitled to the same protection of law.

We cannot compromise on this. The most we might do is work in stages, first enacting a law that recognizes the personhood of the victim of surgical abortions, then also the personhood of the victim of abortifacients. There is some parallel to this in the case of slavery in America. The first stage was freeing the slaves from their bondage, the second stage was granting them equal status as persons in society and under the law. Necessary as this second stage is, it was wise to begin with the first stage if the two could not be accomplished together. Just as it was better that blacks be freed from slavery, but without full civil rights, than continuing to be slaves, which is an even greater violation of their civil rights and their dignity as persons, so too it is better to save many babies by giving them legal protection, than to continue the present horror in which no preborn babies are given any protection of law.

But it must be stressed that in such cases—legal recognition and protection of blacks and preborn persons—there can only be stages, and not compromises of principles. We could never concede that a black person is not fully a person, or that a tiny infant is not fully a person. If it takes time to awaken people to the full impact of the evil in both cases, we must work in stages. The first stage must be accomplished in such a way that it naturally leads to the second. Abortion by D & C, saline, etc. means killing a small child and must therefore be outlawed. Abortifacients also mean killing a child, merely a smaller child, and must therefore also be outlawed.

There is a difference between a rape exception law and the two-stage procedure tentatively suggested here. A two-stage procedure with no compromises on principle goes in the right direction. A rape exception law goes in the wrong direction. The two-stage procedure affirms that any being who is a person must be given equal protection of law; it only leaves open whether a zygote is such a being. The rape exception law must be condemned precisely because it denies the principle that any being who is a person must be given equal protection of law. The two-stage procedure is thus open to full recognition of preborn persons from the very beginning of their existence at conception. The rape exception law, by its exception clause, closes the door to any genuine and effective legal protection for preborn persons.

On the Question of Public Funding of Abortions

It is argued that the government should fund abortions for poor women. "Not to do so is discrimination. The rich can still get abortions while the poor are denied them." Again, it is said, "Abortion is cheaper than welfare. Poor women who want abortions should be encouraged to get them, and supported financially, to ease the welfare burden. Supporting a child on welfare is expensive over many years."

It is clear that government should not fund abortions. Funding abortion means paying for the killing of a small, defenseless child, a child who is singled out for death because he is in the way, and sometimes because it costs too much to support him.

Abortion funding is a triple evil. First, there is the moral evil of abortion itself, as the murder of a small child. Second, there is the additional evil that the government gives this killing its blessing by allowing it under the law. Third, the government even participates in the crime by paying for it.

In reply to the objection that refusal to fund abortions for poor women is a form of discrimination: It is true that there should be no discrimination. But this must be achieved in precisely the opposite direction: neither the rich nor the poor should be allowed, or encouraged, to kill their preborn babies. If poor women are not able to destroy their preborn infants, that is good; rich women should be in the same position. The law must protect all preborn babies, of rich and poor mothers alike.

"Abortion is cheaper than welfare." Indeed it is. So is killing the handicapped, the aged who are unable to take care of themselves. Killing is always cheaper than caring. The Nazis realized this, and put it into practice in their program of mass extermination of handicapped children, the aged, and others who were "useless eaters." Let us not follow that path.

Epilogue

Looking Back and Looking Ahead

When future generations look back at us, what will they see? They will see a society that prided itself on being humane and concerned for human rights, but one that also engaged in the practice of killing small children by dismemberment or poisoning/burning. It did not do this to all its children, just certain ones, who were still in the first phase of their lives. It was a practice called abortion. One would think that such a practice, with its ghastly methods, would be outlawed. It was not; it was perfectly legal. In fact the individual states were forbidden by the Supreme Court to outlaw it and protect these children. Many in the society welcomed this, for they wanted to keep the practice "safe" and legal. Didn't they find it odd to refer to a practice that destroys little children as "safe"?

It was a society that held up very high standards in condemning discrimination against people merely because they were in some way different from those who happened to be the majority, such as in skin color. But it was also a society that treated some of its members very differently from others because they were different: much smaller, much more dependent than the majority, and not in a familiar environment. They were treated differently in that they could be killed if they did not fit into others' plans.

Perhaps that was part of the explanation why a practice that kills a child was called safe: the child doesn't count as a real person because she is different (too small, etc.). In other cases such an attitude would be vigorously condemned as discrimination. Here it was approved, and often strongly supported. Laws that allowed people to murder babies were called liberal, while in other contexts that term referred (among other things) to the protection of those who could not protect themselves.

The child was not taken seriously as a real person. Perhaps that explains how those who favored this practice would vigorously defend "a woman's right to choose." They called themselves "Pro-Choice," thus conveniently avoiding any reference to the killing of the child. They would ordinarily defend choice only in personal matters that did not adversely affect others. They would never defend a right to choose to kill a person, or to discriminate against a person.

It was a society that itself looked back on a horror scene, a holocaust where some six million people were exterminated. It was aghast at what it saw, and kept saying "Never again!" It did not see that essentially the same thing was going on in its own neighborhoods.[1]

This is what they will see. What will they say? Probably many things, one of them being, "Why didn't those people who did see abortion for what it is do something?" That brings us back to the present, where we can look ahead to the future. For us the question is: what must we do now to end the mass abortion killings? Let me suggest the following Call to Action.

(1) We must awaken the American people to what is happening. Two things should be stressed: the reality of the child and how abortion kills the child, the ghastly methods and their results. A major part of this education campaign should be pictures of the child. In so many cases, seeing is believing. If a woman sees her child, she may change her mind about having an abortion. Dr. Bernard Nathanson discusses an article in the *New England Journal of Medicine,* which reported an interview:

> [T]wo women in the early part of pregnancy . . . were privileged to watch their infants on an ultrasound screen. The women were asked if they would still entertain the thought of abortion after having seen their babies move, breathe, and do all those inexpressibly endearing things that all babies do, born or unborn. Both women categorically rejected the abortion option, one stating: "I feel that it is human. It belongs to me. I couldn't have an abortion now."[2]

We must stress that abortion is not a private matter. Joseph Scheidler urges us to "develop an educational program that concentrates on the unborn child as an unseen victim. It is essential that this victim becomes a real person in the mind of the community. The more the unborn is acknowledged, the less tolerant the community will be of taking that person's life."[3]

Why do those who support abortion not see its victim as a real person? I think a major factor is prejudice. We must work to overcome this prejudice where it exists, and a good first step is to understand it. Germain Grisez, in his excellent treatise, "Abortion and Prejudice against the Unborn" explains: "Prejudice takes advantage of a difference" between "those who are prejudiced" and "those against whom there is prejudice." Those who are prejudiced are so for "an intelligible motive" that explains the "development and persistence" of the prejudice.[4] For abortion there is an obvious motive: the desire to terminate an unwanted pregnancy.

> While prejudiced people are not simply dishonest, they act as if they suspected the truth and were trying to avoid facing it. People who are racially prejudiced do not like to be shown facts and have a hard time following arguments that might dislodge their prejudice. This resistance is always surprising, especially when it is encountered (as often happens) in persons who are extremely perceptive and logical in other matters.[5]

The same applies to prejudice against the unborn. Further, "a system built on prejudice is never consistent."[6] People who are pro-abortion are generally very strongly opposed to racial prejudice. Perhaps that helps to assure them that they themselves can't be prejudiced. But, in fact, prejudice is a universal human danger, which any of us can fall into.

To speak of prejudice here is not to level a charge against persons who favor abortion; it is simply a way of trying to understand an aspect of the pro-abortion mentality. How can people favor allowing babies to be killed? The viewpoint of prejudice helps to provide an answer.

There is also, I think, the fact that many people do not support abortion as a conclusion from a process of reasoning. Rather, they first decide that abortion is necessary or desirable, then find reasons to support this view. One such reason is the so-called unreality of the "fetus" as a person. That, in turn, is a prejudice against the unborn.

In addition to those who explicitly favor abortion, there is a large majority who are complacent. They are in between, neither actively pro-abortion nor filled with outrage at this horror. They must be awakened to a response of outrage, and inspired to form a movement to end this mass killing. They must come to see abortion in a new way. According to Brennan:

> As long as abortion remains at the psychologically-remote and abstract level of removing insignificant tissue or contents from the womb, not that many people are likely to get upset. The holocaust perspective, on the other hand, possesses a tremendous potential for breaking through this facade and revealing the harsh realities of large-scale killing, whatever the historical period of their perpetration, and whether the victims be born or unborn. Only when people are allowed

access to the concrete, emotionally repugnant facts of unborn baby killing will they be filled with outrage and motivated to demand an end to the destruction.[7]

One of the most important tasks is devising ways of reaching the American people with a message to awaken them to the reality of the child-killing that is politely referred to as abortion. Perhaps a mass mailing can be arranged. A vital part of this message is a call to action: "If you are outraged at abortion, then _____," specifying what a person should do.

(2) We must prepare a program of political action for ending the mass killing. We must prepare bills to be introduced in Congress. We must devise strategies for reversing court decisions that protect the alleged right to kill instead of the rights of the victim.[8] We can then focus people's energy into specific programs: support this bill, call this government official, etc.

(3) In pursuing the first two steps, our objective must be clear: full membership of preborn children in the community (full status as persons and full protection under the law). There can be no compromise on this. The child can never be killed to benefit the woman or others, any more than the woman or others could be killed to benefit the child.

It is essential that legal protection for preborn persons be written into the Constitution, so that no future court or legislature can ever deprive them of it again. There must be a Constitutional amendment that specifically states that preborn children are persons and entitled to full legal protection. Three elements are essential:

One, the amendment must restore personhood to the unborn child. Two, it must clearly apply from the beginning of life, conception-fertilization. Three, its prohibition of abortion-killing must contain no exceptions.[9]

(4) It will be said that this objective cannot be achieved all at once. If this is so, we should work in stages, doing what we can at each stage and continuing until our task is complete. It is important to be clear on the difference between this approach and one that accepts compromises. We might, for example, start out with a law that bans saline abortions: they are so horrible that it is hard to believe they are used, and even sanctioned by law. Someone who is unclear whether or not the "fetus" is a person could still see the horror of doing this to any living creature, for whom the evidence (presence of nerve endings, etc.) is overwhelming that it feels excruciating pain, and for a considerable time. A law banning the saline method would not condone other abortions; it would simply not mention them. Once this is accom-

plished, we must work in stages to forbid other types of abortion as well.

Working for such a law does not constitute a compromise on principle. It means climbing the first rung of a ladder before climbing the second. If abortions that cause more pain are greater evils than those that cause less pain (or no pain), we should outlaw the greater evil if we cannot outlaw both evils. Incomplete laws are better than no law at all.

However, we must not compromise, allowing an incomplete law that would eliminate or seriously reduce the chances of a complete law later. We must never say that a little bit of murder is acceptable. No murder is acceptable. We must constantly work towards eliminating all abortions.

People who do not understand that a very early abortion is wrong will usually see the wrongness of a late abortion. There are parallel examples in which the wrongness of some abortions is easier to see than that of others. Thus, if we can convince people that certain abortions should be prohibited, we should do so; and then continue our efforts to extend this to all other abortions as well.

Keeping in mind, then, the temporary character of these stages, let me suggest some examples of them.

1. A law, or court ruling, that allows protection for the child; then one that requires it.

2. A ban on all third trimester abortions, then second, then first; or, a ban on killing a viable child, then a previable child.

3. A ban on abortions that cause the worst pain or are more likely to cause pain; then, a ban on others.

4. A ban on all surgical abortions and abortion pills (e.g., RU486); then, one on abortifacients.

5. A denial that there is any right to an abortion. This would mean prohibiting all abortions other than the hard cases (rape, incest, health and life of the woman); then, prohibiting these as well. The first stage would eliminate about ninety-seven percent of all abortions, a great first step, but only a first step.

These five items refer to eliminating all abortions, stage by stage. The remaining nine concern abortions that remain at any stage short of the final stage. They are aimed at reducing the harm done to the child, to the woman, and to the family; at curtailing the number of abortions; and at lessening the inherent evil of abortion (e.g., by banning government funding). There should be no abortions at all, at least no legal abortions, but as long as it is impossible to ban all legal abortions, those that occur must include:

6. Anesthesia for the child in all cases where there is even a slight chance of pain for the child.

7. An informed consent requirement. Any person considering a medical procedure has a right to a full disclosure concerning what that procedure involves and what its possible consequences are. It can be expected that this requirement will significantly reduce the number of abortions. The full disclosure should include all relevant information about the effects of the abortion: (A) What the child looks like, her status of development. (B) What abortion does to the child, the methods of abortion, the high probability of terrible pain for the child, and the length of time of the procedure. (C) What abortion can do to the woman, short term and long term, physically, psychologically, and in regard to future pregnancies; how it can effect her relationships with others. (D) Where applicable, the hazards of eugenic abortions (for eliminating handicapped babies), especially amniocentesis.[10] (E) Alternatives to abortion. (F) Support groups ready to help the woman continue a difficult pregnancy, especially by supporting her in the face of pressure by others to abort.

It is of the greatest importance that the woman be given this information honestly and objectively, that she be encouraged to ask questions. Any kind of pressure in the direction of abortion must be prohibited.

8. A forty-eight-hour waiting period before an abortion can be performed, so that the woman has time to change her mind. Many do. It is a tragedy when a woman is rushed into an abortion, one she may regret bitterly.

9. A requirement that in all live births, the child be given complete medical treatment to maximize his chances for survival and health.

10. Parental consent for minors, something required for all other medical treatments. Making an exception for abortion is outrageous.

11. Spousal consent for married women. Excluding the father is a terrible injustice. The father has obligations of child support; he should also have corresponding rights. For unmarried women, the right of legal intervention for the father of the child.

12. A ban on all government funding of abortion.

13. A ban on all other government participation in abortion. This includes a ban on: offering abortions at government facilities such as military bases, granting tax exempt status to organizations that promote or perform abortions, funding such organizations, promoting abortion in government-sponsored programs, such as family planning.

14. Other measures, such as a ban on all advertising for so-called abortion services, and excluding abortion from health insurance plans.

As many of these proposals as possible should be enacted concurrently, and coordinated with one another.

(5). While working towards this objective, we must continue our efforts to save babies and their mothers from abortion. An excellent guide to this is Joseph Scheidler's book, *Closed: 99 Ways to Stop Abortion*. His first way is sidewalk counseling, in which pro-lifers go to abortion clinics "to intercede for the baby's life":

> Sidewalk counseling is a method of saving babies by talking to their parents in front of the abortion clinic. It is probably the single most valuable activity that a pro-life person can engage in. When pro-lifers counsel in front of an abortion clinic, they are coming between the woman and the doctor, between the baby who is scheduled to be killed and the doctor who will do the killing.[11]

These efforts can be highly successful:

> Women *can* be turned back. In Chicago, in one thirty day period, half a dozen sidewalk counselors at only a few clinics were able to stop ninety women from having abortions. Seventeen were stopped in a single morning at a clinic on Michigan Avenue. While a few of these women may have gone back to have their abortions later, more than ninety percent did not return and they kept in touch with the pro-life counseling center.[12]

As the title indicates, there are many things one can do to fight the evil of abortion. A sample of these include: The Counter-Demonstration, How to Get on Talk Shows, Aids to Effective Lobbying, Call their Bluff: the Legal Threat, and Warn the Garbage Man, "You're Hauling Corpses." All of these ways are non-violent, and there is a chapter, "Violence: Why It Won't Work."[13]

Besides Scheidler's suggestions, especially direct intervention on the sidewalk, there are several other specific things we should do:

We should support women with problem pregnancies. We should encourage them to keep their babies. If they are being pressured by others to kill their babies, we should offer them a haven of support and encouragement. In all these things there should be both spiritual and material assistance.

We should work to encourage adoption as an alternative to abortion for cases where the woman is unable to raise the child.[14]

We should be concerned with women who have had abortions.

> If you or someone you love is suffering from the emotional or physical aftereffects of abortion, you can find compassionate help and support from women who have been through the same experience by contacting any of the WEBA chapters in your state, or any of the other post-

abortion counseling groups which are being formed. If WEBA is not listed in your phone directory, call one of your local or state right-to-life organizations and they will be able to give you a phone number for the post-abortion support group nearest you. Most of these groups have a hot-line that you can call to talk to a sympathetic, non-judgmental member at any time, whenever you need them.[15]

There is also a nationwide toll-free crisis hot line: 1-800-848-5683.

Abortion can be devastating to women, in many ways, as we have seen. We should continue our research into this: How many women suffer? From which problems? For how long? How severely? We should carefully examine the challenges of abortion defenders. Our aim must always be to find the truth.

We must warn women of the hazards of abortion. I see this as a task of the greatest importance. We must protect not only the child, but also the mother. This protection can come from the law, and from an awakened public that realizes the evil of abortion and condemns it. It can also come from an awareness of the terrible things abortion can do to women. The myth of "safe abortions" must be exposed for what it is. We must work towards a general awareness of the threat of abortion to women. "Having an abortion can be hazardous to your health" must become a household phrase.

Saving babies, supporting women before their decision and after it, these are our present tasks. Many organizations exist for these purposes; let us join them, or start new ones where there are none. We cannot merely be against abortion; we must be for the woman and her child, and we should translate this commitment into action. In fact, we are *against* abortion only because we are *for* the child and his mother.[16]

(6). Through all this, we must see ourselves as advocates of the preborn child: voices for those who cannot speak for themselves, who are forgotten because they are unseen. Equally, we must be advocates of women, supporting and encouraging them. For both the child and the woman, we must promote adoption as an alternative to abortion.

These commitments must continue after we achieve our objective of fully recognized personhood for the child. That will be a major step, but it will not be the end of the road. The temptation to succumb to abortion will remain after it has been made illegal. The struggle for justice is an ongoing one.

Finally, I would like to suggest that we work to heal the wounds in our society resulting from the bitter struggle over abortion. If we affirm the personhood of the preborn child and the woman, we must also affirm the personhood of all those who advocate abortion. We must try to help them see abortion in a new way.

Works Cited

AMICUS CURIAE
  1971   Motion and Brief Amicus Curiae of Certain Physicians, Profes-
          sors and Fellows of the American College of Obstetrics and
          Gynecology in Support of Appellees, submitted to the Supreme
          Court of the United States, October Term, 1971, No. 70–18, Roe
          v. Wade, and No. 70–40, Doe v. Bolton. Prepared by Dennis J.
          Horan, et.al. (The List of Amici contains the names of over 200
          physicians.).

ANDRUSCO, Dave
  1983a   To Rescue the Future: The Pro-life Movement in the 1980's. Dave
          Andrusco (ed.) Toronto: Life Cycle Books.
  1983b   "An Insatiable Thirst for Killing," in Andrusco (1983a), pp. 3–16

BAJEMA, Clifford E.
  1974   Abortion and the Meaning of Personhood. Grand Rapids, MI:
          Baker Book House.

BAUER, P. T.
  1981   Equality, the Third World and Economic Delusion. Cambridge,
          MA: Harvard University Press.

BERGEL, Gary
  1980   When You were Formed in Secret. Elyria, Ohio: Intercessors for
          America (pp.I–1 to I–16).
  1985   Abortion in America. This is the same book as Bergel (1980): two
          titles, two parts (I and II), read from opposite ends.

BLECHSCHMIDT, E., M.D.
  1961   *The Stages of Human Development Before Birth.* Philadelphia:
          W. B. Saunders.
  1977   *The Beginning of Human Life.* New York: Springer Verlag, Hei-
          delberg Science Library.
  1981   "Human Being from the Very First," in Hilgers, Horan and Mall
          (1981), pp.6–28.

BLUMENFELD, Samuel L.
  1975   *The Retreat from Motherhood.* New Rochelle, NY: Arlington
          House.

BOLTON, Martha Brandt
  1979   "Responsible Women and Abortion Decisions," in *Having
          Children: Philosophical and Legal Reflections on Parenthood.*
          Onora O'Neill and William Ruddick (eds.). New York: Oxford
          University Press, pp.40–51. See esp. Part II.

BRENNAN, William
  1983   *The Abortion Holocaust: Today's Final Solution.* St. Louis: Land-
          mark Press.

BRODY, Baruch
  1976   *Abortion and the Sanctity of Human Life: A Philosophical View.*
          Cambridge, MA: MIT Press.

BROWN, Harold O. J.
  1977   *Death Before Birth.* Nashville: Thomas Nelson Publishers.

BULFIN, Matthew J., M.D.
  1981   "Complications of Legal Abortion: A Perspective from Private
          Practice," in Hilgers, Horan and Mall (1981), pp. 145–50. Re-
          printed in Hensley (1983), pp.97–105.

CALLAHAN, Daniel
  1970   *Abortion: Law, Choice and Morality.* New York, London: Macmil-
          lan.

CLARK, Colin
  1975   *Population Growth: The Advantages.* Santa Ana, CA: A Life
          Quality paperback.

COHEN, et.al. (eds.)
  1974   Marshal Cohen, Thomas Nagel, and Thomas Scanlon (eds.), *The
          Rights and Wrongs of Abortion, a Philosophy and Public Affairs
          Reader.* Princeton, NJ: Princeton University Press.

COLLINS, et.al.
    1984   Vincent J. Collins, M.D., Steven R. Zielinski, M.D., and Thomas
              J. Marzen, Esq., *Fetal Pain and Abortion: The Medical Evidence.*
              Chicago: Americans United For Life, Inc. Studies In Law and
              Medicine, no. 18.

CROSBY, John F.
    1976   "Evolution and the Ontology of the Human Person: Critique of
              the Marxist Theory of the Emergence of Man," in *The Review of*
              Politics, Vol. 38, no. 2 (April).

DELAHOYDE, Melinda
    1984   *Fighting for Life: Defending the Newborn's Right to Live.* Ann
              Arbor, MI: Servant Books.

DEVINE, Philip
    1978   *The Ethics of Homicide.* Ithaca and London: Cornell University
              Press.

DIAMOND, Eugene F.,M.D.
    1977   "The Deformed Child's Right to Life," in *Death,Dying,and Eutha-*
              nasia. Dennis J. Horan and David Mall (eds.), Washington, DC:
              University Publications of America, pp. 127–38.

DONCEEL, Joseph F.,S.J.
    1970   "A Liberal Catholic's View," in *Abortion in a Changing World,*
              Vol.I, Robert E. Hall (ed.) New York: Columbia University Press,
              pp.39–45. Reprinted in Feinberg (1984). pp. 15–20. References
              are to Feinberg.

DRAMA OF LIFE BEFORE BIRTH
    1965   Reprinted from *Life* (April 30). Life Educational Reprint 27. Pho-
              tography by Lennart Nilsson (Life Educational Reprints. Media
              International, Canaan, NH,03741).

DYCK, Arthur J.
    1972   "Is Abortion Necessary to Solve Population Problems," in Hilgers
              and Horan (1972), pp. 159–76.

ENGELHARDT, H. Tristan, Jr.
    1974   "The Ontology of Abortion," in *Ethics* Vol. 84 (Fall), pp. 217–34.
              Reprinted in *Moral Problems in Medicine,* Samuel Gorovitz et. al.
              (eds.), Englewood Cliffs, NJ: Prentice-Hall, 1976, pp.318–34.
              References are to Gorovitz.

ENGLISH, Jane
   1975   "Abortion and the Concept of a Person," in *Canadian Journal of
           Philosophy*, Vol.5, no. 2 (October). Reprinted in Feinberg (1984),
           pp. 151–60. References are to Feinberg.

ERVIN, Paula
   1985   *Women Exploited: The Other Victims of Abortion.* Huntington, IN:
           Our Sunday Visitor.

FEINBERG, Joel
   1973   *The Problem of Abortion.* 1st ed. Belmont, CA: Wadsworth Pub.
           Co.
   1984   *The Problem of Abortion.* 2nd ed. Belmont, CA: Wadsworth Pub.
           Co.

FINNIS, John
   1973   "The Rights and Wrongs of Abortion," in *Philosophy and Public
           Affairs*, Vol. 2, no.2 (Winter). Reprinted in Cohen (1974), pp.
           85–113. References are to Cohen.

FLANAGAN, Geraldine Lux
   1965   *The First Nine Months of Life.* New York: Simon and Schuster.

FLETCHER, Joseph
   1966   *Situation Ethics: The New Morality.* Philadelphia: Westminster
           Press.
   1979   *Humanhood: Essays in Biomedical Ethics.* Buffalo: Prometheus
           Books.

FOOT, Philippa
   1967   "The Problem of Abortion and the Doctrine of Double Effect," in
           The Oxford Review, no.5. Reprinted in *Moral Problems: A
           Collection of Philosophical Essays*, James Rachels (ed.). New
           York: Harper and Row, 1971, pp. 29–41. References are to
           Rachels.

GALLAGHER, John
   1985   *Is the Human Embryo a Person?: A Philosophical Investigation.*
           Toronto: Human Life Research Institute of Ottawa.

GARTON, Jean Staker
   1979   *Who Broke the Baby?* Minneapolis: Bethany Fellowship.

GILLESPIE, Norman C.
   1977   "Abortion and Human Rights," in *Ethics*, Vol. 87, no.3 (April).
           Reprinted in Feinberg (1984), pp. 94–101. References are to
           Feinberg.

GLOVER, Jonathan
    1977   *Causing Death and Saving Lives.* Harmondsworth, England
           and New York: Penguin Books.

GRAY, Nellie J.
    1989   "Abortion is Homicide," in *March for Life Program Journal,* pp.
           39–48.

GRISEZ, Germain
    1972   *Abortion: the Myths, the Realities, and the Arguments.* New York:
           World Publishing Co., Corpus Books.

HARDIN, Garrett
    1974   *Mandatory Motherhood, The True Meaning of "Right to Life."*
           Boston: Beacon Press.

HEFFERNAN, Bart T., M.D.
    1972   "The Early Biography of Everyman," in Hilgers and Horan
           (1972), pp. 3–25.

HENSLEY, Jeff Lane (ed.)
    1983   *The Zero People: Essays on Life.* Ann Arbor, MI: Servant Books.

HILDEBRAND, Dietrich von
    1950   *Fundamental Moral Attitudes.* New York, London, Toronto:
           Longmans Green.
    1953   *Ethics.* Chicago: Franciscan Herald Press.

HILDEBRAND and HILDEBRAND
    1967   Dietrich and Alice von Hildebrand *The Art of Living.* Chicago:
           Henry Regnery. Includes Hildebrand (1950).

HILGERS, Thomas W., M.D.
    1972   "The Medical Hazards of Legally Induced Abortion," in Hilgers
           and Horan (1972), pp. 57–85.

HILGERS and HORAN (eds.)
    1972   Thomas W. Hilgers, M.D., and Dennis J. Horan, Esq., (eds.)
           Abortion and Social Justice. New York: Sheed and Ward.

HILGERS, HORAN and MALL (eds.)
    1981   Thomas W. Hilgers, M.D., Dennis J. Horan and David Mall
           (eds.), *New Perspectives on Human Abortion.* Frederick, MD:
           University Publications of America, Aletheia Books.

HILGERS, MECKLENBURG and RIORDAN
    1972   Thomas W. Hilgers, M.D., Marjory Mecklenburg, and Gayle Ri-

ordan, "Is Abortion the Best We Have to Offer?" in Hilgers and Horan (1972) pp. 177–97.

HILGERS and O'HARE
1981   Thomas W. Hilgers, M.D., and Dennis O'Hare, "Abortion Related Maternal Mortality: An In-Depth Analysis," in Hilgers, Horan and Mall (1981), pp. 69–91.

HORAN, GRANT and CUNNINGHAM (eds.)
1987   Dennis J. Horan, Edward R. Grant, and Paige C. Cunningham (eds), *Abortion and the Constitution.* Washington, DC: Georgetown University Press.

JOYCE, Robert E.
1981   "When Does a Person Begin?" in Hilgers, Horan and Mall, (1981), pp. 345–56. An adaptation of an article in *The New Scholasticism* 52, no. 1 (Winter 1978), "Personhood and the Conception Event."

JOYCE and ROSERA
1970   Robert E. Joyce and Mary Rosera, *Let Us Be Born: The Inhumanity of Abortion.* Chicago: Franciscan Herald Press.

KALER, Patrick, C.S.S.R.
1984a   "Does the Aborted Baby Feel Pain?" in *Liguorian* (November), pp. 18–22.
1984b   *The Silent Screams: Abortion and Fetal Pain.* Pamphlet. Liguori, MO: Liguori Publications.

KASUN, Jacqueline
1977   "The Population Bomb Threat: A Look at the Facts," in Hensley (1983), pp. 33–41.
1988   *The War Against Population: The Economics and Ideology of Population Control.* San Francisco: Ignatius Press.

KLUGE, Eike-Henner W.
1975   *The Practice of Death.* New Haven, CT and London: Yale University Press.

KOOP, C. Everett, M.D.
1980   "Deception on Demand," in *Moody Monthly,* Vol. 80, no. 9 (May), pp. 24–32.

LADD, John
1979   *Ethical Issues Relating to Life and Death.* New York and Oxford: Oxford University Press.

LADER, Lawrence
 1966 *Abortion.* Boston: Beacon Press.

LENOSKI, Edward F., M.D.
 1981 *The Plight of the Children.* Toronto: Life Cycle Books.

LIEBMAN and ZIMMER
 1979 Monte Harris Liebman, M.D. and Jolie Siebold Zimmer, "The Psychological Sequelae of Abortion: Fact and Fallacy," in Mall and Watts (1979), pp. 127–38.

LILEY, Albert W., Ph.D. (also, Sir A. William Liley, M.D.)
 1972 "The Foetus in Control of His Environment," in Hilgers and Horan (1972), pp. 27–36.
 1981 "A Day in the Life of the Fetus," in Hilgers, Horan and Mall (1981), pp. 29–35.

LOMANSKY, Loren E.
 1982 "Being a Person—Does it Matter?" *Philosophical Topics,* Vol. 12, no.3. Reprinted in Feinberg (1984), pp. 161–72. References are to the latter.

MAHKORN, Sandra K.
 1979 "Pregnancy and Sexual Assault," in Mall and Watts (1979), pp.53–72.

MAHKORN and DOLAN
 1981 Sandra Kathleen Mahkorn and William V. Dolan, M.D., "Sexual Assault and Pregnancy," in Hilgers, Horan and Mall (1981) pp.182–98.

MALL and WATTS (eds.)
 1979 David Mall and Walter F. Watts, M.D. (eds.), *The Psychological Aspects of Abortion.* Washington, DC: University Publications of America.

MALOOF, George E., M.D.
 1979 "The Consequences of Incest: Giving and Taking Life," in Mall and Watts (1979), pp. 73–110.

MANNEY and BLATTNER
 1984 James Manney and John C. Blattner, *Death in the Nursery: The Secret Crime of Infanticide.* Ann Arbor, MI: Servant Books.

MARQUIS, Don
 1989 "Why Abortion is Immoral," in *The Journal of Philosophy* Vol. 86, no. 4, pp. 183–202.

MD GROUP
    1984   "MD Group Claims that Fetuses Suffer Pain," in *American
            Medical News* (pub. by The American Medical Association), Feb.
            24, p. 18. References are to a reprint. Abbreviated "MD Group."

MECKLENBURG, Fred E., M.D.
    1972   "The Indications for Induced Abortion," in Hilgers and Horan
            (1972), pp. 37–56

MONTAGU, Ashley
    1965   *Life Before Birth.* New York: The New American Library of World
            Literature. Signet Books.

MOORE, Keith L.
    1988   *The Developing Human: Clinically Oriented Embryology.* 4th ed.
            Philadelphia: W. B. Saunders, Harcourt Brace Jovanovich.

NATHANSON, Bernard N., M.D.
    1983   *The Abortion Papers: Inside the Abortion Mentality.* New York:
            Frederick Fell.

NATHANSON and OSTLING
    1979   Bernard N., M.D. and Richard N. Ostling, *Aborting America.*
            Garden City, NY: Doubleday. Reprinted, Toronto: Life Cycle
            Books.

NEUHAUS, Richard John
    1983   "A New Birth of Freedom," in Hensley (1983), pp. 283–94.

NEY, Philip G., M.D.
    1979   "Infant Abortion and Child Abuse: Cause and Effect," in Mall
            and Watts (1979), pp. 25–38.
    1983   "A Consideration of Abortion Survivors," in Hensley (1983), pp.
            123–38. Reprinted from *Child Psychiatry and Human Develop-
            ment* (n.d.).

NOONAN John T., Jr.
    1979   *A Private Choice: Abortion in America in the Seventies.* New York:
            The Free Press. London: Collier Macmillan. Reprinted, Toronto:
            Life Cycle Books.
    1981   "The Experience of Pain by the Unborn," in Hilgers, Horan and
            Mall (1981), pp. 205–16. Another version, with the same title,
            appears in Hensley (1983), pp. 141–56.
    1983   "Raw Judicial Power," in Hensley (1983), pp. 15–26. First pub.
            in *National Review.*

PARTHUN, et. al.
    1987   Mary Parthun, Anne Kiss, Heather S. Morris, and Lorraine Williams, *Abortion's Aftermath.* Toronto: Human Life Research Institute.

PATTEN, Bradley M.
    1968   *Human Embryology.* 3d ed. New York: McGraw Hill.

THE POSITION OF MODERN SCIENCE ON THE BEGINNING OF HUMAN LIFE
    1975   No author given. Pub. by Scientists for Life, Inc., Fredericksburg, VA.

POWELL, John, S.J.
    1981   *Abortion: The Silent Holocaust.* Allen, Texas: Argus Communications.
    1983   "The Silent Holocaust," in Hensley (1983), pp. 3–11.

QUAY, Effie A.
    1980   *And Now Infanticide.* 2nd ed. Thaxton, VA: Sun Life.

REARDON, David C.
    1987   *Aborted Women: Silent No More.* Chicago: Loyola University Press.

RICE, Charles E.
    1969   *The Vanishing Right to Life: An Appeal for a Renewed Reverence for Life.* Garden City, NY: Doubleday.
    1979   *Beyond Abortion: The Theory and Practice of the Secular State.* Chicago: Franciscan Herald Press.

ROSS, Steven L.
    1982   "Abortion and the Death of the Fetus," in *Philosophy and Public Affairs,* Vol. 11, no. 3 (Summer). Reprinted in *Moral Issues,* Jan Narveson (ed.) Toronto and New York: Oxford University Press, 1983. Reference is to the latter.

RUE, Vincent
    1983   "The Abortion Decision: A Crisis to be Shared," in Andrusco (1983a), pp. 247–55.
    1986   "Forgotten Fathers: Men and Abortion," Brochure, similar to Rue (1983). Toronto: Life Cycle Books.

RUSHDOONY, Rousas J.
    1975   *The Myth of Over-Population.* Fairfax, VA: Thoburn Press.

SALTENBERGER, Ann
    1983   *Every Woman Has a Right to Know the Dangers of Legal Abortion.* Glassboro, NJ: Air-Plus Enterprises.

SAXTON, Marsha
    1987   "Pre-Natal Screening and Discriminatory Attitudes about Disability," in *Genewatch*, Jan–Feb. 1987, pp. 8–11.

SCHAEFFER, Franky
    1982   *A Time for Anger: The Myth of Neutrality.* Westchester, IL: Crossway Books.

SCHEIDLER, Joseph M.
    1985   *Closed: 99 Ways to Stop Abortion.* Westchester IL: Crossway Books

SCHWARZ, Balduin
    1975   "Ideological Sources of the Loss of the Respect for Life," in *Persona y Derecho*, Vol II, pp. 103–10.
    1984a   "Von der Würde des Menschen," in *Theologisches*, no. 166 (February), pp. 5629–38.
    1984b   "Die Würde des Menschen als Rechstgut," in *Rechtstheorie*, Beiheft 6, pp. 19–26.

SHETTLES, RUGH and EINHORN
    1971   Roberts Rugh, Ph.D., Landrum B.Shettles, Ph.D., M.D., and Richard N. Einhorn, *From Conception to Birth: The Drama of Life's Beginnings.* New York: Harper and Row.

SIMON, Julian L.
    1981   *The Ultimate Resource._*Princeton, NJ: Princeton University Press.

SINGER, Peter
    1979a   *Practical Ethics.* Cambridge, England: Cambridge University Press.
    1979b   "Unsanctifying Life," in Ladd (1979), pp. 41–61.

SPECKHARD, Anne
    1987   *The Psycho-Social Aspects of Stress Following Abortion.* Kansas City, MO: Sheed and Ward.

SUMNER, L. W.
    1981   *Abortion and Moral Theory.* Princeton, NJ: Princeton University Press.
    1984   "A Third Way," in Feinberg (1984), pp. 71–93. A revised version of chap. 4, pp. 124–60, of Sumner (1981).

SUNDBERG, et. al.
   1965   Axel Sundberg-Ingelman and Cloes Wirsen, with photographs by
           Lennart Nilsson, *A Child is Born.* New York: Delacorte Press.

THOMSON, Judith Jarvis
   1971   "A Defense of Abortion," in *Philosophy and Public Affairs,* Vol. 1,
           no. 1 (Fall). Reprinted in Cohen (1974), pp. 3–22, Feinberg
           (1973), (1984), and Wasserstrom (1979). References are to
           Cohen.

TOOLEY, Michael
   1972   "Abortion and Infanticide," in *Philosophy and Public Affairs,*
           Vol.2, no. 1 (Fall). Reprinted in Cohen (1974), pp. 52–84.
           References are to Cohen.
   1973   "A Defense of Abortion and Infanticide," in Feinberg (1973), pp.
           51–91.
   1979   "Decisions to Terminate Life and the Concept of a Person," in
           Ladd (1979), pp. 62–93.
   1983   *Abortion and Infanticide.* Oxford: Clarendon Press.
   1984   "In Defense of Abortion and Infanticide," in Feinberg (1984), pp.
           120–34.

VAN DE VEER, Donald
   1984   "Justifying 'Wholesale Slaughter'," in Feinberg (1984), pp.
           65–70. Excerpted from an article with the same title, *Canadian
           Journal of Philosophy,* Vol. 5, no. 2 (October, 1975).

WALDSTEIN, Wolfgang
   1982   *Das Menschenrecht zum Leben.* Berlin: Duncker and Humblot.

WALLING, Regis
   1987   *How Abortion Affects Men: They Cry Alone.* Pamphlet. Liguori,
           MO: Liguori Publications.

WARDLE, Lynn D.
   1983   "Restricting Abortion Through Legislation," in Andrusco (1983a),
           pp. 101–117.

WARREN, Mary Ann
   1973   "On the Moral and Legal Status of Abortion," in *The Monist,* Vol.
           57, no. 1 (January). Reprinted in Wasserstrom (1979), pp.
           35–51; "Postscript on Infanticide" was added especially for this
           volume. Also reprinted in Feinberg (1984). References are to
           Wasserstrom.

WASSERSTROM, Richard A. (ed.)
1979   *Today's Moral Problems.* 2nd ed. New York: Macmillan, London: Collier Macmillan.

WEBER, James A.
1977   *Grow or Die!* New Rochelle, NY: Arlington House.

WEISBORD, Robert G.
1982   "Legalized Abortion and the Holocaust: an Insulting Parallel," *The Jewish Veteran*, January–February–March 1982, pp. 12–13.

WERNER, Richard
1979   "Abortion: the Ontological and Moral Status of the Unborn," in Wasserstrom (1979), pp. 51–74. Revised, from the article in *Social Theory and Practice*, Vol. 3, no. 4, 1974.

WERTHEIMER, Roger
1971   "Understanding the Abortion Argument," in *Philosophy and Public Affairs.* Vol. 1, no. 1 (Fall). Reprinted in Cohen (1974), Feinberg (1973), (1984). References are to Cohen.

WHITEHEAD, K. D.
1972   *Respectable Killing: the New Abortion Imperative.* New Rochelle, NY: Catholics United for Faith.

WILLIAMSON, Laila
1978   "Infanticide: An Anthropological Analysis," in *Infanticide and the Value of Life*, Marvin Kohl (ed.). Buffalo: Prometheus Books, 1978, pp.61–75. Original source: G. W. Steller, *Beschreibung von dem Lande Kamtschatka* (1774), as quoted in George Devereux, *A Study of Abortion in Primitive Societies* (New York: Julian Press, 1955, p. 252.).

WILLKE, J. C., M.D.
1984   *Abortion and Slavery: History Repeats.* Cincinnati: Hayes Pub. Co.

WILLKE and WILLKE
1979   J. C. Willke, M.D., and Mrs. J. C. Willke, *Handbook on Abortion.* Cincinnati: Hayes Pub. Co.
1985   J. C. Willke, M.D., and Mrs. J. C. Willke, *Abortion: Questions and Answers.* Cincinnati: Hayes Pub. Co.

YOUNG, Curt
1983   *The Least of These: What Everyone Should Know about Abortion.* Chicago: Moody Press.

Notes

1. Only the basic organs are present; they are not yet developed as they will be in the future. I am indebted to Dr. Roy Heyne for his many helpful suggestions on medical and scientific matters in this chapter and chapters 2, 3, and 6.

2. *Amicus Curiae*, pp. 8-25. See Heffernan (1972) for a similar, partly equivalent statement. Other descriptions of the developing child in the womb include Blechschmidt (1961), (1977), (1981); Moore (1988); Patten (1968); Shettles and Rugh (1971); Flanagan (1965); Nathanson (1979), pp. 197-205, esp., 202-203; Willke (1979), pp. 5-27, (1985), pp. 5-6, 33-35; Young (1983), pp. 74-80; Bergel (1985), pp. I-2 to I-13; *Drama of Life Before Birth*. See also Albert W. Liley, "The Foetus in Control of his Environment" (1972) which shows the fetus as an active dynamic being; and "A Day in the Life of a Fetus" (1981).

   (In the quotation from *Amicus Curiae*, and in all subsequent quotations containing footnotes, these references have been omitted.)

3. Particularly fascinating is the fact that in a baby girl, "by the day 46 . . . the 600,000 potential ova of a lifetime already exist in" her. She is just starting her own life, and is already being prepared for eventual (possible) motherhood! Nathanson (1979), p. 202.

4. *Amicus Curiae*, p. 21.

5. Nathanson (1983), p. 150. He also discusses fetal surgery which is already occurring and soon will be commonplace. The child in the womb is treated as a patient, a distinct being in his own right, with his own ailments. p. 143, passim. See also *Amicus Curiae*, "The Doctor Treats the Unborn Just as He Does Any Patient." (pp. 26-32).

6. More precisely, "I who now *validly* remember . . . " Invalid memory experiences, in which I seem to remember having an experience that I actually never had, are an exception to the general rule, that we now have a memory experience of something because we really did experience it in the past. The existence of some invalid memory experiences does not destroy the usefulness of the general rule for bringing out the meaning of personal identity, since (a) the vast majority of cases, valid memory, fit directly under it; and (b) even the invalid cases fit in terms of what is meant by the memory claim. That is, when I say "I remember . . . ," what I mean is that I, the same person, had a certain experience in the past. The meaning of personal identity implied in this memory claim remains intact even if, in a particular case, what I seem to remember didn't actually happen.

7. The idea that a human "embryo" or "fetus" is not a child but merely something that develops into a child is widespread among abortion advocates. See, for example, Hardin (1974): "The question...is whether an embryo . . . *should* be given the right to live and develop into a child, . . ." (p. 17; see also p. 75). Also Lader (1966), " . . . whether or not a fetus shall become a child affects the population charts." (p. 2).

8. Donald Van De Veer's article (1984) is typical of this misunderstanding of the Continuum Argument. He assumes (A) that the anti-abortion position is based on the idea that one "can't find a clear cut-off point"; and (B) that pointing out the fallacy of insisting on such "clear cut-off points" is sufficient to discredit the anti-abortion position. "The Conservative [anti-abortion person] is restrictive; he permits attention only to consecutive stages." (p. 69). Van De Veer is mistaken on both points, A and B.

9. Nathanson affirms the continuum of human life when he says: "It is a continuous spectrum that begins in utero and ends at death—the bans of the spectrum are designated by words such as fetus, infant, child, adolescent, and adult." *New England Journal of Medicine*, "Sounding Board" Section, Nov. 28, 1974. Reprinted in his *Aborting America* (1979), p. 165. Also, (1983), p. 137.

10. See Grisez, "Abortion and Prejudice against the Unborn" (1972), pp. 467-70 (epilogue of his book). He lists six aspects of prejudice, each of them applicable to the attitude of defenders of abortion toward the preborn, victims of the prejudice. For example, taking advantage of a difference between oneself, or one's own group, and the class of victims of prejudice.

11. *Amicus Curiae*, p. 15. See also Liley (1972).

NOTES TO CHAPTER 2

1. *Life or Death.* Brochure depicting the results of abortion (Hiltz Pub. Co.: Cincinnati, 1972). Description under picture and caption, "D & C abortion at 12 weeks." Essentially the same description appears in the 1981 edition, which also describes D & E abortions.

2. Based on Bergel (1985), p. II-4.

3. "Babies who survive abortion challenge limits of law, ethics." *The Providence Sunday Journal,* Feb. 19, 1984, p. A-15.

4. Bergel (1980, 1985), p. II-4.

5. *Life or Death* (1972,1981). Description under picture and caption, "Salt Poisoning Abortion at 19 Weeks."

6. Saltenberger (1983), p. 33.

7. Bergel (1980), p. II-4. A similar description is in the 1985 edition.

8. Bergel (1980, 1985), p. II-4.

9. Ross (1982), p. 243.

10. Data for this table are taken mostly from *Amicus Curiae*, pp. 8-21. Data for weeks 9 and 10 are also from Flanagan (1965), pp. 80-81. Data for week 4.5 is from a brochure, *Life? When did your life begin?* (Value of Life Committee, Inc.: Brighton, MA). Data assembled by physician members of this committee, using a number of standard scientific texts, including Shettles and Rugh (1971). Some items appear in more than one place.

11. The moral equivalence of abortion and infanticide applies also in the reverse direction: if abortion is accepted, infanticide follows (logically and historically). See: Brennan (1983), pp. 81-90; Delahoyde (1984); Manney and Blattner (1984), pp. 115-29. ("If you could kill someone five days before he was born, why not five days after?") Quay, (1980); Willke (1985), pp. 203-215 ("Abortion Leads to Infanticide like Night Follows Day . . . Same Patient / Same Problem / Same Solution.") Willke (1979), pp. 111-23. Among those who defend abortion, Fletcher says, "It is reasonable, indeed, to describe infanticide as post-natal abortion." Quoted in Brennan (1983), p. 82. A similar position is that of Tooley: "In Defense of Abortion and Infanticide" (1984); I will carefully examine this position in chapter 7.

12. Williamson (1978), p. 62

13. It is sometimes thought that an evil motive is essential for murder. Thus, Bajema (1974) lists "Four Ingredients of Murder." They are: "(1) A person is killed. (2) He is killed intentionally. (3) The person killed is innocent. (4) There is unlawful or sinful motive involved in the killing." That (4) is not essential will become clear in what follows. See also note 14.

14. For a similar analysis, including a similar example, see Devine (1978), p. 15. It should also be noted that Bajema's "sinful motive" (see note 13) refers to what is true of *persons* rather than of *actions* in *themselves*, and is therefore out of place here, where the question is whether abortion as an action is murder. Bajema holds that abortion is murder, except for what he calls "critical abortion," abortion to save the life of the woman (pp. 47-48).

15. Or similar phrases. See, e.g., Reardon (1987), pp. xvii, 184, 280, and 304.

16. *Ibid.*, pp. 181, 277, 304, 309.

17. He will "never know the difference" as far as *this life* is concerned; and if death is annihilation, he will simply "never know the difference," as he will simply "not be." But if there is a life after death, he may well come to realize that he was killed and thereby deprived of what would have been the rest of his life. It will then not be true that if he is killed "in his sleep," he will "never know the difference." This point applies equally to a born person killed in his sleep and to a pre-born child

killed in the womb. Or, perhaps it applies with greater devastation to the pre-born child: he would realize that he was deprived of his *entire life* after birth! This is one more reason for not making the assumption that "he will never know the difference."

18. The reprint has that title and is published by National Right to Life Educational Trust Fund, Washington, D.C. The original article is by Liz Jeffries and Rick Edmonds, and appeared in the *Inquirer*, August 2, 1981. It is reprinted in Schaeffer (1982), pp. 155-87.

19. *Ibid.*, front page, before beginning of the article.

20. *Ibid.*, p. 2 (second page; no pagination in the reprint).

21. *Ibid.*, p. 3b (Schaeffer, p. 163).

22. *Ibid.*, p. 1d (Schaeffer, p. 159).

23. *Ibid.* (Schaeffer, p. 160).

24. *Ibid.*, p. 3a-b (Schaeffer, p. 163).

25. *Ibid.*, p. 6b (Schaeffer, p. 176).

26. *Ibid.*, p. 4c, bottom (Schaeffer, p. 183).

27. *Ibid.*, pp. 4a and 7c-d (Schaeffer, p. 180).

28. Besides deliberately killing the child by active means and letting her die through neglect, there is also deliberately doing nothing so that she dies, intentionally letting her die. Morally, this is like the first, behaviorly, it resembles the second.

NOTES TO CHAPTER 3

1. Kaler (1984a), p. 21; (1984b), p. 15.

2. Collins (1984), p. 8.

3. Young (1983), p. 89.

4. "M.D. Group Claims that Fetuses Suffer Pain" (1984), 4th column.
    Hereafter, "M.D. Group."

5. Collins (1984), p. 9.

6. Kaler (1984a), p. 22; (1984b), p. 17.

7. See Collins (1984), p. 5.

8. *Ibid.*

9. *Ibid.*, p.6.

10. *Ibid.*

11. *Ibid.*, p. 7.

12. *Amicus Curiae*, p. 23 Italics in original.

13. Collins, p. 7.

14. *Amicus Curiae*, pp. 15 and 17.

15. Collins, p. 7.

16. "M.D. Group," 3rd and 4th columns.

17. Collins, p. 7.

18. Noonan (1981), p. 211; in Hensley (1983), p. 149.

19. Kaler (1984a), p. 22; a similar passage, (1984b), p. 22.

NOTES TO CHAPTER 4

1. Proposals and defenses of birth as the critical point include Cisler in
    "Unfinished Business: Birth Control and Women's Liberation," in
    Robin Morgan (ed.), *Sisterhood is Powerful* (New York: Random
    House, 1970), p. 274. Quoted in Sumner (1981), p. 51; Hardin (1974)
    p. 100; Lader (1966), p. 168; and Lomansky (1982), p. 172. Rejections
    and refutations include Devine (1978), pp. 87-88; Glover (1977),

pp. 125-26 and 159, last lines; Nathanson (1979), pp. 210-11 (see below, p. 44); Singer (1979a) p. 108; Sumner (1981), pp. 52-53; Tooley (1973), pp. 74-75; and Werner (1979) p. 55. The last four (as well as Glover) all defend abortion: Sumner and Werner "draw the line" at sentience, Singer and Tooley after birth.

2. Nathanson (1983), p. 132. He states:

> [In] fetoscopy . . . an exquisitely fine optical instrument is inserted into the uterus through the mother's abdomen, and the child can be viewed directly . . . The instrument itself is about a foot long, and is about one-twelfth of an inch in diameter. There is a light at the far end and an eyepiece at the observer's end . . . Sometimes the light is so strong that the child flinches when the light is switched on (p. 132).

> With fetoscopy . . . the skin can be observed, and skin diseases have been diagnosed in utero . . . We can thread a fine needle which we can insert into a blood vessel of the unborn child and actually carry out blood tests on it, even as we can in adult patients. Thus, we can diagnose hemophilia, clotting disorders, sickle cell disease, anemia, and a host of other blood disorders. We can also thread through the length of the instrument a biopsy forcep, an instrument which can take a piece of tissue for analysis. In this way, we have been able to actually take a biopsy of the liver of the unborn child and study that organ with its enzymes and complicated chemistry (p. 133).

> Another technology which has allowed us to perceive the unborn child directly is hysteroscopy. A hysteroscope is a long slender optical instrument, similar to the fetoscope, . . . with a light at the far end and an optical eyepiece at the observer's end. . . . This instrument is pushed up through the cervix in *early* pregnancy at four, five, or six weeks. Peering through the eyepiece with the light on at the opposite end, one can see the six week old infant clearly. We can even study the face, . . . in fact, the entire young child . . . One can see the eyes, count the fingers and toes, and even see the blood vessels of the child through its incredibly fine, translucent skin! (pp. 134-35).

See also Andrusco (1983a), Part IV.

3. Nathanson (1979), pp. 210-11.

4. Rejections and refutations of viability as the critical point include Blumenfeld (1975), p. 150; Devine (1978), pp. 86-87; Glover (1977), p. 124-25; Kluge (1975), pp. 30-32; Nathanson (1979) pp. 211-13,

and (1983), p. 148; Noonan (1983), p. 23; Singer (1979a), pp. 108-110; Tooley (1973), p. 74; and Werner (1979), p. 55. In the literature on abortion that I have studied, I cannot recall a single instance where viability was proposed or defended. The closest thing that comes to mind is the U. S. Supreme Court decision, *Roe v. Wade* (Jan. 22, 1973), in which the Court said: "With respect to the State's important and legitimate interest in potential life, the 'compelling' point is at viability." [Quoted in Feinberg (1973), p. 186 and (1984), p. 196.] It did not assert that a person exists after viability. It went on to say that "if the State is interested in protecting fetal life after viability, it may go so far as to proscribe abortion during that period except when it is necessary to preserve the life or health of the mother" (Ibid.). After viability, there is "fetal life," not a "person," according to the Court. What line viability is supposed to mark remains unclear. The "fetus" is a person neither before nor after, according to the Court. If the "fetus" is not an actual human person before viability, as the Court maintains, it is surely a potential human person then, for "it" obviously develops into an actual human person. If "it" is a potential person both before and after viability, and an actual person neither before nor after, what significant point is viability supposed to represent? On what logical basis does a change in regard to "State's compelling interest" rest? See Singer (1979a), pp. 108-109 for another criticism of *Roe v. Wade* on this point.

Though hardly defended in the literature, viability plays a great role in popular thinking. For those who defend abortion, probably the two most commonly assumed lines are birth and viability. Hence, the need for an extensive refutation here.

5. *Amicus Curiae*, p. 11.

6. *Aborting America*, p. 208. He points out that "all discussion of viability and survival rates must be based upon weight in grams, not weeks."

7. *Ibid.*, p. 213. See also Singer (1979a), p. 109.

8. Blumenfeld (1975), p. 150.

9. Devine (1978), p. 86.

10. *Amicus Curiae*, p. 19. Other refutations of quickening include Singer (1979a), pp. 108-110 and Kluge (1975), pp. 27-28.

11. Werner (1979), Section III, p. 63.

12. *Ibid.*, p. 64, quoting W. K. Frankene, *Ethics*, 2nd ed. (Englewood Cliffs, N.J.: Prentice Hall, 1973), pp. 44-45.

13. Werner, p. 64. Another defense of sentience is Sumner (1981), Chapter 4 and (1984).

14. Sentience marks a very significant line in terms of a person's ability to think, decide, communicate, etc.; what I have called *functioning* as a person—in contrast to *being* a person, which is the all-important category for the question of abortion, and our theme here. The distinction is explained and developed in chapter 7.

15. Drawing the line at the emergence of human form is also rejected by Kluge (1975), pp. 32-33 and Tooley (1973), p. 77.

16. Brody (1976), pp. 108-109.

17. *Ibid.*, p. 83.

18. *Ibid.*

19. *Ibid.*

20. *Ibid.*

21. Whether the loss of certain brain waves really does imply death, and, if so, under what conditions, is a complex and disputed question, which I shall not enter upon here. If such loss does not imply death, or not in all cases, this is further evidence for the invalidity of Brody's argument, further proof of the falseness of his conclusion. If I assume the (possible) truth of the theory that loss of brain waves implies death, it is only to give Brody's argument every possible benefit of the doubt.

    See Paul A. Byrne, M.D., Sean O'Reilly, M.D., Paul M. Quay, S.J., and Peter W. Salsich, Jr., "Brain Death: The Patient, the Physician, and Society" in *Gonzaga Law Review*, Vol. 18, no. 3 (1982/83), pp. 429-516. Also, Paul A. Byrne, M.D. and Paul M. Quay, S.J., Ph.D. *On Understanding "Brain Death."* (Omaha: Nebraska Coalition for Life Educational Trust Fund, n.d.). "Cessation of total brain function, whether irreversible or not, is not necessarily linked to total destruction of the brain or to the death of the person." (*Ibid.*, p.5. This is from a quotation from, or a reference to, the *Journal of the American Medical Association.* JAMA 242: 1985-1990, 1979)

22. Cf. Devine (1978), p. 85.

23. A full development of this point will be presented in chapter 7.

24. Joyce (1970), p. 15. Italics in original.

25. Nathanson (1979), p. 216. I am not sure whether Nathanson still holds this position.

26. *Amicus Curiae*, pp. 13-14.

27. Joyce (1970), p. 15. See also the section on "The Problem of Twinning," pp. 31-33.

28. That is, it would be a radical break if (and only if) the frog ceased to exist and was replaced by the prince, one being really transformed into another; the other actually coming into existence at that moment. (This is precisely what happens at conception-fertilization, the "frog" corresponding to "sperm and ovum," the "prince" to the newly conceived child, in the zygote phase of her existence, as will be shown in Chapter 6.) If, on the other hand, the frog and the prince are supposed to be the same being; that is, one being assuming different forms (a prince disguised as a frog), then the frog-prince story cannot be used as it is above. In using it, I am assuming the first (transformation) interpretation.

NOTES TO CHAPTER 5

1. The Agnostic Position is adopted, or assumed, mainly in popular discussions of the moral question of abortion, and the question of what should be its legal status. It is rarely adopted or defended in the literature on the subject. An instance of this position, or something similar to it, can be found in Wertheimer's article (1971), though I am not sure that it is his final position. See pp. 44-45. Rejection of the Agnostic Position is implicit in most of the literature on the morality of abortion. Most writers are concerned with the question of "the

status of the fetus," whether "it" is a "person," or "it's humanity." They advance and try to defend theses that they claim to know; hence, a rejection of the view that "no one knows when human life begins." Most theories advanced in the literature are precisely theories as to when "human life," in the morally relevant sense, begins; when the claims of the "fetus" become serious claims or rights that must be respected; or when "it acquires moral standing." (Judith Jarvis Thomson's article, to be discussed in chapter 8, is a notable exception.)

An explicit rejection of the Agnostic Position is found in Sumner (1981), pp. 73-81, esp. pp. 78-79. For example: "Why should the moral status of the fetus be less decidable than other moral questions?"

2. Foot (1967), p. 29. Similar sentiments are expressed by Sumner (1984), p. 73; and Gillespie (1977), p. 96, in which he quotes a part of the passage from Foot.

3. Devine (1978), p. 77. (See note 4.)

4. *Ibid.* Devine rejects the Gradualist Position; the quotations are from his presentation of it (pp. 77-82). It is a position which is often assumed or advocated by defenders of abortion in popular discussions. In the literature on the subject, different versions have been proposed and defended; they include Gillespie (1977); Sumner (1981); Sumner (1984); Callahan (1970); and Kluge (1975).

5. For a similar refutation see Gallagher (1985), p.21. The absolute impossibility of a gradual process in the *being* of a person is clearly and convincingly shown by John Crosby in his excellent article (1976).

> If we reflect on the kind of being which we call human being, we will find that it admits of no degrees, of no more or less. It makes no sense to speak of one man as being more a human being than another. It is not just that this does not work linguistically, but rather the impossibility to say the thing, reflects an impossibility in the thing itself (p. 219).

> A child whose spiritual and rational powers are just beginning to develop certainly has many potentialities which are yet to be developed; but its very being as a human being is not one of these

> potentialities; that being is not actualized out of a state of potency as the child grows up. And so it is that man as this kind of being either exists entirely, or does not exist at all; there is only this alternative, and there is no sliding scale of degrees of being human (p. 220).

Also, I am always *myself,* the same person:

> If we just think of our speaking in the present of what I did or thought earlier, we see that an identity of my present self with my self at that earlier time is implied. There is a self-identitical self present in all the experiences of a given person, a self enabling him to call these experiences *his own;* if this self were to change and develop as other dimensions of a person do, then this self-identity would be unintelligible (p. 222).

6.   See Gillespie (1977), p. 96, and Sumner (1984), p. 83.

7.   For readers unfamiliar with the logic of the *Reductio ad Absurdum* argument, I offer the following. Whatever implies an absurdity, or a falsehood, must itself be false. For example, "If we get home by sundown, we will have traveled at 100 miles per hour." Since (in this instance) "we get home by sundown" implies an absurdity, it must be false.

8.   Devine (1978), p. 79.

9.   The thesis that a child is not a person until some time after birth has been advanced by some philosophers; for example, Michael Tooley, who holds, in his book [(1983), p. 411], that personhood is not reached until about three months after birth. I shall consider Tooley's theory in chapter 7.

NOTES TO CHAPTER 6

1.   *Drama of Life Before Birth* (1965), p. 5.

2.   Patten (1968), p. 43a. Emphasis added, except for "*fertilization.*"

3.   "*Problems of Fertilization,*" quoted in Patten (1968), p. 41b.

4.   Flanagan (1965), p. 19.

5. Blechschmidt (1981), p. 7. This is in the context of his critical discussion of the thesis of Ernst Haeckel (1866), that "in the course of its individual development," a human being repeats "the entire process of phylogenetic history in abbreviated form." That is, that "the human conceptus passes first . . . through nonspecific (nonhuman) early stages and only thereafter, at about the beginning of the third month, shows characteristically human differentiations." (*Ibid.*, p. 6). Remnants of this thesis linger on, in the idea that humans pass through certain animal-like phases (e.g., a fish-like phase because of gill-like organs). Through the techniques of modern science, Blechschmidt tells us, this thesis has been refuted. "Ontogenesis [the development of an individual] is a homogeneous, continuous process in which there are no breaks." (*Ibid.*, p. 7)

6. Montagu (1965), pp. vii and 12.

7. Joyce (1981), p. 350.

8. Joyce makes the same point: "There really is no such thing as a fertilized ovum. Once fertilization occurs, the ovum has ceased to be." Ibid., p. 346. Also (1970), p. 23.

9. As Joyce puts it: "I am a developed zygote." *Ibid.*, p. 17. Other statements of conception-fertilization as the beginning of a person's existence include Grisez (1972), Heffernan (1972), Liley (1981), and Willke (1979, 1985). See also *The Position of Modern Science on the Beginning of Human Life* (1975) for numerous statements in support of this. Denials include Callahan (1970), chapters 10 and 11; Donceel (1970); Glover (1977), pp. 123-24; Hardin (1974), pp. 46-55; and Singer (1979a), pp. 106-107.

10. See chapter 5, refutations of the Gradualist Position.

11. Hardin advances this objection, (1974), pp. 59-64.

12. See Willke (1979), p. 11, (1985), p. 36, for another, brief refutation of the "blueprint" objection. Also Joyce (1970), p. 16 and Grisez (1972), pp. 275-76.

13. The "acorn" objection is frequently raised, in popular discussions and in the literature; for example, Thomson (1971), p. 4, though she does not discuss it.

14. I am indebted to Roger Goos, Professor of Botany at the University of Rhode Island, for his assistance on the scientific aspects of this matter. For further details, see Peter Kaufman, et. al., *Plants: Their Biology and Importance* (New York: Harper and Row, 1989). For a similar refutation of the "acorn objection" see Devine (1978), p. 52. See also Joyce (1970), pp. 20-22.

15. Bent G. Boving, letter to the editor, *Science*, vol. 213, p. 154.

16. Shettles and Rugh (1971), p. 20. See also Sundberg, et. al. (1965), pp. 38-49.

17. Shettles and Rugh (1971), p. 20.

18. Hardin advances this objection, (1974), p. 48.

19. Joyce (1981), p. 350.

20. Moore (1988), p. 28a.

21. *Ibid.*, p. 28b.

22. *Ibid.* See also Flanagan (1965), p. 19-34.

23. Nathanson (1979), p. 214.

24. *Ibid.*

25. Joseph Donceel, S.J., defends a version of this view in "A Liberal Catholic's View," (1970). He terms it "*the theory of mediate or delayed animation*" (p. 16), in contrast to "*the theory of immediate animation*," that "a human being . . . [with] a spiritual soul" exists from the moment of conception (p. 15). Donceel's view is that "there is no human soul, hence no human person, during the first few weeks of pregnancy, as long as the embryo remains in the vegetative stage of its development" (p. 18). He does not espouse the view that this being can simply be killed, but rather that "it deserves a very great consideration, because it is a living being, endowed with a human finality, on its way to hominization." And thus, "that only very serious reasons should allow us to terminate its existence." (pp. 19-20).

26. Donceel, in trying to support his theory, appeals to what was taught "during long centuries," namely, "that the human soul was infused into the body only when the latter began to show a human shape or outline and possessed the basic human organs. Before this time, the embryo is alive, but in the way in which a plant or an animal is alive. It possesses . . . a vegetative or an animal soul, not yet a human soul. . . . It has reached the physiological or the psychological, not yet the spiritual level of existence. It is not yet a human person; it is evolving, within the womb, toward hominization."

Let me offer some reasons for rejecting this theory. (1) Regarding "human shape and outline": See chapter 4, sec. 6; present chapter, objections and replies 1-3. (2) Regarding "basic human organs": See chapter 4, sec. 7, 8; this chapter, objection and reply 2; next chapter, pp. 94-97. That which is to become the developed organ is already present in the zygote. The development occurs in one and the same being who is there all along. Born people need these organs in their developed form, the zygote does not, for she is in a different phase of her development. Each, the born person and the zygote, has what she needs; level of development is irrelevant. (3) Regarding the claim that the zygote or embryo has not yet reached the spiritual level of existence: This can mean only that she cannot yet function as a person, not that she lacks the being of a person. A full analysis of this follows, in the next chapter. (4) Regarding the claim that the zygote or embryo is alive only in the sense in which a plant or animal is alive: We are human beings, alive *as human beings* from the very beginning of our existence, all the way through pregnancy. Recall the Continuum of human life (chapter 1). "I was once a small child in my mother's womb, beginning as a tiny zygote." I was always *myself*, a person. *I was never an animal!* See also chapter 5, refutation of Gradualist Position. (5) Regarding the claim that the zygote or embryo is evolving towards hominization: On the contrary, a zygote is *already* human, in every sense of the term. A zygote does not "evolve" into a person; she *is* a person, a small person at the beginning of her existence, and development. See again Gradualist Position, the section below ("Is the zygote a person?"),and chapter 7.

27. For another criticism of this view, see Grisez (1972), pp. 282-83.

28. A possible exception to this would be cases of identical twins, if either (a) they came from a single-celled "parent," who then died, or (b) the second was begotten by the first, who was begotten by the adult

parents (as was the single-celled "parent" in (a)). But even here, what is begotten is, in each case, a human person, and not a mere biological organism into which the soul, or being of a person, is later infused. So the essential point remains.

29. Joyce (1981), p. 346.

30. See Weisbord (1982), p. 13.

31. This is the way it is generally presented. See, e.g., Weisbord (*Ibid*), where it forms part of his claim that "legalized abortion" is not parallel to the Nazi holocaust.

NOTES TO CHAPTER 7

1. Fletcher (1979), p. 144.

2. Tooley (1973), p. 54. See also (1984), p. 122.

3. Tooley (1979), pp. 80-81.

4. Warren (1973), p. 43.

5. *Ibid.*

6. *Ibid.*, pp. 43-44.

7. *Ibid.*, p. 45.

8. *Ibid.*

9. *Ibid.*, p. 50.

10. *Ibid.*

11. *Ibid.*, p. 51.

12. Tooley (1972), p. 82. Also (1983), p. 121 and (1984), p. 130. Essentially the same point is made by Engelhardt (1974), pp. 321-23.

13. *Amicus Curiae*, pp. 11-13.

14. *Ibid.*, pp. 13-14.

15. Engelhardt (1974), p. 322. He says this of the fetus in general. The context is a comparison of the fetus and a sleeping person.

16. Blechschmidt (1981), p. 8.

17. Joyce (1970), p. 22.

18. Joyce (1981), p. 347.

19. The Functioning Person Theory, especially in its emphasis on the distinction between being "merely human" and being a "person" (meaning a functioning person), is held by a number of contemporary writers in different forms. See: Tooley (1972), pp. 55-69, *passim*; (1973), pp. 54-73, *passim*; (1979), pp. 84-92; (1983), pp. 50-157, *passim*; (1984), *passim.* Warren (1973). Fletcher (1979), chapters 1, 10, 11. See also Engelhardt (1974). Speaking of a "fetus," he says "there may be merely human life present but not a person" (p. 321). Also Glover (1977), pp. 127, 138-40, and chapters 3, 9, 11 and 12, *passim*; Singer (1979a), chapter 4 and (1979b); Sumner (1981), pp. 90 ff. Finally, Kluge (1975), pp. 88-95, esp. 91, where the Theory is more restricted in scope than in authors such as Tooley, Singer and Warren.

20. Tooley (1983), p. 77. This is the conclusion he reaches in section 4.2, entitled "The Moral Irrelevance of Species Membership," pp. 61-77. See also (1979), p. 67, and (1972), p. 70.

21. Singer (1979a), p. 117. Also (1979b), p. 47.

22. Adherents of the Functioning Person Theory recognize that the term "human" may be used in a sense other than that of designating a mere biological category. It may mean, as the *Oxford English Dictionary* says, "of, belonging to, or characteristic of man," or "having or showing the qualities or attributes proper to or distinctive of man." [Singer (1979b), p. 48]. The term "man" in this context is, of course, interpreted by adherents of the Functioning Person Theory as meaning "functioning person." It would then include only beings who had the (present immediate) capacity to function as persons; that is, who had "qualities or attributes we think characteristic of, proper to, or distinctive of man" [*Ibid.*], for example, the "characteristic . . . [of

having] a capacity of self-awareness or self-consciousness" [*Ibid.* p. 49]. This would mean that "we will not count severely retarded infants as human beings even though they are clearly members of *homo sapiens* [the biological species human] (*Ibid.*)." Thus, the term "human" is taken by adherents of the theory to be ambiguous between "functioning person" and "member of the biological species 'human.'" See also Singer (1979a), pp. 74-76. In this connection, Tooley says that "the tendency to use expressions like 'person' and 'human being' interchangeably is an unfortunate one" (1972), p. 56. See also (1973), p. 56 and (1983), p. 50.

My criticism of the Functioning Person Theory in this section is therefore directed to it in so far as it uses the term "human" in one of the two meanings just described, namely, "member of the biological species 'human.'" It is in this sense that the term is claimed to be "a mere biological category."

23. Tooley (1983), p. 175; see also 193. See Marquis (1989) for another refutation of views such as those of Tooley that try to justify abortion by claiming that the "fetus" is not a person. Marquis argues that abortion is wrong because it denies the "fetus" a valuable future, regardless of whether "it" is a person.

24. Warren (1973), section 4, p. 48.

25. *Ibid.*, p. 49.

26. *Ibid.*

27. Joyce (1981), p. 351.

28. *Ibid.*, p. 350.

29. *Ibid.*

30. An explicit endorsement of the Achievement View is found in Sumner: "The future awaiting a human fetus is not relevant to its moral status; that status is based on what it has already achieved. The threshold [when "it" achieves moral status, namely at sentience] is a moral quantum leap, for it is the stage at which the fetus joins the class of

beings whose rights are secured by our network of positive laws and conventional moral rules" [(1981), p. 227]. When Sumner says that "the paradigm bearer of moral standing is an adult human being with normal capacities of intellect, emotion, perception, sensation, decision, action, and the like" [(1984), p. 74], he is expressing the Achievement View. The normal human adult has achieved these capacities, so he "counts" as a full moral being, a "paradigm bearer of moral standing." The "fetus" has not achieved them, at least not before sentience, so he lacks moral standing; or at least full moral standing. See also (1981), p. 10. Another explicit advocate of the Achievement View is Ashley Montagu. Devine tells us that "another possible account treats personhood, as Ashley Montagu once said, not as an endowment but as an achievement [Letter to the *New York Times*, March 9, 1967], an achievement (like the earning of a university degree) which confers a certain status on someone as long as he is" [(1978), p. 93]. See pp. 93-95 for Devine's criticism of this view. See also Grisez (1972), pp. 278, 281 for a criticism.

31. Tooley acknowledges this. After listing fifteen "proposals [that] have been advanced as to what . . . properties are required" for being a "person," in addition to consciousness, he observes that "these alternatives, and various combinations of them, provide one with quite a bewildering selection of candidates for the properties that should enter into the definition of the concept of a person" [(1983), p. 90].

32. Singer (1979a), p. 76.

33. Fletcher (1979), pp. 12-15.

34. Tooley (1973), pp. 59-60.

35. Tooley (1983), p. 90.

36. *Ibid.*

37. *Ibid.*, pp. 90-91.

38. *Ibid.*, p. 121.

39. *Ibid.*, p. 132.

40. Tooley's discussion of the notion of a "person," in his book, is mainly in chapter 5, "The Concept of a Person" (pp. 87-164). See also chapters 4 and 6, "Persons and Human Beings" (pp. 50-86) and "Potential Persons" (pp. 165-241).

41. Warren, "reasoning"; Singer (1979a), p. 76; Tooley (1983), pp. 134-38 and 299.

42. Warren, "the presence of self-concepts and self-awareness." Singer (1979a), p. 76. Fletcher, "self-awareness." Tooley (1972), p. 59; (1973), pp. 59-60 and 72; (1979) p. 91, "at least . . . the *capacity* for self-consciousness."

43. Tooley (1983), pp. 144-46.

44. *Ibid.*, pp. 138-42. It is probably also affirmed by Warren, "self-motivated activity."

45. Section 11.54, "The Scientific Evidence: Human Neurophysiological Development," Tooley (1983), pp. 372-407.

46. English (1975), p. 152. All quotations are from Part I of her paper.

47. *Ibid.*

48. *Ibid.*, p. 153.

49. *Ibid.*, p. 154.

50. Where would Tooley "draw the line" after birth? In each of his three articles on abortion he says: "The practical moral problem can . . . be satisfactorily handled by choosing some short period of time, such as a week after birth, as the interval during which infanticide will be permitted" [(1972), p. 79; (1973), p. 91; (1984), p. 133]. In his book this period is considerably extended. "New-born humans are neither persons nor even quasi-persons [see sec. 11.6, pp. 407-12], and their destruction is in no way intrinsically wrong. At about the age of three months, . . . they probably acquire properties that are morally significant, and that make it to some extent intrinsically wrong to destroy them" [(1983), pp. 411-12]. Even at three months, the killing of a child is not as wrong as killing an adult, according to Tooley. The killing of

infants, he says is only "eventually . . . comparable in seriousness to the destruction of a normal adult human being" [*Ibid.*, p. 412].

51. This is reflected in Sumner's question: "To which creatures should we distribute (some degree of) moral standing?" [(1981), p. 128]. As if "moral standing," the right to be treated with respect as a person, were something we could distribute at will!

52. For a profound analysis of reverence, see von Hildebrand, "Reverence" [(1950), pp. 1-15; reprinted, (1967), pp. 1-9]. The dignity of a person is closely related to the intrinsic value of a person as person, which von Hildebrand calls the ontological value of the person. See his analysis, (1953), pp. 129-39.

53. For an analysis of the notion of the dignity of the human person, see Balduin Schwarz, "Von der Wurde des Menschen" (1984a).

54. *Ibid.*, p.5638.

NOTES TO CHAPTER 8

1. Thomson (1971).

2. Bolton (1979).

3. *Ibid.*, p. 42.

4. Thomson (1971), p. 4.

5. See Foot (1967), p. 31. Based on "the story . . . of the fat man stuck in the mouth of the cave."

6. I am indebted to John Barger for calling the central idea behind this refutation of Thomson to my attention, and for helpful suggestions in formulating it.

7. Thomson (1971), p. 5.

8. *Ibid.*, pp. 15-16.

9. *Ibid.*, pp. 14-15.

10. See Finnis (1973), p. 110 for a similar criticism of Thomson.

11. See, e.g., Sumner (1981), pp. 65-73, in which he endorses the view that the child is a parasite on the woman, and discusses Thomson's arguments from this point of view. See also (1984), p. 88.

12. Finnis (1973), p. 109. Italics in original.

NOTES TO CHAPTER 9

1. See the excellent book by David Reardon (1987) on this subject, especially the twenty-one stories by women devastated by their abortions (foreword and eight profiles).

2. See Reardon (1987); e.g., pp. 74-75, 86, 148.

3. Brennan (1983). See also Powell, *Abortion: The Silent Holocaust* (1981); also (1983).

4. Brennan (1983), pp. 1-3. Used with permission of Landmark Press.

5. *Ibid.*, pp. 37-38.

6. *Ibid.*, p. 45.

7. *Ibid.*, p. 44.

8. *Ibid.*, p. 105.

9. *Ibid.*, p. 114.

10. *Ibid.*, pp. 114-115.

11. Andrusco (1983b), p. 6. Used with permission of Life Cycle Books.

12. Tom Bethell to Joseph Sobran. From the latter's column, "Washington Watch," *The Wanderer*, November 10, 1988., p. 5.

13. For an extensive comparison, see Willke, *Abortion and Slavery: History Repeats* (1984).

14. Andrusco (1983b), p. 4.

15. Reardon (1987), p. 114. See also p. 292.

16. *Ibid.*, p. 110. See also Saltenberger (1983), p. 51. This is admitted by the Center for Disease Control "which is strongly pro-abortion in its editorial opinions." (Reardon, p. 110).

17. "Wie die Erfindung der Atombombe" [Like the Invention of the Atom Bomb], by Norbert Martin, in Deutsche Tagespost Nr. 4, 10 January 1989, p. 8.

18. *Ibid.*

19. Andrusco (1983b), p. 3.

20. "Baby Boys, to Order," by John Leo. *U.S. News and World Report*, January 9, 1989, p. 59b.

21. *Ibid.*, p. 59a.

22. Brennan (1983), p. 3.

23. Andrusco (1983b), pp. 14-15.

NOTES TO CHAPTER 10

1. Brody makes this point when he urges us to reflect that "however unjust the act of rape, it was not the fetus who committed or commissioned it. The injustice of the act, then, should in no way impinge upon the rights of the fetus, for it is innocent" [(1976), p. 38]. Also Kluge: "As to . . . pregnancy resulting from rape, in this case, too, abortion will be an act of murder . . . "[(1975), p. 98].

    In addition to Brody, Kluge, Reardon, McCormack and Willke, (see notes 3, 4, and 6), other authors who recognize that abortion is not justified in the case of pregnancy due to rape include Brown (1977), pp. 28-29; Garton (1979), pp. 75-79; Griscz (1972), p. 343; Joyce (1970), pp. 42-44; Rice (1969), pp. 37-39; (1979), p. 94; Whitehead (1972), pp. 109-110; and Young (1983), pp. 206-210.

2. I am indebted to Fritz Wenisch for calling my attention to this principle.

3. Ellen McCormack, "Is Abortion a Solution for Rape?" *Christian Crusade*, April 18, 1976, p. 9.

4. Wertheimer makes this point, (1971), p. 47.

5. Willke (1979), p. 44; (1985), p. 152.

6. Reardon (1987), p. 188. See also Young (1983), p. 206.

7. See Reardon (1987), pp. 190-191. Mahkorn (1979), pp. 55-56.

8. The metaphysical refers to the essential nature of reality; for example, the nature of time (that it is directional, that one cannot go back in time, that one cannot undo the past), the nature of causation, the nature of a person (e.g., that a person is one and cannot be split), the nature of freedom.

9. From "'I Had an Abortion'—The Agonizing Aftermath." *All About Issues*, November 1982, pp. 18-19. Reprinted with permission from American Life League. *All About Issues*, P.O. Box 1350, Stafford, VA 22554.

10. Reardon (1987). Another very important book in this area is Ann Saltenberger's *Every Woman has a Right to Know the Dangers of Legal Abortion* (1983). Other works include Bulfin (1981); Ervin (1985); Hilgers (1972); Liebman and Zimmer (1979); Mecklenburg (1972); Parthun *et. al.* (1987); Speckhard (1987); and Willke (1979), pp. 78-97; (1985), pp. 90-131. There are several articles on this subject in Hilgers, Horan, and Mall (1981), Part I.

11. Reardon (1987), p. xxiii.

12. *Ibid.*, p. 25. Quotes from Reardon used with permission of Loyola University Press.

13. *Ibid.*, p. 118.

14. *Ibid.*, p. 93.

15. *Ibid.*, p. 75.

16. *Ibid.*, p. 90.

17. *Ibid.*

18. *Ibid.*, p. 119.

19. *Ibid.*, p. 23.

20. *Ibid.*, p. 120. Emphasis added.

21. *Ibid.*, p. 127.

22. *Ibid.*, p. 20.

23. *Ibid.*, p. 94.

24. *Ibid.*

25. *Ibid.*, p. 96.

26. *Ibid.*

27. *Ibid.*, pp. 220-21. Italics in original.

28. *Ibid.*, p. 101.

29. Saltenberger (1983), p. 23.

30. Reardon (1987), p. 109.

31. *Ibid.*, p. 111.

32. *Ibid.*, p. 221.

33. *Ibid.*, p. 106.

34. *Ibid.*, p. 113.

35. Hilgers and O'Hare (1981), p.89.

36. *Ibid.*, p. 90. Italics in original.

37. Saltenberger (1983), p.52.

38. Reardon (1987), p. xvI.

39. *Ibid.*, p. xxv.

40. *Ibid.*, p. 163.

41. *Ibid.*, p. 169.

42. *Ibid.*, p. 167.

43. Mahkorn and Dolan (1981), pp. 192-93.

44. Mahkorn (1979), p. 67.

45. *Ibid.* See p. 66.

46. *Ibid.*, p. 69.

47. *Ibid.*, p. 65.

48. *Ibid.*, p. 66.

49. *Ibid.*, p. 67.

50. *Ibid.*, see p. 67.

51. Young (1983), p. 208.

52. Mahkorn (1979), p. 68.

53. Young (1983), pp. 207-208.

54. Reardon (1987), p. 199.

55. *Ibid.*, p. 201.

56. *Ibid.*, p. 202.

57. Maloof (1979), p. 101.

58. Reardon (1987), p. 164.

59. Koop (1980), p. 26. See also Rice (1969), pp. 48-49, and Young (1984), p. 205.

60. U.S. Supreme Court, *Roe v. Wade*, No. 70-18, 410 US 113, Jan. 22, 1973, note 54, pp. 157-58.

61. Reardon (1987), p. 164.

62. Thomson (1971), pp. 8-9.

NOTES TO CHAPTER 11

1. Thus Fletcher says that "*no unwanted and unintended* baby should ever be born" [(1966), p. 39. Italics in original]. See also Lader (1966), ch. XVII, "The Century of the Wanted Child," esp. pp. 155-57.

2. Hilgers, Mecklenburg, and Riordan (1972), p. 181.

3. Saxton (1987), p. 9b.

4. *Ibid.*

5. *Ibid.*, p. 9c.

6. Jean Garton makes this point, (1979), p. 30.

7. Lenoski (1981), p. 7 (seventh page; no pagination).

8. *Ibid.*

9. *Ibid.*, p. 5.

10. Reardon (1987), p. 225.

11. *Ibid.*

12. *Ibid.*

13. *Ibid.*pp. 225-26.

14. Lenoski (1981), p. 7.

15. Ney (1979), p. 32.

16. Reardon (1987), p. 226.

17. Ney (1979). He lists seven points in all; the others are included in other parts of this discussion.

18. Reardon (1987), p. 225.

19. As reported in *The Providence Journal,* March 9, 1989, p. A-10.

20. Diamond (1977), p. 133.

21. Garton (1979), pp. 79-80. Diamond's letter appeared in *Newsweek,* Dec. 3. 1973.

22. Ney (1983).

23. *Ibid.,* p. 128.

24. *Ibid.,* p. 130.

25. Ney (1979), pp. 28-29.

26. *Ibid.,* p. 29. See also Rice (1969), p. 43.

27. See Noonan (1979), pp. 90-95 for this, and the succeeding point.

28. *Ibid.,* p. 95. For the effect of abortion on the family, see also: Allan C. Carlson, "The Abortion Culture and the Disappearing Family in America" *A.L.L. About Issues* (Pub. by American Life Lobby), May 1989, pp. 12-14. See also Andrusco (1983a), Part V.

29. Walling (1987), back cover

30. *Ibid.,* p. 4.

31. Rue (1986), first and second page. See also (1983), p. 250.

32. Walling (1987), p. 7.

33. Rue (1986), first page; (1983), p. 250.

34. Bauer (1981), pp. 43-44.

35. Weber (1977), p. 161.

36. *Ibid.*, p. 165.

37. Kasun (1977), pp. 35-36.

38. *Ibid.*, p. 38. Kasun quotes Francis P. Felice, "Population Growth," *The Compass*, 1974. First item in brackets inserted here; second item is in Kasun's text.

39. *Ibid.*, pp. 33-34. See also Willke (1985): "There isn't overpopulation at all. The problem is too low a birth rate and an aging population." (p. 153; discussion of this, pp. 153-61). See also (1979), pp. 64-77. Other works arguing against the threat of overpopulation include Clark (1975); Dyck (1972); Kasun (1988); Rushdoony (1975); Simon (1981); and Whitehead (1972), pp.136-53.

NOTES TO CHAPTER 12

1. Balduin Schwarz (1984a), p. 5635. "*Die Wurde des Menschen ist das hochste Rechtsgut.*"

2. *Ibid.* See also Schwarz (1975).

3. Schwarz (1984b), esp. pp. 22-24.

4. *Ibid.*, p. 24. For a discussion of abortion in this context, see pp. 24-26. See also Schwarz (1975).

5. See Noonan (1979), pp. 80-89. And Willke, *Abortion and Slavery: History Repeats*, (1984).

6. See Franky Schaeffer, "The Case for Rape," in *The Christian Activist*, vol. 1, no. 4 (Winter 1985), p. 39. With tongue in cheek, the author

shows that all the standard arguments advanced for legalizing abortion apply with equal logic to legalizing rape. Legalizing one is as absurd, and as morally outrageous, as legalizing the other.

7. Reardon (1987), p. 314.

8. *Ibid.*, p. 299.

9. *Ibid.*, pp. 319-20.

10. *Ibid.*, p. 291.

11. *Ibid.*, p. 13.

12. *Ibid.*, p. 15.

NOTES TO CHAPTER 13

1. Noonan (1979), pp. 1-2.

2. Neuhaus (1983), p. 288.

3. I am indebted to Kiki Latimer for bringing this point to my attention.

4. William James, "The Will to Believe," Section IV. First pub., 1896. Reprinted in *The Will to Believe and Other Essays on Popular Philosophy* (New York: Dover, 1956), p. 11. Italics in original.

5. See Waldstein (1982), pp. 20-21. See also Rice (1969), pp. 41-42. He quotes the Roman poet Ovid: "Women, why will you thrust and pierce with an instrument and kill your children not yet born? That neither the tigress has done . . . nor did the lioness ever have it in her heart to destroy her unborn young."

6. See, e.g. Brennan (1983), p. 134.

7. *Ibid.*, p. 137.

8. In its *Roe v. Wade* decision of Jan. 22, 1973, the Supreme Court legalized abortion during the time prior to viability, banning all restrictions that would protect the child. In the second trimester, there could be regulations, but only to protect "maternal health," not to

protect the child. After viability, protection of the child was made an option for "the State" and abortion could be forbidden "except where it is necessary . . . for the preservation of the life or health of the mother." [410 U.S. 113 (1973). Excerpts are reprinted in Feinberg (1984), pp. 192-98. See p. 197.] The phrase "health of the mother" is broad enough to encompass any situation; a woman need only find a doctor willing to certify that the abortion is "necessary for her health."

9. From a NARAL brochure, "Do you want to return to the butchery of self-induced or back-alley abortion?" (National Abortion Rights Action League).

10. Mary Ann Warren (1973), p. 36.

11. Reardon (1987), p. 292.

12. *Ibid.*

13. *Ibid.*, p. 293.

14. *Ibid.*, p. 110.

15. *Ibid.*

16. *Ibid.*

17. *Ibid.*, p. 235.

18. *Ibid.*, pp. 235-36.

19. *Ibid.*, p. 237.

20. *Ibid.*

21. *Ibid.*, pp. 242-43.

22. *Ibid.*, p. 243.

23. *Ibid.*, p. 15.

24. *Ibid.*, p. 321-22.

25. J.C. Willke, M.D., "Those 'Back Alley' Abortions," in National Right to Life News, Feb. 16, 1989, p. 3d. See also Willke (1979), pp. 104-110; and (1985), 162-69.

26. Nathanson (1979), p. 193.

27. *Ibid.*

28. Reardon (1987), p. 299. Italics added.

29. "Prohibition" of alcohol in the United States was made the law of the land through the adoption of the 18th Amendment to the Constitution, in 1919. The amendment said that ". . . the manufacture, sale, or transportation of intoxicating liquors within, the importation thereof into, or the exportation thereof from the United States . . . for beverage purposes is hereby prohibited." It was repealed in 1933 by adoption of the 21st Amendment.

30. NARAL brochure, "Constitutional Amendments: The Effort to Outlaw Safe Abortions." Prepared by Carol Werner, April 1, 1979. See also Hardin (1974), pp. 90-94.

31. NARAL brochure (note 30).

32. *Ibid.* See also Hardin (1974), p. 91.

NOTES TO CHAPTER 14

1. See Gray (1989) for an excellent analysis of abortion as homicide and murder, and a discussion of the question of penalties. I am indebted to this article for some of the points made above.

NOTES TO EPILOGUE

1. See chapter 9, Pictures of the Results of Abortion and The Abortion Holocaust. See also Brennan's excellent book, *The Abortion Holocaust: Today's Final Solution* (1983).

2. Nathanson (1983), p. 136.

3. Scheidler (1985), p. 211.

4. Grisez (1972), p. 467. The section on prejudice against the unborn is the epilogue of the book.

5. *Ibid.*

6. *Ibid.*, p. 468.

7. Brennan (1983), pp. 4-5.

8. See Horan, Grant and Cunningham (1987). Part III is entitled "Strategies for Reversal of *Roe v. Wade.*" See also Wardle (1983).

9. See Rice (1979), pp. 106-107 for an essentially similar statement.

10. See Reardon (1987), pp. 171-77.

11. Scheidler (1985), p. 19.

12. *Ibid.*

13. *Ibid.*, pp. 277-79, Chap. 81

14. See *Adoption: A Loving Choice* a brochure pub. by Life Cycle Books, P.O. Box 420, Lewiston, NY 14092-0420.

15. Reardon (1987), p. 327.

16. See Andrusco (1983a), Part IV, "The Pro-Life Alternative: Helping *Both* Mother *and* Child," pp. 259-87.

Index